THE SOCIAL WORLD OF PUPIL ASSESSMENT

Also available:

Sandra Acker: *Realities of Teachers' Work*
Patricia Broadfoot, Marilyn Osborn, Claire Planel and Keith Sharpe: *Promoting Quality in Learning*
Paul Croll (ed.): *Teachers, Pupils and Primary Schooling*
Gordon Lloyd: *How Exams* Really *Work*
Marilyn Osborn, Elizabeth McNess and Patricia Broadfoot, with Andrew Pollard and Pat Triggs: *Policy, Practice and Teacher Experience*
Andrew Pollard, Patricia Broadfoot, Paul Croll, Marilyn Osborn and Dorothy Abbott: *Changing English Primary Schools?*
Andrew Pollard with Ann Filer: *The Social World of Children's Learning*
Andrew Pollard and Ann Filer: *The Social World of Pupil Career*
Andrew Pollard: *Reflective Teaching in the Primary School*
Andrew Pollard: *Readings for Reflective Teaching in the Primary School*
Andrew Pollard: *An Introduction to Primary Education*
Andrew Pollard and Pat Triggs: *Reflective Teaching in Secondary Education*
Andrew Pollard and Pat Triggs, with Patricia Broadfoot, Marilyn Osborn and Elizabeth McNess: *Policy, Practice and Pupil Experience*

The Social World of Pupil Assessment

Processes and Contexts of Primary Schooling

Ann Filer and Andrew Pollard

CONTINUUM

London and New York

Continuum

Wellington House   370 Lexington Avenue
125 Strand   New York
London WC2R 0BB   NY 10017-6503

First published 2000

British Library Cataloguing-in-Publication Data
A catalogue record for this book is available from the British Library.

ISBN 0 8264 4790 2 (hardback)
       0 8264 4799 6 (paperback)

Typeset by York House Typographic Ltd, London
Printed and bound in Great Britain by Redwood Books, Trowbridge, Wiltshire

Contents

Acknowledgements

We would like to express our gratitude to the children, parents, teachers and governors of Albert Park Primary School, where most of the research presented in this book was conducted. We would similarly like to thank the children, parents and staff of Greenside Primary School on whose data we also draw. In this, we acknowledge a profound debt to so many people who have freely given their time and effort and maintained a consistent interest in the project, and trust in us as researchers, over the years of the study. Without the continued commitment they have shown, this study would not have been possible.

We would like to thank the Economic and Social Research Council for the necessary funding to extend Ann Filer's PhD study. The funding provided for the continued development of an existing longitudinal data set, tracking the class cohort through three more years to the end of their primary schooling at Albert Park.

Also, our thanks go to Sarah Butler and Jacquie Harrison for their work on, and interest in, the project as a whole. Especially we thank them for the care and many hours devoted to the transcription of interview tapes.

In drawing on the full data sets and analytic development of the longitudinal ethnographies from 1987 to the present, we have needed to include materials that we have previously published elsewhere. Thus we are pleased to acknowledge the original sources of the following and thank publishers for permission to reproduce extracts:

Figure 3.1, Figure 12.2 and data from 'William's Story', 'Harriet's Story' and 'Robert's Story' in Chapters 3 and 12, first appeared in *The Social World of Pupil Career* (Pollard and Filer, 1999). Data from 'Mary's Story' in Chapter 12 first appeared in *The Social World of Children's Learning* (Pollard with Filer, 1996). Figure 5.2 was originally published in *The Social World of the Primary School* (Pollard, 1985). Data and some aspects of the analysis in Chapter 6 first appeared in Filer's (1993c) PhD thesis and in the *British Educational Research Journal*, **19**(1). Figure 8.1 and an earlier version of the analysis presented in Chapter 8 were first published in *Children and their Curriculum* (Pollard *et al.*, 1997). Figure 10.1 and some aspects of the data and analysis in Chapter 10 were first published in Filer's (1993c) PhD thesis and in *International Studies in Sociology of Education*, **3**(2).

Introduction

The assessment of educational performance has become one of the most significant areas of interest in educational policy development worldwide. Official assessment procedures and techniques are commissioned and sanctioned to provide 'hard evidence' on which governments, parents and the media evaluate educational policies and hold educational institutions to account. Pupil and student learners are classified and counselled on life-course decisions on the basis of assessment outcomes. Educational and employment opportunities hinge on assumptions of their predictive powers for future success.

Underpinning such confident practices is a belief that educational assessments are sufficiently objective, reliable and impartial to be used in these ways. But is this belief well founded? Can routine assessment evidence be treated as being factual and categoric?

This book is about the ways in which social processes and taken-for-granted practices influence the production of pupil performance, its assessment and the interpretation of such judgements. Through an exploration of the social world of pupil assessment we will show that the notion of the possibility of 'objectivity' in assessment practices and outcomes is an illusion. More specifically, we will suggest that:

- individual performances cannot be separated from the contexts and social relations within which they are embedded;
- assessment techniques are social processes and are vulnerable to bias and distortion;
- the 'results' of assessment take their meaning for individuals via cultural processes of interpretation and following mediation by others.

Our argument thus highlights various ways in which social processes *inevitably* intervene in assessment procedures. It is thus intended as a contribution to penetrating the 'myth of assessment' (Broadfoot, 1996) and to understanding assessment as a social practice and product (Filer, 2000). As our title suggests therefore, our purpose is not to contribute to the endless pursuit of technical 'fixes'. Rather it is to develop sociological understandings of classroom processes and interaction and, hence, of the social influences on assessment.

The research we report is part of what we have called the *Identity and Learning Programme*, which has developed through a series of our parallel or collaborative studies. Whilst influenced by Andrew Pollard's early book, *The Social World of the Primary School* (1985), the programme really began to take shape when we began work on two parallel ethnographies of children's learning and school experiences at contrasting primary schools. Children at the two schools, Greenside Primary and Albert Park Primary, were eventually studied throughout their primary school education and on up to their GSCE examinations at age 16. The figure, above, shows the relationship between our work in the two schools.

	Greenside Primary	Albert Park Primary
1987/88	Reception	
1988/89	Year 1	Reception
1989/90	Year 2	Year 1
1990/91	Year 3	Year 2
1991/92	Year 4	Year 3
1992/93	Year 5	Year 4
1993/94	Year 6	Year 5
1994/95	Secondary education	Year 6
1995/96		Secondary education

Longitudinal ethnographies in two primary schools

We have published two other books from the programme. *The Social World of Children's Learning* (Pollard with Filer, 1996) is focused on social influences on young children's approach to learning and their sense of themselves as learners. It is based on data gathered and analysed by Andrew Pollard at Greenside Primary School. *The Social World of Pupil Career* (Pollard and Filer, 1999) extends this analysis to look at the 'strategic biographies' of children throughout their primary school careers at Greenside. This study was supported by the Leverhulme Trust and uses data gathered and analysed by us both.

The present book has its direct origins in Ann Filer's PhD, *Classroom Contexts of Assessment in a Primary School* (1993c), for which Andrew Pollard and Patricia Broadfoot were advisers. When this work started, we began to realize the potential for comparative longitudinal ethnographic studies of young children moving through compulsory schooling and we were fortunate to obtain funding from the Education and Social Research Council (ESRC) for an extension to Ann's PhD, which enabled the Albert Park study to be continued in parallel with the Greenside work. Whilst completing the analysis and writing up of this work, Ann Filer also edited a significant collection, *Assessment: Social Practice and Social Product* (2000), and all these sources have been drawn on in the production of our analysis here. Three chapters of the present book (6, 8 and 10) are derived specifically from Ann's single-authored work, and original sources are indicated as appropriate.

The secondary phase of the *Identity and Learning Programme*, funded by ESRC, will conclude in 2001. Its major theme will be how social experiences in contrasting schools, families and communities influence attitudes to learning and produce highly differentiated life chances.

Part One

Setting the Scene

Chapter 1

Theory, Method and the Sociology of Assessment

1.1   INTRODUCTION

In this chapter we describe the ways in which we have been influenced by symbolic interactionism as the underlying theoretical framework for the *Identity and Learning Programme*, and for this book. We also provide an overview of the research design, methods of data-gathering and forms of analysis used in our ethnographic work. Most substantively, however, through a preview of our major arguments, we suggest how the present book contributes to an emergent 'sociology of educational assessment'.

1.2   SYMBOLIC INTERACTIONISM

Symbolic interactionism provides strong theoretical continuity across the *Identity and Learning Programme*, supporting the themes in relation to teachers and their individual pedagogies, as well as in relation to pupils' experiences in family, peer-group and classroom contexts.

Symbolic interactionism originated in the theories of Mead (1934) through which he developed the idea of an individual's self-concept being acquired through social interaction. Actions of others, especially 'significant others', are interpreted as having meaning. It is through these meanings that the internalization of how others construe oneself and the regulatory aspects of self develops.

'Identity' presents a core analytic theme through the *Identity and Learning Programme*, connecting and integrating the major themes of 'learning', 'pupil career' and 'assessment'. In Chapter 3 we elaborate more fully on the relationship between symbolic interactionism and ways in which we have conceptualized 'identity' through the programme. Here, however, we might usefully cite Jenkins' (1996) interpretation of Mead. In everyday terms, he suggests:

> We cannot see ourselves at all without also seeing ourselves as other people see us. (Jenkins, 1996: 21)

We suggest that this interpretation of Jenkins represents very important elements of symbolic interactionism. It emphasizes the development of meaning through significant relationships and events and the development of important aspects of the individual sense of 'self' as a social product. In this the role of parents, friends, teachers or imagined others from television or other media is important, as young children develop their sense of who they are as learners and pupils. Also of key importance in this is the role of formal and informal assessment events, through which capacities are deemed to be measured, behaviours and attitudes evaluated and both labelled and classified in relatively categoric, authoritative and public ways.

We have, of course, used and developed many analytic and theoretical perspectives through the *Identity and Learning Programme*. However, in their concern for the interpretive nature of experience and individual and group construction of 'meaning' within social and cultural contexts, they all share a common approach to conceptualizing experience with the more general sociological theory of symbolic interactionism. Such complementary theories include, for example, those of Vygotsky (1978) and socio-cultural theories of learning (Pollard with Filer, 1996), Bernstein's (e.g. 1971, 1996) work on pedagogic codes and the framing of educational knowledge and Halliday's (1978, 1982) perspectives on the socio-linguistic contexts and culture of classrooms (both in this book).

From the earliest years of study, through to the present, we have been influenced by, and used, symbolic interactionism in many ways. Thus *The Social World of the Primary School* (1985) focused on how children and teachers negotiate classroom understandings and 'good relationships'. Andrew Pollard argued that each party has particular 'interests-at-hand' but, with a shared concern to protect their sense of self, teachers and pupils negotiate ways of getting along together – a working consensus. Each year, teachers and pupils negotiate from their relative positions of power until the classroom settles around a broad set of understandings about 'how we do things here'. In ideal circumstances, this enables a mutual exchange of dignity as the 'coping strategies' of teachers and different social groupings of pupils become meshed together. In her PhD, *Classroom Contexts of Assessment in a Primary School* (1993c), Ann Filer argued that teacher assessments are products of such negotiated classroom environments and are thus inevitably related to their specific context. As we further argue in this book, the classroom contexts which teachers create, and the subsequent interrelation of teacher–pupil strategies within those contexts, has consequences for the performance of individuals and groups of pupils and for the assessments of them made by teachers. Both can be seen as products of the patterns of symbolic interaction and meaning that have developed in the lives and biographies of teachers and pupils and within particular classroom and school settings. Thus, in *The Social World of Children's Learning* (1996) the argument was broadened to include the influence of parents, siblings and friends as well as teachers and the focus was turned towards how very young pupils made sense of themselves as learners and developed a 'learning identity'. More recently, *The Social World of Pupil Career* (1999) extended the analysis longitudinally to trace how children evolve and maintain their 'pupil identities' as they negotiate their way through the expectations and interpretations of successive teacher and classroom contexts. In this we analysed the dimensions, and tracked the dynamics, of the children's strategic action, thus mapping the 'strategic biographies' of their primary school careers.

On completion of the secondary phase of the *Identity and Learning Programme* in 2001, our tracking and analysis of the school experience of the two cohorts of pupils will have covered some fourteen years of study. Over those years, and in some of the ways we have described above, our theoretical analysis and thinking about symbolic interactionism has continued to develop in the context of debates on meaning, action and interaction, language, culture and social structure. The interactive and 'micro' focus of symbolic interactionism has taken place in the context of, and incorporated implications of, an ongoing analysis of the structural, material and 'macro' factors which shape the lives and experiences of individual pupils, families, teachers, schools and local communities. As we discuss in Chapter 3, any satisfactory account of 'identity' has to synthesize the internal and personal concerns of individuals with the external influences and mediations of culture. It has to consider the differential distribution of material, social and linguistic resources which give rise to the socio-economic and cultural circumstances that position expectations of, and for, particular social groups and communities. Thus we would reject some historic criticisms of symbolic interactionism for its failure to address structural, material and 'macro' influences on the experience and interpretations of individuals and groups. Rather, we believe our evolving use of symbolic interactionism shows how it is possible to focus on detailed and holistic case studies and patterns of interaction, whilst also addressing the deep-rooted affects of social position, political economy and socio-historic circumstance.

From a postmodern position, it is also possible to generate a critique of symbolic inter-actionism for adopting a now outdated and unidimensional view of identity and self. Some argue that, in the complexity and diversity of modern, global societies, individuals develop multiple identities, embedded within associated forms of discourse, so that the notion of a singular self becomes almost redundant. We have some sympathy with this illuminative perspective. Indeed, it has influenced our analysis with respect to the dynamics of continuity and change as meanings and interpretations change across classroom contexts and relationships. However, we believe that the emphasis on multiple identities can be pushed too far and Chapter 3 (and Pollard and Filer, 1999) gives our position and research findings on the flexibility and continuity of social and, particularly, pupil identities and the dynamics of change.

Of course all theoretical approaches have particular characteristics, strengths and weaknesses. A key research judgement, therefore, evaluates possible theoretical frameworks and decides which would be *most appropriate* in terms of the aims of the research. Amongst the criteria that may be applied, a theoretical framework should be consistent with research aims, the available evidence and methodological approaches adopted. It should enable key issues, patterns and findings to be identified, represented, communicated and understood. In the form of symbolic interactionism that we have developed we have much in common with other UK 'interactionist ethnographers' (see Hammersley, 1999) and find that it continues to be a valid and appropriate theoretical framework for our purposes. It has certainly proved sufficiently flexible to underpin evolving analysis and re-analysis of our longitudinal data and to address that in the light of the continuously generated theoretical discourse of the wider academic community. In particular, it yields a communicable set of analytic concepts with which to illuminate key aspects of taken-for-granted social processes in schools. It has the potential to make direct connections with the lived experiences of children, teachers and parents and to facilitate the development of social awareness and reflexivity.

1.3   RESEARCH DESIGN, DATA GATHERING AND ANALYSIS

As indicated in the Introduction, our overall research design for this phase of the *Identity and Learning Programme* was based on two longitudinal ethnographies of primary schools. Much of the detailed work connected with assessment was conducted at one, Albert Park, with the other, Greenside, providing a comparative case study.

Ethnography is a classic anthropological method which is compatible with the methodological implications of symbolic interactionism (Blumer, 1969). It was developed as a way of attempting to understand the beliefs, cultures and practices of traditional communities and tribes. The key data-gathering method was that of participant observation, in which the anthropologist lived in the community for a significant period of time, participated in daily life and tried, appreciatively, to identify and record significant aspects of the culture. Since its early beginnings, ethnography has been considerably developed, but the goal of achieving a holistic and appreciative understanding of a group of people remains fundamental. Ethical, representational and analytical issues are now far more significant than they were in the past and particular methods, initially developed by ethnographers, have been extracted and taken in new directions by other researchers dealing with qualitative data. Ethnography has thus become a popular approach for sociologists wishing to document perspectives and 'agency' among particular social groups.

Our work at Greenside and Albert Park Primary Schools illustrates many of the characteristics of more modern, sociological ethnography and some aspects of older traditions. For instance, whilst explaining the analytic goals of the study, we sought access to the schools and families in ethically aware ways. At all times, we have tried to be appreciative of the concerns and perspectives of children, teachers and parents and, in a context where we have had to present multiple and often conflicting perspectives, have had to consider their inevitable sensitivities to some parts of our analysis. At all times, our concern for the feelings and responses of the children in the study and for presenting their perspectives has been paramount. However, perhaps our continued association with families and schools across the years is some testimony to the ways in which we have negotiated some of the difficult issues that we have met (see Filer with Pollard, 1998).

As in traditional ethnography, we committed ourselves to long-term and holistic study and our initial aim was to build up 'thick descriptions' of what we found. Thus we used field notes to record observations and conversations, collected examples of children's work and diaries from parents, videoed and recorded, sat in classrooms, roamed playgrounds and attended school events, visited homes and conducted successive interviews with pupils, teachers and parents. Such data-gathering was informed by a carefully constructed annual schedule, but it was also subject to pragmatic adjustments as circumstances, funding and pressures of other work forced adjustments as the programme developed.

At Greenside Primary School, Andrew Pollard began data collection in the autumn of 1987 with a Reception class cohort. He focused on the ten children, five boys and five girls, who, close in age, were thought likely to (though they didn't) stay together within classes through the school. The school's intake was predominantly drawn from children of affluent, white, middle-class professional or self-employed families. In 1991, with support from the Leverhulme Trust, Ann Filer took over the main data-gathering role at Greenside.

At Albert Park Primary School, Ann Filer began her work in the autumn of 1989 with a Year 1 cohort. Of the initial 26 children, there were 10 girls and 16 boys, all of whom were white. The classroom settings that these children experienced were studied intensively, as part of Ann's PhD fieldwork, until the summer of 1992. This period of time was of considerable significance, with the National Curriculum being introduced into England from 1989, the cohort of pupils being studied was thus the first to experience the new National Curriculum and assessment arrangements and Key Stage 1 SATs in 1991. A 'link-study' kept contact alive with the pupils and school during 1992/3 during the writing up of Filer's PhD. When, from 1993 to 1995, ESRC funding became available, the number of children being studied was reduced to allow more individual pupil, rather than class cohort, data-gathering and to extend the depth of work with parents. These changes enabled more direct comparisons with the Greenside data-set.

Over the period of study, whilst gradually moving from a descriptive to a more analytic priority, data were analysed in a variety of ways. In the early stages of our parallel work, analysis was relatively independent. However, a progressive integration of our thinking took place as our collaboration grew. An initial attempt at formal coding and sorting of the topics and themes embedded in our wide-ranging material was abandoned, both for technical reasons and because it fragmented the meaning which we felt was contained within the data. We preferred to try to get close to the *overall* developing story of each child or class of pupils as they moved through successive classroom contexts. Thus annual data-sets were compiled and we read and re-read them both longitudinally and comparatively, trying to appreciate the lives of the pupils as a whole. We regularly discussed our emergent understandings, challenging major propositions with evidence or interpretations which might undermine them and progressively developing more confidence in our basic, *descriptive accounts*. In most cases, these draft case-study accounts were read by the major participants and their comments were taken into account in subsequent revisions. As a second, interrelated element of our analysis we worked on ways of representing our analysis more abstractly. Our explicit intention in this *theoretical modelling* was to stand back from the specific details of our cases and to present the essence of our understanding and the key issues in ways which would be accessible to a wider audience. In this respect, we sought to fulfil the aspiration of ethnography to provide conceptual tools which might be helpful in reflecting on everyday practice. Our models, such as that in Figure 1.1 introduced on page 9, are intended to facilitate this. Finally, having achieved descriptions and theoretical representations which we felt to be valid and secure, we selected interview quotations, field notes of incidents and documentary evidence which would illustrate them most effectively. The result is sets of narrative developmental 'stories' about individual children, or detailed analytic accounts of classroom practices and their consequences, which are designed to complement and illustrate our more theoretical arguments.

Of course, whilst specific empirical generalization from ethnographic case studies is not warranted, readers will see that those presented here are embedded in wider understandings generated over the years of our own continuing research and that of others. Through the theoretical chapters in the book we contextualize our research within wider theoretical and research findings relating to classroom processes, pedagogy and assessment generated over some 30 years of academic study, particularly in this country and in the USA. Thus, whilst we hope that our case-study analyses will resonate with the experience of readers and offer insights for classroom practice, the theoretical chapters offer conceptual tools and models which may be applicable in other settings. The possibility of such theoretical inference is an important product of qualitative work, and contributes to awareness and professional judgement. We do not believe that there is anything particularly unusual about the schools, teachers, families and children in our studies and their experiences may thus have a wider audience.

For more detailed information of our research design and methods please see Pollard with Filer (1996, Chapter 10); Filer with Pollard (1998) and Filer (1993c, Chapter 11).

1.4   THE SOCIOLOGY OF EDUCATIONAL ASSESSMENT

In writing this book we have sought to contribute to an emergent sociology of assessment. This relatively underdeveloped approach exists in a field that has been dominated by technical discourse of assessment and testing procedures, measurement and applications. More specifically, the present book can be located within the framework of Ann Filer's collection, *Assessment: Social Practice and Social Product* (2000), which identifies key 'themes' within a sociological discourse of educational assessment. Such a discourse presents insights into the fact that, as well as having educational purposes, assessment fulfils a range of political and social functions within modern societies. These wider functions are concerned with social differentiation and reproduction, social control and the legitimizing of particular forms of knowledge and culture of socially powerful groups. In this the discourse has a critical role in examining some of the myths and assumptions embedded in the activity of educational testing. It critiques the 'science' of testing and offers insights into the fact that assessment, from the most formal to the most informal, takes place within social contexts. Thus the social and cultural values, perceptions, interpretations and power relations of assessors and assessed carry important implications for processes and outcomes. Such a discourse is, therefore, particularly concerned with the social impact of assessment, the perpetuation of educational and social disparity and its cumulative effects in shaping ways in which individuals and groups in society come to be seen and to see themselves (Filer, 1993c; 1995; 2000).

One of Filer's key themes in the collection concerns the 'socio-cultural and historical contexts of policy'. The theme draws attention to the fact that assessment policies, requirements and prescriptions are culturally, structurally and politically embedded in particular societies at particular times. Comparative and historical studies (e.g. Broadfoot, 1996) have demonstrated significant variations over time and place, but it is also the case that modern, technologically and competitively driven societies are showing remarkable convergence in deploying the results of educational assessments as an evaluative and accountability device for the modern centralist state. Thus in the present book we locate the analytic implication of our model of 'the social influences on assessment' (Figures 1.1 and 4.1) within specific socio-cultural contexts of state policy, region and community. That is to say, we ask the question 'Where and when is the assessment taking place?' In this case the contexts in question are those of two southern English primary schools in the early 1990s, serving what we would contrast as white, middle-class and skilled, working-class families. Thus the case studies illustrating the model are particular to their time and place. However, as we describe above, theoretical chapters address more generalizable theoretical understandings and research findings within which they are embedded. In addition, of course, the *questions* raised through the model (Figure 1.1) are considered to be relevant to an enquiry into the social influences on assessment in any setting at any time.

A second theme of a sociological analysis of assessment scrutinizes the 'technologies and testing' that are used in assessment processes. In our case, we have been particularly concerned with the introduction of Teacher Assessment (TA) and Standard Assessment Tasks and Tests (SATs) into primary schools. Many aspects of assessment practice draw on a scientific discourse and, in so doing, make claims for the legitimacy and objectivity of results. Thus 'tests', 'instruments', administration, marking and moderation 'procedures' are 'standardized'. Results are scrutinized from year to year to ensure that consistent standards are being maintained – though most years produce a moral panic about the 'dilution of standards', for which 'expert' rebuttal is required. Through such processes, established assessment practices are legitimated, myths and assumptions of impartial objectivity are sustained and the social control and distribution of life chances that educational assessment underpins remain unchallenged.

Exploration of the third and fourth of Filer's themes, 'classroom contexts of assessment' and 'assessment as lived experience' lie at the core of this book. Thus we are concerned with the sociocultural interpretations which pupils and teachers bring to their interaction, and the differentiating consequences of classroom processes. There then follows the issue of how assessment outcomes are interpreted, contested or otherwise mediated by learners and significant others and how the consequences of such outcomes are incorporated into future lives.

As indicated above, to tackle such issues, we have identified some key questions and, drawing

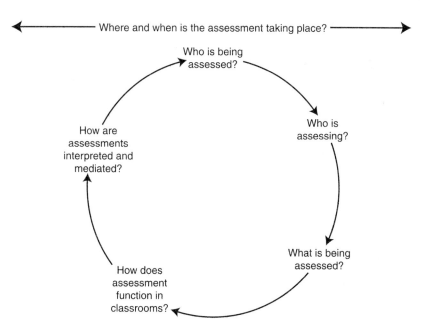

Figure 1.1   *A simplified model of questions concerning social influences on assessment*

on a model developed through our previous work (Pollard with Filer, 1996), we set these out in Figure 1.1 above.

This model is the organizing device for the book as a whole and is presented in this chapter in a simplified form. The main chapters of the book are focused on the five major questions within the cycle and are arranged in pairs. As described above, in each case a theoretical or conceptual chapter is followed by an empirical illustration of its application. A model of greater sophistication (Figure 4.1) thus gradually emerges and is elaborated as the book progresses.

Who is being assessed?

Regarding identity, we see self-perceptions held *by* individuals and judgements made *about* individuals as being inextricably linked to the social relationships through which they live their lives. Of course, there certainly are factors that are internal to the individual in terms of capacities and potentials, but their realization is a product of external social circumstances and social relationships to a very significant extent. Amongst these are assessments, of various forms, which constitute formalized, partial but very powerful representations of children as social beings, as learners and as pupils. Chapter 3 elaborates our view of identity and problematizes what it is for a teacher to know 'the whole child' for assessment purposes. The application of this perspective to assessment issues is illustrated in Chapter 4 through the story of a pupil, Elizabeth, and her primary school career.

Who is assessing?

Having argued that pupil identity can only be understood in context, we clearly need to focus on teachers – since they are undoubtedly the most powerful classroom participants with whom pupils must interact. In particular, we need a sociological conception of pedagogy and its link to each teacher's own sense of personal identity. For this, we have deployed the concept of 'coping strategy' (Woods, 1977; Hargreaves, 1978; Pollard, 1982) and traced how satisfying role expectations and the constant pressures of teaching must be balanced with maintaining a sense of personal integrity and fulfilment. In the immediacy of classroom dynamics, this can be seen as teachers juggle their 'interests-at-hand'. At the level of the school, it is played out through negotiation between different interest groups and the formation of taken-for-granted institutional assumptions. Chapter 5 discusses such issues and relates them to ways in which teachers have 'coped' with National Curriculum and assessment requirements which have progressively challenged their autonomy and traditional practices through the 1990s. In Chapter 6, a case study of one teacher and her classroom practice demonstrates the detailed application of this analysis. In particular, it shows how Marie Tucker's coping strategies, classroom organization and associated pedagogies produced particular contexts with which pupils had to cope, in turn, and it documents how Mrs Tucker began to perceive and assess pupils in terms of their actions in relation to her personal strategic criteria.

What is being assessed?

An official answer to such a question might point to the subject content of a test, or to listed criteria of judgement, and would draw conclusions in terms of the 'attainment' of pupils. More colloquially, inferences about the particular 'abilities' of children may be legitimated by faith in the objectivity and categoric techniques of 'standardized assessment'. In Chapter 7 we argue that such confident conclusions are misplaced because pupil knowledge, skills and understandings are embedded in particular sociocultural understandings and conditioned by factors such as gender, ethnicity and social class. We particularly focus on the influence of peer-group relationships and the ways in which peer culture and the sociocultural identity of each pupil can condition performance. Thus, whilst pupils' subject knowledge, skill or understanding may seem to be 'objectively' revealed by the neutral, standardization technique of a test or by a classroom task or teacher questioning, tests and tasks also reveal the facilitation or constraint of sociocultural influences and forms of understanding. Chapter 8 is focused around a Year 3 'news' session at Albert Park Primary School and shows how classroom meanings were created through interaction of circumstances, strategies and identities and how language was used to satisfy pupil agendas as well as in response to teacher-led instruction. Assessment, the analysis suggests, can never tap pure knowledge or capability – any result will also always reflect the wider sociocultural circumstances of its production. Assessment is an interpretive process – thus, beyond academic subject matter, we must ask 'what *else* is being assessed?'

How does assessment function in classrooms?

In Chapters 9 and 10 we address the links between assessment and other sociologically important influences on classroom life – ideology, language and culture. As a whole, these factors are played out through particular power relations between teachers and pupils and have significant consequences for social differentiation. We explore these ideas drawing on some of Basil Bernstein's work. This highlights the ways in which classroom language is conditioned by patterns and forms of control, which are embedded in teachers' routine and everyday practices. The consequence is that it is not possible for teachers to be 'neutral' either in their impact on pupil performance or in their assessment of pupil performance. Irrespective of intentions, each teacher generates a *particular* set of circumstances in which interaction with each child takes place. The scope for variability in the overall effect is enormous.

How are assessments interpreted and mediated?

Chapters 11 and 12 introduce the concept of the 'audience' of assessment, with particular reference to families and, to a lesser extent, peers. These are the 'significant others' whose influence we have traced throughout the *Identity and Learning Programme*, but their response to seemingly official assessment results is particularly important. Most specifically, we consider how families interpret, mediate and give meaning to assessment outcomes, so that their impact on their child is shaped and filtered. Once again then, we will argue that the outcomes of assessment cannot be seen as categoric and direct in their consequence. Rather, their meaning is malleable and is likely to be drawn into existing frames of reference, relationships and patterns of social interaction. For each learner, this is an extremely important process in the development of further phases of their personal narrative and in the construction of identity.

Overall then, in relation to each of the five major questions set out in our cyclical model in Figure 1.1, we emphasize the influence of social factors on assessment. Learner, assessor, focus, process and interpretation are all embedded in their sociocultural contexts and caught up in webs of social relationships. In such circumstances, we believe that the technical 'objectivity' of assessment is a myth too far. Indeed, we will go further and argue that presently established practices yield patterns and systematic effects which are fundamentally divisive. As the policy-makers configure the education system to meet the demands of international competition, they may also unwittingly reinforce social divisions and widen the life-chance gaps which children already face.

1.5   CONCLUSION

In this chapter, we have seen how the *Identity and Learning Programme* has been influenced by symbolic interactionism and how our empirical work was conducted. We remain focused on how people, particularly children, teachers and parents, construct meaning and interpret their lives in the circumstances of modern schooling. The present book has been particularly interesting to work on because it crystallizes the tension between the individual and the state. Both our theoretical perspective and our research design highlight 'identity' as the central organizing device for personal meaning and yet, in relation to education, assessment can be represented as the most penetrating form of state classification and control. In our focus on the assessment of pupils, we thus have a paradigm case of the classic tension between agency and constraint, action and structure, biography and history. We have tried to use the sociological imagination (Mills, 1959) to investigate the ways in which these tensions are played out and mediated by social practices in schools, classrooms, playgrounds, homes and families. The consequences of such arguments are significant; we will return to these larger themes in Chapter 13.

We begin, in Chapter 2, by setting the contextual scene for our fieldwork in more detail.

Chapter 2

The Contexts and Research Settings

2.1   INTRODUCTION

This chapter provides background information on the contexts within which our research took place. As we indicated in Chapter 1, the theoretical framework that we have adopted recognizes the considerable significance of both time and place. The specific manifestation of social relationships, actions and behaviours are seen as intimately connected to the histories, locations and circumstances of families, teachers and schools. In particular, we see such socio-historical factors as a strong influence on the social positions, interests and cultural assumptions that are played out in classrooms, homes and playgrounds on a day-to-day basis – and hence, on social practices of assessment.

In *The Social World of Pupil Career* (1999) we provided an analysis of policy developments from successive national governments and the local education authority, some of which we have drawn on below. In that book we provided an extensive description of Greenside Primary School, its head teacher and the class teachers encountered by our sample of children. In the present book, our major analyses are based on the cohort of pupils that Ann Filer studied at Albert Park Primary School, and that school is thus our major focus here.

We begin, however, with a revised account of the national and local policy contexts, with particular emphasis on assessment issues. As in our previous accounts, names of people and places within the local context have been changed to protect the anonymity of individuals and institutions.

2.2   THE NATIONAL POLICY CONTEXT

The childhood years of the children in this study were lived exclusively under the Conservative governments of Margaret Thatcher and John Major. They were years which combined nationalism and materialistic individualism – a synergy which was underpinned by New Right arguments that Britain's strength was dependent on the existence of free-market competition in every sphere of life. Teachers were among the professional groups which successive governments of the 1980s and early 1990s sought to challenge. Primary school teachers, steeped in 'child-centred' commitments, were particularly vulnerable to new demands for accountability and 'reform'. The introduction of 'objective' assessment and inspection procedures were seen as major strategies to provide overt evidence of pupil, teacher and school performance. Such information was essential for the decision making of parents as 'consumers' and for mounting effective challenges to the vested interests and taken-for-granted practices that were felt to be endemic amongst teachers.

In *The Social World of Pupil Career* we identified three phases in the development of national education policy over the period.

The first phase, 'gathering forces for change', began in the 1980s by taking forward the arguments for a National Curriculum which had previously been advanced by Jim Callaghan in his Ruskin Speech of 1976. In essence, the post-war partnership of education professionals in schools and local education authorities was seen as having failed to produce an economically relevant education service of consistent quality. Government had been excluded from the 'secret garden' of the curriculum and, under the shield of teacher autonomy, both primary and secondary education were deemed to be suffering from various 'progressive' ideologies. The DES (1984) White Paper, *Better Schools*, set out a new conception of how curriculum, assessment, teacher effectiveness and school governance could be developed within a national system.

The second phase, 'state control and the free market', began following the 1987 General Election – just before the pupils in our research were to start in school. The Education Reform Act, 1988 was designed to introduce a standard national system for curriculum and assessment. Ten subjects plus religious education were specified, along with national tests to be held at ages 7, 11, 14 and 16, and reporting to parents so that schools could be held accountable. This standardization of 'product' and the degree of central control exercised by ministers and new quangos for curriculum and assessment was unprecedented in English education. Meanwhile, the rights of the parental 'consumer' were set out in a new Parents' Charter (DES, 1992), and school budgets became based on numbers of pupils on roll. Schools were, in effect, to be placed in market competition with each other for pupil numbers and would subsequently be encouraged to maximize this 'choice and diversity' by opting out of their local authorities by applying for grant maintained status (GMS).

The introduction of the National Curriculum presented primary schools with tremendous problems as provision for each subject was developed with little overall coordination or reference to the whole. Subjects were introduced over several years, with a different schedule for each Key Stage and follow-on arrangements for the assessment of each subject. The net result was a National Curriculum of huge complexity, massive subject overload and inconsistent presentation. Teachers, many of whom had welcomed the concept of a National Curriculum on grounds of entitlement, began to wilt and protest under the strain. However, the pace of government policy change did not slacken. A new system for regular school inspection, with publication of results to parents, was introduced in the 1992 Education Act. Additionally, primary school teachers' previously accepted forms of teaching and classroom organization were questioned (Alexander *et al.*, 1992) and became the subject of a 'discourse of derision' in some parts of the media.

The development of standardized assessment procedures brought particular problems since it was both central to the government's purpose and a direct challenge to the beliefs and value commitments of many primary school teachers. When pilot rounds of national assessment began, teachers drew the sympathy of many parents in arguing that they were stressful to children and would have the effect of distorting the curriculum. However, the government pressed ahead with the testing programme until, prompted by a teacher boycott, they called on Sir Ron Dearing to review the situation.

The third phase that we identify, of 'pragmatism in the new hegemony', was a period of some compromise by both government and teachers. However, the educational landscape remained very significantly altered. The main concessions from government came in the form of the Dearing Reports of 1993/4. The National Curriculum was simplified and reduced in form and content. There was a particular attempt to reduce overload at Key Stage 2 and standardized testing became limited to English, mathematics and science.

However, the fundamental framework and conceptualization of the National Curriculum, assessment, inspection and accountability remained. Teacher autonomy had been replaced by national requirements, LEAs had been weakened and parents as 'consumers' were, in principle at least, able to exercise market choice amongst competing schools. Teachers and schools had become externally accountable in ways that were almost unimaginable before the provisions of the Education Reform Act and successive legislation started to take effect (see Pollard *et al.*, 1994). Yet, strangely, the very intensity of the experience seemed to lead many teachers to accept its apparent inevitability. For many, the initial attempts to assimilate new requirements into old practices gradually waned (Osborn *et al.*, forthcoming) and a significant number retreated from the fray to contribute to an exceptional number of early retirements. Teachers in post gradually came to terms with the national requirements made of them and the accountability systems to which they were now subject – and new teachers knew no other system. The new hegemonic 'reality' was simply that pupils had to be taught the prescribed curriculum and their progress measured. Assessment had been established as the technical means of producing the key indicators of educational 'standards' and 'performance' – on which individual pupils, teachers, schools, local education authorities and, ultimately, the nation would be judged.

2.3   EASTHAMPTON AND ITS LOCAL EDUCATION AUTHORITY

Easthampton was a city with a population of about one million in the south of England. It had a long history of manufacturing, though during the 1980s and 1990s there was considerable diversification into new technology based companies and finance. Additionally, many major international companies were attracted to the city over the period. During the period of study Easthampton and associated towns nearby grew steadily, with several major new housing developments and shopping centres.

The Local Education Authority had had a very good reputation for much of the 1970s but during the 1980s and 1990s it was rocked by successive rounds of financial cutbacks and a lack of stable political control. We have identified four phases of LEA policy in relation to primary education in the city over the period of study.

First, there was a period in which the LEA sought to promote 'good practice'. For most of the 1980s educational leadership in Easthampton primary schools was provided by the two Senior Primary School Advisers and their teams. There were strong commitments to particular forms of classroom practice, important networks within the LEA and elements of patronage in advancement. Two interconnected forms of practice were particularly promoted, both based on 'active learning'. First, for the younger children the principles of the High/Scope Project were introduced. High/Scope is an early years 'cognitive curriculum' project which was first set up as part of the US Headstart Project. Based on 'key experiences' and a 'plan-do-review' planning sequence, children are encouraged to engage in classroom activities in aware and reflective ways.

Second, addressing similar issues but for an older age group, the concept of the 'negotiated curriculum' was advanced. It was suggested that children should exercise a significant degree of control over their learning as topics of study are negotiated and understanding and capability are established. These approaches were promoted very effectively, with cross-LEA events, courses, national speakers, workshop and discussion groups and advisory visits to schools. In the absence of national requirements, the specialist LEA Advisers were able to work with schools to develop a distinctive educational philosophy. The head teacher of Greenside School played a key role in the development and dissemination of this approach to active learning. Its development within that context, and staff and parental responses to it, can be tracked through our books *The Social World of Children's Learning* (1996) and *The Social World of Pupil Career* (1999). However, by 1987/8, with a general election over and the Education Reform Act looming, a new phase of the LEA's development was about to begin.

In 1987, a second phase began in which an attempt was made to build a 'new professionalism'. A self-confident and forceful Principal Adviser was appointed to the Easthampton Education Authority. Dr Castle had risen from a primary education background, maintained a considerable interest in teaching and learning issues and promoted his role as being directly concerned with the improvement of professional practice across the authority. The vehicle which he chose for this improvement was action research. Setting out his philosophy in his first meeting with headteachers, he referred to Stenhouse (1975) and the need to develop professional expertise in the new era of accountability which he foresaw. Over next few years, Dr Castle created a significant programme for continuous professional development based on action research and 'reflective practice'. However, scope for autonomous LEA initiatives was reducing and by the autumn of 1989, with the National Curriculum beginning to be introduced and local management of schools anticipated, Dr Castle began to apply his 'new professionalism' to the evolving circumstances.

We characterize this third phase of the development of the LEA as 'mediation and incorporation of national policy'. As the consequences of the Education Reform Act began to be felt, Dr Castle sought to assert some control over the new agenda. Thus, with Local Management of Schools (LMS) looming he began a major initiative to introduce reflective forms of school management planning based around curriculum, teaching and learning objectives. A new system of 'Institutional Development Plans' was introduced and management training was offered to all head teachers. With the responsibilities of head teachers beginning to grow, the overall process was received with remarkable enthusiasm. Further, the head teachers who had acted as 'trainers' became strongly bonded and were to remain influential opinion leaders in the years ahead – including Mrs Davison, the head teacher of Greenside Primary School.

Dr Castle's initial strategy was to incorporate new government requirements into the professional framework which he had been creating. This was particularly explicit with regard to new assessment regulations which required massive INSET programmes during 1990–1. Building on the opportunities legitimated by the TGAT Report (Task Group on Assessment and Testing, 1988), a programme was constructed based around formative assessment as a means of refining and applying professional judgement in the teaching–learning process. With action research and reflective practice at its heart, this was elaborated both in terms of gathering evidence in classrooms and regarding 'profiling' – the compilation of an annotated portfolio of pupil work. 'Tick-list' assessment systems were frowned upon, but the LEA supported pilot schemes to draw pupils into the assessment process.

The fourth phase that we have identified, 'accommodation and resistance', began during 1992. By then, Local Management of Schools was well established, OFSTED inspections were beginning and it was apparent that the powers of the LEA were beginning to wane. Ironically, however, Dr Castle was promoted to become Chief Education Officer. The LEA provided advice and INSET for teachers as the National Curriculum was introduced, with a strong line that they should attempt to accommodate the new requirements into their existing practices. For his part, Dr Castle resolutely encouraged head teachers to focus on teaching and learning issues and avoid being exclusively drawn into management concerns. The LEA continued to promote formative assessment whilst increasingly being required to prepare schools for SATs. It also provided covert support for a group of primary school head teachers which formed to oppose the government threat to publish league tables of SATs results. This group, building on their management training experience, their networks across the LEA's school clusters and the principles which had been publicly espoused by Dr Castle, formed one of the largest oppositional head teacher groups in England. They engaged in extensive lobbying of government ministers and opposition spokesmen, stiffened head teacher resolve regarding the SAT boycott of 1993 and, when league tables were eventually published, took advertisements in the local press to explain what they saw as the inadequacies of the information provided and the weaknesses in the educational principles on which the league tables were based.

Overall, however, such acts of resistance were rare. Dr Castle wrestled with the implications of a finely balanced political control on Easthampton's City Council and began to network both within the government and opposition parties. However, the reality was that the LEA's powers had been considerably reduced. The initiative on curriculum, assessment, pedagogy, inspection, accountability and school finance now all rested with central government or its agencies. Operational power lay with schools. The LEA, seen as an interruption in the free market which would raise education standards, was searching for a new role.

The early LEA support for active pupil learning and the later efforts of Dr Castle to encourage teacher professionalism and school autonomy were important in providing the context for Albert Park and Greenside Primary Schools and their staffs. In these ways the LEA was a key mediating force (Broadfoot and Pollard, 1996), both promoting a particular learner-centred conception of teacher professionalism and actively seeking to defend it against new national requirements.

Tables 2.1 and 2.2 below provide an overview and summary of developments in English education policy during the period of the study, with particular reference to primary education, and of the responses and actions of Easthampton LEA and its officers.

2.4   ALBERT PARK AND ITS PRIMARY SCHOOL

Albert Park was an established urban area, on the edge of Middleton, that had been an old market town a few miles to the north of Easthampton. Middleton was mentioned in the Doomsday Book and had historically been an administrative and trading town of regional importance. It enjoyed an expansion during Victorian times, hence the development of the area known as Albert Park along one of the roads serving the town. The park itself was lost to development some years ago. Indeed, over the past century the area between Middleton and Easthampton had become increasingly built up, so that Middleton's early identity was somewhat compromised as it became absorbed into the city. Nevertheless, it remained a significant centre for shopping, local services and administration and provided a wide range of modestly priced private housing.

The primary school, set beside a narrow but now busy road, was flanked by compact Victorian terraces, a few small shops and some industrial buildings. However, its further surroundings, from which many of its pupils were drawn, also consisted of some rather more spacious houses

Table 2.1 *National education policy and LEA developments 1984–90*

Greenside cohort: Academic year, teacher and pupil age	Albert Park cohort: Academic year, teacher and pupil age	National education developments	LEA developments
1984–5 Age 1/2	1984–5 Year of birth	Keith Joseph Secretary of State *Better Schools* White Paper *The Enquiring Classroom* (Rowland)	Dr Jones, CEO, takes benevolent pride in schools' achievements within the LEA – but then retires
1985–6 Age 2/3	1985–6 Age 1/2	Education Act established new rights of governing bodies *The Curriculum 5–16* (HMI)	Mr Sutcliffe, a CEO 'systems man', manages bullishly and with political effectiveness, but remains distanced from schools Junior Schools Adviser promotes the 'negotiated curriculum'
1986–7 Pre-school Age 3/4	1986–7 Age 2/3	*Achievement in Primary Schools* (House of Commons) Teachers industrial action over pay and conditions *The National Curriculum 5–16: A Consultation Document (DFE)*	Early Years Adviser promotes High/Scope for pre-school and infant schools LEA developments through adviser-backed projects Strong adviser influence on senior promotions in school
1987–8 Reception Mrs Powell Age 4/5	1997–8 Pre-school Age 3/4	General Election Kenneth Baker Secretary of State TGAT report published Education Reform Act passed: National Curriculum Council and School Examination and Assessment Council	Dr Castle appointed Principal Adviser Recommends Stenhouse to headteachers and emphasizes developing professional expertise for classroom practice and new accountabilities Concept of subject curriculum co-ordinators is promoted
1988–9 Year 1 Miss Scott Age 5/6	1988–9 Reception Mrs Joy Age 4/5	LMS circular issued John MacGregor Secretary of State, July Caldwell and Spinks publish *The Self-managing School*	Dr Castle introduces comprehensive LEA inset, all based on action research Early Years Adviser retires
1989–90 Year 2 Miss George Miss Sage Age 6/7	1989–90 Mrs Tucker Year 1 Age 5/6	NC KS1 English, Maths and Science introduced	Dr Castle advises Heads to buy Caldwell and Spinks and to consider curriculum-led school planning LMS budgeting introduced

built during the 1930s, as well as a number of small or moderately sized post-war homes. The children's families were predominantly skilled working class, but with some lower middle-class families as well – though such definitions hide a wide range of family circumstances and class identities (see Filer, 1993c for more details). Most children attending Albert Park Primary School transferred to the nearby Riverwood Comprehensive School, situated to the north of Albert Park School, where urban development gradually gave way to green belt countryside and a popular riverside recreational area. A few children transferred to Middleton Comprehensive School, further away from Albert Park School on the south-western edge of the town of Middleton.

Table 2.2   *National education policy and LEA developments 1990–5*

Greenside cohort: Academic year, teacher and pupil age	Albert Park cohort: Academic year, teacher and pupil age	National education developments	LEA developments
1990–1 Year 3 Mr Brown Age 7/8	1990–1 Year 2 Mrs Major Age 6/7	NC KS1 Technology introduced NC KS2 English, Maths, Science and Technology introduced Parents' Charter circulated to schools, September Kenneth Clarke Secretary of State, September John Major replaces Mrs Thatcher as Prime Minister, November NCC/SEAC powers and significance grows National assessment KS1 English, Maths and Science, May	Management skills training for all head teachers Institutional Development Plans are promoted, requiring evidence of performance 'Assessment for Learning' and 'Profiling' training for all schools All phase school 'clusters' set up across the LEA, with associated link advisers Junior Schools Adviser retires
1991–2 Year 4 Miss King Age 8/9	1991–2 Year 3 Ms Luke Age 7/8	NC KS1 History and Geography introduced NC KS2 History and Geography introduced Revised teacher appraisal scheme Hargreaves and Hopkins publish *The Empowered School* Alexander's Leeds report – media furore Alexander *et al.* publish 'Three Wise Men' report on pedagogic 'orthodoxies', January Education (Schools) Act sets up inspection system and OFSTED John Patten Secretary of State, April White Paper, *Choice and Diversity* published KS1 SAT reports published	Dr Castle appointed CEO, commits to reflective practice and school development planning New School Development Planning scheme introduced based on 'priority setting', 'targets' and 'success criteria'
1992–3 Year 5 Miss French Mr Brown Age 9/10	1992–3 Year 4 Mrs Robinson Age 8/9	NC KS1 Art, Music and PE introduced NC KS2 Art, Music and PE introduced Secondary school 'league tables' published Dearing review of NC announced Grant Maintained Schools introduced NCC and SEAC abolished, School Curriculum and Assessment Authority set up Teacher boycott of pilot national testing, May	OFSTED inspections begin nationally Easthampton advisers reject 'inspection' role Head teacher campaigning group against assessment league tables flourishes, with tacit LEA support

Table 2.2 *Continued*

Greenside cohort: Academic year, teacher and pupil age	Albert Park cohort: Academic year, teacher and pupil age	National education developments	LEA developments
1993–4 Year 6 Mrs Chard Age 10/11	1993–4 Year 5 Ms Luke Age 9/10	SEN Code of Practice introduced Dearing reports National Curriculum overloaded New OFSTED Handbook and Guidance for school inspection OFSTED publishes 'Primary Matters' on pedagogy Gillian Shephard Secretary of State, July	Governors', parents' and quango powers grow as LEA powers continue to weaken Dr Castle campaigns against schools opting out of the maintained system Announcement of plans for the break-up of Easthampton LEA, and establishment of unitary authorities
1994–5 Children move to secondary schools	1994–5 Year 6 Mrs Hutton Age 10/11	External assessment markers introduced to reduce teacher workload Publication of revised National Curriculum Blair declares support for 'league tables, high standards and discipline' Chief HMI Woodhead urges 'whole class teaching' Baseline assessment of 5-year-olds encouraged National assessment at KS2, English, Maths and Science Labour Party publishes 'Diversity and Excellence', indicating policy continuity Department for Education and Employment established	Schools encouraged to commit to the Investors in People standard Local government reorganization produces considerable confusion, repositioning and planning blight within the LEA Middleton to be separated from Easthampton into new unitary authority LEA advisers struggle to maintain continuity in support to schools

With some 400 pupils it was large for a school of its type and was the product of a recent merger of the former infant and junior schools and the addition of a nursery class. Architecturally it was impressive, with elaborate wrought-iron gates and railings facing the road. Overall the large Victorian buildings of the infant and junior departments and the perimeter walls and railings created a somewhat austere impression, as did the interiors, each consisting of a hall surrounded by high-windowed, high-ceilinged, rectangular classrooms. However, the rear of the school opened on to extensive playing fields where more recent extensions provided a staff room and administrative offices for the head teacher and school secretary and a conversion of old classrooms had also created a dining room and the Nursery Unit.

Over the period of the research, two clear phases can be identified in the school's development.

First, the long-standing head teacher, Mrs Clegg, strongly emphasized traditionalism and formal approaches to teaching. She had previously been responsible for the infant school, had been appointed as head teacher to the new school at the time of the merger and was nearing retirement when Ann Filer began her data collection. As Ann describes in Chapter 6, on the one hand, Mrs Clegg was viewed by many of her staff as being 'old fashioned and authoritarian'; on the other, she was also aware of new initiatives stemming from the 'active learning' philosophy of the key LEA advisers and set in train their incorporation into teachers' practices. However, some critical teachers felt that the head just wished to be 'seen' to be involved with the latest LEA initiatives. In reality she mediated and subverted the expectations and resources of the LEA and would not let their latest initiatives undermine her commitment to the 'basics' of a structured 'three Rs' approach and an emphasis on 'presentation'. That was what she 'checked up on' and the approaches to which staff knew they had to respond. However, this gave rise to a lack of overall coherence and direction. As described in greater detail in Chapter 6, teachers struggled to integrate often short-lived initiatives lacking support and evaluation whilst maintaining the too frequently contradictory approaches of Mrs Clegg's true commitments.

Parents appeared to feel somewhat in awe of and intimidated by Mrs Clegg, as did many teachers. The teachers, moreover, were mostly well established, several having taught at the previous schools for over twenty years. There was thus little questioning of the school's policies or provision, although many teachers in fact found their own ways of doing things. Indeed, some teachers had taught the same age group for many years and had established particular teaching repertoires to which they were committed and through which they could accommodate the head teacher's requirements. Organizationally, the school maintained a policy of having single-age year-groups, with two parallel classes in each year. This, together with the structuring of hierarchical and graded systems for pupils individual progression through maths and phonics work cards, reading and maths schemes across the school provided considerable stability and eased curriculum planning. The school had a house point system which teachers used in accordance with their particular classroom aims (see Chapter 6) and it was expected, though not always the case, that children come to school in the uniform of a green sweatshirt and grey skirts and trousers. Chapter 6, describing one teacher's practice in detail, provides a further and more detailed picture of the school ethos and curriculum management as it stood prior to the introduction of the National Curriculum.

The demands of the new National Curriculum and assessment procedures were considerable in the early 1990s but were tackled pragmatically within Albert Park. Most staff, including the long-standing and influential school secretary, were cynical about initiatives from national government and the LEA. Whole school planning and coordination for curricular and educational purposes were limited, and many learning materials and resources were in need of updating. Many teachers still felt bruised by the merger and devalued by the criticisms of teachers that then dominated the media. As was the case with many head teachers at that time, the necessity for radical change in a context of long-established practice contributed to Mrs Clegg's decision to retire.

The second phase of Albert Park's history, which is of relevance to our study, followed the appointment of Mrs Foster as the new head teacher for the 1993/4 school year. We might term this the phase of the 'new broom'. However, Mrs Foster had previously been a head teacher for only a short period before being appointed to Albert Park and her new role in this large school in need of development was thus a significant challenge.

Despite these circumstances, Mrs Foster took up her new responsibilities with great energy. She immediately updated the decorations in the foyer and tried to develop a productive working relationship with her classroom teachers. A curriculum review was instituted and discussions slowly began on whole school issues. Some progress was made but staff communications were not always easy. However, Mrs Foster developed a close link with her School Adviser. New school policies on topics such as discipline were established in an effort to improve continuity, and the production of new schemes of work for all National Curriculum subjects gradually began. At about this time Dr Castle, now Chief Education Officer, began to promote the Investors in People Programme and its adaption for schools. Mrs Foster felt that this could be good for Albert

Park and, after enlisting the support of the governors, committed the school to achieving the Investors in People standard. A 'Mission Statement' was produced and a number of new systems and procedures were introduced. The IIP standard was awarded in the summer of 1994.

Unfortunately, however, the adoption of the Investors in People Programme produced some criticism from teachers and parents for being 'too flash and business orientated' and the ubiquitous demands of the National Curriculum, new assessment requirements and School Development Planning Programme still had to be addressed. The pressures on Mrs Foster were thus very considerable – but the equally significant constraints had not really been resolved by her previous strategies. In the summer of 1995, just as the cohort of children in this study were leaving the school, Mrs Foster began a period of sick leave and, after a prolonged period during which the deputy head took responsibility for the school, Mrs Foster took early retirement. In early 1997 this difficult history was unfortunately reflected in a very poor report from OFSTED inspectors and a more fundamental reappraisal of the school began.

The pupils, on whom much of our analysis in this book focuses, thus initially experienced a very traditional primary school pedagogy. This was focused on the 'three Rs' and was highly routinized. At both classroom and school levels, there were clear evaluative and differentiating processes and structures. As Mrs Clegg moved towards her retirement, relatively pragmatic and superficial responses were made to National Curriculum and assessment requirements and problems in adapting to the new circumstances accumulated. When Mrs Foster was appointed and energetically tried to sweep the school towards a new future, she found it impossible to win the confidence and develop the skills and commitment of her staff. Mrs Foster's innovative presentation of the school moved ahead of the reality and old practices continued, expectations were modest and coherence was limited.

2.5   GREENSIDE AND ITS PRIMARY SCHOOL

Greenside and its primary school has been described in some detail in *The Social World of Children's Learning* and *The Social World of Pupil Career*, so relatively brief details will be given here.

Greenside was an affluent, 'leafy' suburb just south of Easthampton's city centre. Most of the properties had been built in the 1920s and 1930s and comprised of high-quality detached and semi-detached houses, each with large gardens – as was the fashion at the time of their construction. In addition, there were also some roads with very substantial houses. The 'village', with shops, church and hall, provided a focus and sustained an idyll of rural community, despite the clearly suburban character of modern Greenside. The families living in Greenside were almost exclusively white, well off and middle-class, with at least one parent employed in business or the professions.

The primary school was a single-storey, post-war development with large playgrounds and playing fields. The classrooms were large and opened both to the outside and to wide corridors in which shared resources and activities could be organized. Overall, the school had excellent facilities. Many of the Greenside families sent their children to Greenside Primary but they then often preferred nearby independent schools for secondary education, rather than 'risk' the local comprehensives.

We characterized the development of Greenside Primary School as having passed through three phases during our study. During the 'old school' phase, prior to the appointment of a new head teacher in 1985, the school was extremely highly regarded by Greenside families. It was seen as reliably traditional with good, old-fashioned values. There was a house system, competitive sports, high-quality music and clear expectations about uniform and behaviour. Teaching was very traditional and provided the right preparation for entry into independent secondary education. The influence of the LEA was weak at that time.

The second phase, 'the battle for good practice', began on the appointment of Mrs Davison as head teacher. With the strong support of the LEA Primary Advisers, Mrs Davison wanted a more modern school which would 'really challenge the children and get them to think'. In due course, therefore, she ended the house system, introduced 'active learning' and a 'negotiated curriculum', challenged the classroom teachers to review their practice and introduced more proactive, whole-school management. There was a period of considerable staff turnover and significant dissent from parents. Many middle-class parents began to send their children to a neighbouring school. Numbers on roll decreased for a while, leaving room for an influx of children from the considerably poorer, working-class area of Damibrook which was adjacent to Greenside. However, despite the controversy and considerable challenges she faced, the LEA and school governors continued to support Mrs Davison's goals and a new settlement gradually emerged.

In 1989 Greenside Primary entered a third phase as Mrs Davison managed a period of 'assimilation and mediation' regarding national policy. She first attempted to assimilate the National Curriculum through a sophisticated approach to curriculum planning which apportioned the Attainment Targets of each subject to sequentially designated 'topics' covering each of the primary school years. This approach was widely admired in the LEA and other schools but, in combination with other internally generated initiatives and other new national requirements, the complexity and work-load consequences for Greenside staff became severe. The piloting of standardized assessment tasks for Year 2 pupils in 1991 was a particular pressure point and led Mrs Davison to re-evaluate and moderate her expectations and ambitions. Her strategy in relation to government requirements thus explicitly became one of mediation. Working in consultation with her staff, Mrs Davison sought to satisfy external requirements while also preserving her commitment to active learning. As each issue arose, a principled compromise was sought.

This strategy of assimilation and mediation was actually very successful. Enrolment grew in the years following our data gathering and in 1997 the school was very highly rated by OFSTED.

2.6   CONCLUSION

This chapter has described the contexts within which the social practices reported in this book developed. The lives and school experiences of children at Albert Park and Greenside were dramatically different in many respects. The majority of skilled, working-class families at Albert Park had far less material, cultural and linguistic resources than the far more affluent professionals and business people of Greenside. Albert Park families were generally accepting and supportive of the teaching in their community primary school and were unaware of the far higher expectations, resources, professional knowledge and management skills being deployed at Greenside. Indeed, in terms of the new conventional wisdoms of school management and effectiveness, the two schools could not have been further apart. Whilst Albert Park suffered traditionalist drift, incoherent development and an ultimately ineffective change in leadership over the period of our study, Greenside benefited from a single, strategically sophisticated head teacher using a clear set of educational principles to adapt to new legislative challenges.

Nevertheless, the two schools also had much in common. Located in different parts of Easthampton they shared something of the culture, history and economy of the city. Both experienced new head teachers attempting radical change to long-standing practices and a traditional ethos. Through this process, both were simultaneously responding to the same policies and practices of the local education authority and the national government and its quangos. In the initial stages of our studies LEA advisers were the greatest external influence but they were soon superseded by successive statutory requirements and 'guidelines' concerning the National Curriculum and assessment. As our studies progressed, so the pressure of such categoric forms of prescription, assessment and inspection increased. The teachers and pupils lived through the same period of history and, by the end, the teachers, governors, pupils and parents of both schools were extremely concerned about the 'standards' achieved by the children in the annual SATs and about the outcome of their OFSTED inspections.

In conclusion, two points can be highlighted. First, the social circumstances, cultures, histories, resources and expectations of each school and the families and local communities they served were very different. Unsurprisingly, such factors create unique social practices in relation to many aspects of school life, including, as we shall demonstrate in this book, routine and standardized assessment. Second, we need to note that in the public debates of recent years the educational performance of pupils and schools has been officially 'measured' and judged without reference to the influence of such contextual factors. We thus know circumstances to be different but we choose to compare performance as if circumstances are the same.

Our argument in this book builds from an even more detailed, interactionist analysis of classroom processes to show that 'performance' itself is partially a social product. We argue, therefore, that we cannot assess the performance of a pupil without also considering the context and pattern of social relations and practices from which it has originated.

In Chapters 3 and 4 we begin this argument by focusing on pupil identity. We pose the question, 'Who is being assessed?' How, in their web of social relationships and social practices, are particular children understood and known to themselves and to others? Such perceptions are key to the social conditions from which assessed performance derives.

Part Two

The Social World of Assessment

Chapter 3

Who is being Assessed? – An Introduction

3.1   INTRODUCTION

In this chapter we review the ways in which we have conceptualized 'identity' through *The Social World* books and also position our ideas with reference to other related work. Throughout our longitudinal studies of children's school experience, 'identity' represents a core analytic theme, connecting and integrating the major themes of 'learning', 'pupil career' and 'assessment'.

In addressing here the question of 'Who is being assessed?' we also explore issues relevant to 'whole child' approaches to assessment. Using case study data from *The Social World of Pupil Career* we compare different ways in which teachers experienced and interpreted the identities of three children through successive classroom contexts at Greenside School. We then go on to problematize the question of what might be involved in a teacher 'knowing' a child.

The account is intended to further sensitize the reader to our theoretical interpretation and to some key issues concerned with pupils' identity, prior to engagement with the 'assessment career' of Elizabeth at Albert Park School in Chapter 4. Though the case study of Elizabeth can be read independently, this chapter should help to inform and structure that reading.

3.2   WHAT IS 'IDENTITY' AND WHY IS IT IMPORTANT IN CLASSROOM ASSESSMENT?

The question of 'Who is being assessed?' is central to our conception of the social world of pupil assessment. How do children come to see themselves as learners and as pupils? How do others see them as they strive, and are encouraged, to fulfil their potential and demonstrate competencies within the social context of their classroom? In *The Social World of Children's Learning* and *The Social World of Pupil Career*, we suggested that this question raises the core issue of 'identity'. There, in relation to case studies of children at Greenside School, we posed the question 'What is identity?'

Any theoretical discussion concerning the hugely complex topic of 'identity' is problematic. Reviewing the difficulties in 1986, Breakwell wrote about the impossibility of comparing definitions across theories of identity. On the one hand theorists use a variety of terms relating to phenomena within a broadly similar conceptual territory. The choice of term, for example, 'the self', 'ego', 'personality', 'self concept', 'self image', will depend on the methodological or philosophical foundations of particular disciplines, as well as on the role the definition has to perform within the theory. Alternatively, where theorists do use the same term, 'identity' can mean completely different things to different writers (1986: 10). If that were not complex enough, the problem of defining identity has intensified through the 1990s. For instance, Jenkins (1996) in discussing the difficulty declares:

> Everybody, it seems, has something to say about it: sociologists, anthropologists, political scientists, psychologists, geographers, historians, philosophers. The prospectus is crowded. ... At every turn we encounter discourses about identity. (Jenkins, 1996: 7)

Indeed, Jenkins asserts, identity seems to be 'the touchstone of our times' (1996: 8), as much the 'stock in trade' of journalists, politicians, the advertising industry and popular culture as of intellectuals. This wide interest, of course, serves to further fuel the theoretical interest of academics. Jenkins describes how contemporary discourses of identity are much concerned with multiple positionings of difference and similarity between individuals and groups and with change. Thus identity can be a matter of individual or community self-definition and of re-definition; it can be a matter of local and indigenous distinctions or of identification on a global scale. Hence new identities can emerge, existing ones transform and old identities resurge (1996: 10).

Thus the conclusions we have reached through the *Identity and Learning Programme* regarding 'What is "identity"?' are necessarily shaped by the particular theoretical and methodological perspectives we brought to the study and by the patterns of understandings we derived from the longitudinal tracking of children's learning and school careers. 'Identity', in relation to how children come to see themselves and how others see them as learners and pupils, therefore entails a fairly tight focus around particular issues of relevance to those research questions, to our analysis and to our developing understanding. We position our conclusions in relation to other related work which takes a similarly sociological or social-psychological approach to understanding 'identity'. Such is the nature of the conceptual territory that our focus may exclude any number of potentially interesting insights which others, coming from other perspectives or disciplines, might bring to bear on the issues.

How then, for our analytic purposes, do we conceptualize 'identity'? We can begin with Breakwell's (1986) suggestion that, in part, the concept embodies three key principles of individuality, which people strive to sustain in their daily lives:

- distinctiveness and uniqueness;
- continuity across time and situation;
- self-esteem and a feeling of personal worth.

However, from a social-psychological perspective, awareness and maintenance of individual differentiation is only part of the story. Thus, Breakwell suggests, an adequate model has to attempt to link intrapsychic experience with socio-political processes. In this way, identity is:

> a dynamic social product, residing in psychological processes, which cannot be understood except in relation to its social context and historical perspective. (Breakwell, 1986: 10)

Thus, for instance, structural position in the family, school or workplace, cultural knowledge, socio-political structures and policy and particular forms of discourse represent social influences which impact on all individuals.

Jenkins, writing from 'the borders of social anthropology and sociology' (1996: 12), makes similar links between identity as individually experienced and the wider society. Jenkins' model

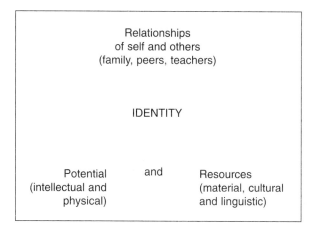

Figure 3.1   *Relationships, potential and resources: three factors in identity.* (Reproduced from Pollard and Filer, 1999, *The Social World of Pupil Career*, Cassell)

of identity sees 'an internal–external dialectic of identification' (1996: 20) as the process whereby all identities, individual and collective, are constituted. He explains that, if having an identity is necessary for social life, then the reverse must also be true that:

> Individual identity – embodied in selfhood – is not meaningful in isolation from the social world of other people. Individuals are unique and variable, but selfhood is thoroughly socially constructed. (1996: 20)

Thus, from what we might term a broadly sociological perspective, any satisfactory account of identity has to synthesize the internal and personal concerns of individuals and the external influences of cultures and expectations of appropriate social groups and the wider society. It can be argued therefore that, ultimately, we can only make sense of individuals in the context of their social relationships. This suggests a measure of flexibility, as well as continuity, which given the uncertainties and unpredictability of life is a vital aspect of social identities. Thus social identities can be 'neither remorselessly permanent nor frivolously malleable' (Jenkins, 1996: 62) since:

> the dialect of identification is, in principle, never wholly closed. (1996: 62)

Indeed, given the complexity, change and uncertainties of modern society, this dialect is likely to be played out continuously (Giddens, 1991).

In exploring the question 'Who is learning?' in *The Social World of Children's Learning* and *The Social World of Pupil Career* we focused on three groups of factors contributing to children's evolving identities as learners and as pupils. The factors, shown here in Figure 3.1, were those of 'potential', 'resources' and 'relationships'. Together they reflect identity as individual biological and family differentiation in dynamic relationship with the wider social world as we have described above. In the above publications, we showed how these factors were played out in respect of each case-study child.

In identifying *potential*, we drew attention to the interrelation of biological endowment and social learning in identity formation. In our everyday lives, speculation on the relative contributions of 'nature' or 'nurture' are endlessly fascinating as we observe the developing physical, intellectual and social capacities of children in our families. Such issues, however, are clearly beyond the scope of our work here, belonging rather in the realms of biological and psychological disciplines (see e.g. Rutter, 1989; Kagan, 1992; Meadows, 1993; Clarke and Clarke, 1996). Whilst recognizing, as do these authors, that physical, intellectual affective dispositions are not fixed, we have used the concept of 'potential' to identify some important factors in exploring questions of children's evolving identities. In *The Social World of Children's Learning* and *The Social World of Pupil Career*, year-on-year tracking of children's learning, interests and social relations in the contexts of home, playground and classroom enabled some understandings of key strengths and potentialities of individuals. More importantly for our purposes though, that longitudinal tracking enabled us to analyse patterns of learning and affective responses through classroom contexts which varied in supporting those potentialities.

Through *resources*, we focus on the differential distribution of material, cultural and linguistic factors which give rise to socio-economic and cultural circumstances and positions. The consequence, for individuals and particular social groups, is a differential flow of opportunities, living conditions, commodities, social experiences, cultural capital, concepts and linguistic forms and skills. Linguistic resources are identified here because of the enormous significance of language in early learning in understanding the language of classroom culture and expectations and thus in 'becoming' a pupil (see e.g. Tizard and Hughes, 1984; Bruner, 1986; Edwards and Mercer, 1987; Wells, 1992; Dunn, 1996). However, notwithstanding these differential consequences, postmodern theory would reject explanations of a predictable interrelation of such distributions. Such a position, rather, views individual identities as full of contradictions, inscribed by multiple and contested discourses. We might consider, for instance, the contradictions that abound in the position of being white, male, homosexual and working class. Postmodern theorizing, therefore, sees distributions of resources as being located within the multiple positionings that each of us takes up based on the intersections of race, class and gender (see e.g. Adams, 1997; Marshall, 1997). Opportunities to deploy resources vary across settings and are influenced by attitudes towards difference. For example, schools may view the social, linguistic and ethnic identities of pupils affirmatively or through the lens of disadvantage and deficit (Tsoldis, 1988). We can also question whether the values and expectations embodied in the assessed curriculum act to legitimize the lived experience of pupils. Do they include them or exclude them as the assumed subjects and subject matter of schooling? (Yates, 1997: 48). For some children, their material, cultural and linguistic resources may be relatively consistent with those of their teachers. This was the case among families and teachers in the more middle-class setting of Greenside School in our study. On the other hand, as we shall see, such family resources among Albert Park children were more likely to contribute to identities which were dissonant with the lived experiences of their teachers.

The third aspect of 'identity' in Figure 3.1, *Relationships of self and others* is a direct reference to Mead (1934) and the symbolic interactionist conception of self. As Berger and Berger (1976) put it:

> identity ... is appropriated by the individual through a process of interaction with others. Only if an identity is confirmed by others is it possible for that identity to be real to the individual holding it. In other words, identity is the product of an interplay of identification and self-identification. (Berger and Berger, 1976: 73)

Or, as Jenkins interpreting Mead (1934) in everyday terms puts it:

> We cannot see ourselves at all without also seeing ourselves as other people see us. (Jenkins, 1996: 21)

These interpretations represent very important elements of the symbolic interactionist position in that they emphasize the development of self-awareness and the construction of meaning through interpersonal relationships. With regard to young children, this is undoubtedly an extremely significant level of social awareness. Wider and more diverse cultural forms of understanding will be embedded in such interactions, and grow in significance, through member-ship or identification with different social groups, categories or positions within particular sociocultural contexts. In our study, for instance, the social identities of 'boy', 'girl' and 'pupil' took particular forms in respect of the English, middle-class location of Greenside and that of the skilled, working-class location of Albert Park. Social identities were further modified by the positioning of the children in terms of attainment and participation in schools and the positioning in families and the community.

Parents, carers, siblings and other family members also exert influence over what it means to be a pupil. Though the sources of information available to them may be weak, parents and other carers tend to maintain a constantly evolving image of their child as a pupil. This image forms as they both monitor and support the social, emotional and intellectual progress of their child. If concerns emerge, then further information will be sought and a visit to the school may take place to consult with the teacher. The image held in the family at any particular point in time offers the child a significant mirror back on themselves as a pupil. As we argued in *The Social World of Children's Learning* and *The Social World of Pupil Career*, parents are key mediators of children's experience. They assist in interpreting and making sense of new challenges – and this includes understanding oneself as a 'pupil'.

The question of 'Who is being assessed?' therefore highlights likely conceptions of the 'pupil', and one of the first challenges which any child faces on entry to his or her school is to learn the role as interpreted within that particular setting (see e.g. Jackson, 1968; Willes, 1983; Torrance and Pryor, 1998). Initially teacher guidance is likely to be very direct, with explicit attempts being made to induct new children into the established routines, procedures and rules. Individual children will respond to this in different ways. By drawing on their accumulated experience and biographical resources, they will act strategically in accommodating to the demands of the new situation. As we have seen, there are many sites of engagement as a pupil identity is developed. In relation to teachers, curricular activity, academic performance, social relationships and behaviour are likely to be particularly important. In relation to peers, participation within child culture and the development of appropriate friendships may well precede acceptance. Addition-ally, variations in the expectations and behaviour of both teachers and peers are likely in relation to gender, social class, ethnicity, etc. The resulting positioning of each child as a 'pupil' will be mediated by wider cultural and political influences and will be constantly evaluated by teachers, peers and parents. From the resulting understandings, children experience, shape and negotiate their status and sense of self as a pupil; they accomplish their 'strategic biography' (Pollard and Filer, 1999).

What then are the implications of the above analysis for teachers in the day-to-day assessment of their pupils? Certainly if we ask 'Who is being assessed?' of primary school teachers in England and Wales we can be sure of being provided with in-depth knowledge of individual pupils across a range of academic, social and extra-curricular settings in school. In addition, teachers often hold detailed knowledge of families and local communities and often have frequent contact with parents, sometimes on an almost daily basis when children are young. Furthermore, notwithstanding national requirements for 'evidence' and pressure to formalize and make transparent their assessment practices, research shows that teachers continue to value and use this kind of holistic knowledge of pupils in their day-to-day classroom assessments (Pollard *et al.*, 1994; Gipps *et al.*, 1995; Torrance and Pryor, 1998).

However, our analysis of 'identity' above leads us to raise questions concerning the nature of the holistic knowledge that teachers develop in relation to their pupils. We have analysed pupils' identities as being continuously and dynamically shaped through the complexities of biography and experience, relationships and strategies for coping in school settings. These contexts and the expectations they embody are in turn shaped by the particular teacher biographies, professional expectations and strategies for coping that are brought to day-to-day acts of assessment. In the light of this interactive complexity we are therefore led to problematize what might be involved in a teacher 'knowing' a child. Drawing on data relating to individual children's case studies and our findings from *The Social World of Pupil Career* we address this issue in the next part of this chapter.

3.3   WHAT IS INVOLVED IN KNOWING A CHILD?

Despite pressures to formalize their classroom assessment practices and the need to produce 'evidence', teacher use of 'whole child' approaches for contextualizing pupil progress and informing the next stage of teaching have remained strong (Pollard *et al.*, 1994; Torrance and Pryor, 1998). The following primary teacher's view, cited by Broadfoot (1996), illustrates the confidence that most primary teachers continue to hold in their all-round knowledge of the children that pass through their school.

> Because I think, you see, if you've already got a good team you don't need all this formalization and paper work, because we've always talked to each other and every member of staff knows every child in the school, not just by name but we know their talents and we recognize them. (Key Stage 1 teacher, Broadfoot, 1996: 72)

'Whole child' approaches to assessment not only involve direct knowledge of a pupil's attainments and efforts across a range of settings, but can also embody, explicitly or implicitly, a number of social, emotional and physical characteristics of students. In this, a vast assortment of behavioural, attitudinal, socio-economic, cultural and family characteristics often constitutes a 'social diagnosis' (Filer, 2000) in accounting for students' progress, fulfilment of potential or application to tasks. A Year 1 teacher cited by Torrance and Pryor (1998) described just such a diagnosis in relation to the possible emotional state of a pupil.

> I've got a child at the moment who's got a lot of problems at home and so I will plan an activity for that child and if that child can't see themselves to the end of the activity I record what they have achieved but I suppose I'm giving them the benefit of the doubt and thinking they could have achieved more if they hadn't been going through all these emotional turmoils at home. (Year 1 teacher, Torrance and Pryor 1998: 36)

As Torrance and Pryor suggest, to take account of previous effort and achievement, reflecting and making allowances, seems a legitimate, even laudable use of a teacher's previous knowledge of a child. However, our findings through the *Identity and Learning Programme* have led us to question what it means for a primary school teacher to 'know' the child they are assessing. What assumptions are embedded in notions of a 'whole child' approach to learning and assessment, with its suggestion of a child as a knowable entity, accessible for teacher interpretation? For instance, some of the above kinds of diagnostic judgements that teachers make have been shown to arise, and be inseparable from, particular teacher-created classroom settings (Leiter, 1974; Filer, 1993c and see Chapter 6). It is perhaps not surprising, therefore, that our longitudinal tracking of children's experience in home, playground and classroom contexts at Greenside and Albert Park School has generated a wealth of data concerning the *different ways* in which teachers 'knew' the same children. Consider, for example, three classmates at Greenside School,

William, Harriet and Robert, whose case-study stories appeared in *The Social World of Pupil Career*:

William had an autonomous, fun loving, communicative identity that was experienced and interpreted very differently by his successive teachers at Greenside School. For some teachers he was an 'ideas man' and as such seen as a stimulating challenge to teachers' own thinking and expectations. In these contexts, William's classroom identity was perceived, and valued, as integral to the learning process; his own and that of the class as a whole. For other teachers, this same autonomous, fun loving and communicative identity was variously seen as a threat to teacher–pupil relationships, as a source of ill-discipline and as a hindrance to William's own learning. Though he was always well liked by his teachers, he could be perceived as a marginally deviant, noisy nuisance in the classroom. In the latter contexts William's usual easy negotiative relationships could be transformed into critical opposition to staff and withdrawal of effort. The individuality and flair he brought to curriculum tasks in other contexts were replaced by low-risk, minimalistic response to teacher expectations.

Harriet's distinctive interests and independent identity did not often conform to classroom and playground norms. However, in classrooms where she could incorporate her out-of-school interests in horses and other animals and her imaginative identity into curriculum tasks she enjoyed school. In those contexts she liked her teachers and, importantly, felt liked and valued by them. In such classrooms her teachers viewed her as 'intelligent', 'creative' and 'co-operative'. In years when her interests and individual identity were not accommodated, she felt marginalised by a classroom and girls' peer culture with which she did not identify. In those contexts, though she remained popular with peers, she disliked school and her teachers and was convinced that teachers disliked her. Indeed this latter was to some extent true as in those classes she was viewed by her teachers with, at best incomprehension and irritability; at worst, with clear hostility. Throughout these less appreciative and less supportive contexts she was viewed by teachers as 'underachieving', 'lacking enthusiasm' and 'stubborn'.

Robert's creativity, self-direction in learning and absorption in his own learning agenda were admired by some of his teachers, valued as an inspiration to others and positively incorporated into his classroom learning. Over time, through a series of such settings, he was able to develop a distinctive pupil identity of 'computer expert' and construct for himself a supportive role in relation to other children's work. His status as 'Einstein' and 'a genius' and the approval among his peers that flowed from this role were important to Robert as he did not identify with the predominant boisterous and football orientated boys' playground culture. However, in other years Robert's qualities of self direction and independence in learning were viewed problematically by teachers and enthusiasms that diverged from set tasks and teacher expectations were curbed. These teachers variously stated that he failed to listen to, or do, what was expected of him, were somewhat disappointed with his work and contribution to classroom tasks and generally cast doubt on his reputation of being extremely able, if not 'gifted'. Curtailment of his freedom to negotiate supportive classroom roles and relationships in these contexts meant a marked loss of peer group integration and status. At home during these years, his mystified parents told of bouts of weepiness and complaints that he had 'no one to play with' at school. At the same time his teachers were of the opinion that Robert was 'a loner by choice'. (Case-study summaries based on data first published in Pollard and Filer (1999) *The Social World of Pupil Career*)

Of course, the kinds of active, independent or challenging strategies that some pupils present can cause difficulties for teachers. Certainly, as other of our case studies show, pupil conformity and the search for teacher approval are often more comfortable strategies for teachers to live with. However, it has not been the case in our longitudinal studies that particular teachers consistently succeeded in responding positively to each child's individual identity and strategies where others failed. That is to say, we found no pedagogic 'formula' for achieving rapport and understanding individual pupils across the class. Rather it was the case that different teachers *experienced* and *interpreted* the identities of individual children in different ways. For example, the Greenside children's very popular Year 4 teacher, interpreted Robert's autonomous respon-ses as belonging to a child who 'doesn't listen', 'likes to do his own thing' and 'doesn't work co-operatively with other children'. However, the same teacher enjoyed the autonomous approaches of Harriet and William. She liked Harriet's independent personality and struck a close rapport with her. She also delighted in William's communicative, humorous and autonomous approach. Important to our understandings of this difference is the fact that the curriculum in this class was organized and presented in ways that provided Harriet with plenty of opportunities to incorporate horses into her talk, reading, art work and writing. It also provided William with outlets for his humour and personality. Those same curricular and organizational frameworks, however, did not allow Robert the kind of freewheeling opportunity to follow his own agenda and *do*, *discover* or make what interested *him*. Nor did it allow him scope to establish peer relationships on *his* terms, which were necessarily different from those of his peers. What these case studies begin to illustrate, therefore, is that teachers' experiences of pupils and the different interpretation they put upon their behaviour, relationships, attitudes to work and intelligences are, in part, features of the classroom contexts that teachers themselves create. Further chapters in this book present detailed case studies of ways in which teachers' presentation of educational knowledge and the social, emotional and organizational aspects of classroom life they create can have dramatic effects upon pupils' engagement with learning and classroom relationships, and hence upon the assessments that flow from those engagements and relationships.

We have, then, begun to problematize what is involved for teachers in 'knowing' a child and thus begun to problematize 'whole child' approaches to classroom assessment. In this we have set out some of the complex sources and dynamic influences of people and settings on pupil identities and strategic responses. Might this appear to be leading to the conclusion that teachers should abandon attempts to identify the background and causes of individual pupils' underachievement or disaffection? This is certainly not the case. Indeed, a major finding from the *Identity and Learning Programme* as a whole concerns the importance of valuing and respecting children's individual identities and distinct approaches to learning. As the above examples suggest, children's case studies demonstrated the significance of allowing individual children to incorporate and maintain distinct identities within and through their classroom learning. This was especially important where a child's identity is distinctly different from, or in tension with, those of the mainstream girls', boys' or other peer cultures. These findings clearly suggest the value of teachers' attempts to understand the 'whole child' which is each pupil. In particular, our studies and others (Nicholls *et al.*, 1996; Filer, 1993b and 1997; Collins, 1996; Pollard with Filer, 1996; Pollard and Filer, 1999) suggest the particular value of trying to access the perspectives of those children who experience and present difficulties through their acts of resistance and withdrawal. These studies show that changes to aspects of the learning context or relationships that are problematic for a child can have dramatic effects upon a pupil's engagement in learning and relationships. Whilst we have observed such changes through our longitudinal case studies, the late American researcher John Nicholls actually sought to bring them about (Nicholls *et al.*, 1996). Nicholls, as researcher, liaised with a child's teacher and family in exploring the child's resistance to tasks and withdrawal from classroom relationships. Their growing understanding of the 8-year-old's sense of self informed their explorations in presenting the curriculum in ways that were personally relevant for him. Through this process, they were able to look beyond easy assumptions concerned with 'lack of ability' or 'social inadequacy' to seek more holistic understandings.

In addressing the question of 'What is involved in knowing a child?', therefore, we begin to see that there is a distinction between the 'holistic' understandings that we have problematized above and those arrived at through classroom research. What we have problematized are assumptions that knowledge of individual pupils' attitudes, motivations and emotions can be 'read off' in some straightforward way by teachers from however many classroom responses and interactions. The kind of 'holistic' knowledge described in the above research involves, rather, an *active intent* on the part of teachers to understand a child's responses and relationships *in the context of classroom settings*. That is, it involves teachers in reflection on their own practice, in accessing pupil perspectives and in a readiness to experiment. However, we acknowledge that such changes are not easy to enact where teachers have to accommodate many ever-changing demands on their time and attention. These issues and others relating to the classroom contexts which teachers create are discussed further in Chapters 6 and 10 where case-study data presents the perspective of some teachers at Albert Park School.

Finally, however, we return to the question which we posed at the beginning of section 3.2 concerning why 'identity' is important in classroom assessment. Our initial conclusions, presented above, can be summarized in the assertion of Lloyd and Duveen that

> individuals are so inextricably interwoven in the fabric of social relations within which their lives are lived, that a representation of the 'individual' divorced from the 'social' is theoretically inadequate. There is no pure 'individuality' which can be apprehended independently of social relations. (Lloyd and Duveen, 1990: 20)

To borrow the words of these authors, we can say that assessments, whether relating to pupils' achievements, their behaviour, their relationships or their attitudes to work, are quite literally 'representations of the individual'. Through Elizabeth's story (which follows) and through the subsequent chapters of this book, our aim is to show those representations of pupils as 'inextricably interwoven in the fabric of social relations' of children's and teachers' lives.

3.4   CONCLUSION

This chapter has addressed the first of our 'Questions concerning social influences on assessment', posed in Chapter 1, concerned with 'Who is being assessed?' We have explained the key importance of 'identity' in addressing this question and its core analytic role in the *Identity and Learning Programme* as a whole. We have described ways in which we have conceptualized 'identity' in our earlier writing in *The Social World of Children's Learning* and *The Social World of Pupil Career* and positioned our ideas in relation to some related work. In the second part of the chapter we described how conceptions of identity and our case-study findings led us to problematize what is involved in a teacher 'knowing' a child. This problematizing arises because such knowledge is bounded by the context and social relations through which it is formed.

The account is intended to further sensitize the reader to our theoretical interpretation and to some key issues concerned with pupils' identity, prior to engagement with the following chapter. Thus in that chapter we continue our exploration of the question 'Who is being assessed?' with an account of the assessment experience of one child, Elizabeth, and the ways in which her identity as a pupil was experienced, interpreted, shaped and maintained through her years at Albert Park Primary School.

Chapter 4

Who is being Assessed? – Elizabeth's Case Story and a Model of Assessment in a Social Context

4.1   INTRODUCTION

This is the second of a pair of chapters concerned with the question of 'Who is being assessed?' Chapter 3 represented our attempt to sensitize readers to ways in which we have theorized 'identity' in relation to individual pupils and, hence, to what might be involved in 'knowing' a child. In this chapter we track some of the social influences shaping the assessment experiences of one child, Elizabeth, through successive classroom contexts at Albert Park Primary School in order to illustrate some of the issues raised.

Of course, it is impossible to present here more than a small proportion of the data relating to seven years of Elizabeth's schooling which support our analysis. However, we also provide matrices which summarize year-by-year assessments, experiences and interpretations of Elizabeth's academic and social identity in the context of her classroom, home and peer-group relationships.

The important question concerning 'Where and when is the assessment taking place?' has been set out in Chapter 2. There we described some of the impact of extensive changes affecting all aspects of teachers' work in primary school classrooms through the period of the study. These changes were experienced at Albert Park, as they were in schools throughout the country, as challenges to teachers' ideologies, established ways of working and ways of assessing the learning of their pupils. Elizabeth's class cohort, which Ann Filer began to track for her PhD in 1989, were the first to experience the National Curriculum and its assessment provision and the first cohort to experience SATs at Key Stage 1 when they were seven years old. The impact of those changes and challenges were therefore most profoundly felt by the teachers of this year group, especially by their Year 1 and Year 2 teachers. The data relating to ways in which Elizabeth's identity, her classroom relationships and approach to classroom tasks were experienced and interpreted by teachers and the ways they recorded and reported them have to be viewed in the context of that history of change.

We conclude the chapter by presenting a model of the social influences on classroom assessment, processes and outcomes. Whilst this chapter can be read independently of Chapter 3, the theoretical perspectives and concepts which inform it, our own and those of others, are not to any great extent rehearsed again here.

4.2   WHO IS BEING ASSESSED?

Identity: potential and resources

Elizabeth was the only child of Eleanor and John Barnes who lived in an immaculately kept, small, modern terraced house, somewhat further away from Albert Road School than most of its intake. Though Elizabeth's parents had a choice of several primary schools nearer to their home, Albert Park was chosen mainly for the nostalgic and intuitive appeal that it held for Eleanor:

> There was something about Albert Park. It reminded me of the school I went to when I was four. And even the smell of the pencils! It brought everything back. I had a happy time at that school. Instead of looking at the school in a way that you think – 'Oh yes, I think Elizabeth would like this' – I was thinking more – 'Oh yes, I remember!', – you know. It made me feel comfortable. And John said, 'Well Albert Park is quite a way'. But I said, 'I think it's lovely'. And that was the reason why she went to Albert Park. I mean, isn't that awful really? (Ann Filer interview with Eleanor Barnes, December 1994)

Thus in the autumn of 1988, Elizabeth entered Barbara Joy's Reception class with about 27 other children and began her schooling at Albert Park. She was a physically healthy, attractive and lively child and assessments made during that first year relate to such characteristics, as well as to her intellectual and linguistic competence. These assessments made by Barbara Joy, as well as those of other teachers, are summarized in the first column of the matrices of Elizabeth's assessment experience presented below. Below also are examples of data extracted from Barbara's teacher records relating to a range of Elizabeth's communication, physical and intellectual skills.

> Vocabulary good – a clear ability to express herself – confident – can communicate with adults. Can concentrate and talk about her observations.
> Good language and fine motor skills – reading now enthusiastic – writing good.
> Can organise herself, is able to take turns.
>   (Profile for Nursery and Reception-age children, summer 1989, Reception)

The above offers a brief impression of some of Elizabeth's 'potential' and 'resources' with which she embarked on school life. In relation to Figure 3.1, 'three factors in identity', a third factor invites a consideration of Elizabeth's important relationships as she began school.

Identity: relationships between self and others

In contrast to the above positive expressions of Elizabeth's physical and intellectual skills, Barbara Joy perceived Elizabeth's classroom relationships in a more negative light, as her records from the time also show:

> Elizabeth is loud during class activity time – she never looks particularly happy unless doing something she shouldn't be – Elizabeth is a loud boisterous child who needs constant correction of negative behaviour. When corrected she often cries and becomes morose for a short period.
>   Elizabeth doesn't mix well with the girls and disrupts them at any given opportunity – she prefers the company of boys, particularly Adrian and Sam. This mix is not encouraged. (Teacher records, Reception, 1988–9)

In the second column of the matrix relating to Reception (see overleaf) there is a summary of some of the data relating to the relationship between Elizabeth and her parents. We see there that Eleanor describes herself as 'strict' and 'watchful' and that she was concerned for Elizabeth's

Matrix 4.1   *Elizabeth's assessment experience in Reception and Year 1: a summary matrix*

TEACHER RELATIONSHIPS AND ASSESSMENTS	FAMILY RELATIONSHIPS AND INTERPRETATIONS	PEER-GROUP RELATIONSHIPS AND INTERPRETATIONS
Reception: Mrs Joy		
Skills and progress in maths, reading and writing are 'good'. Communication skills and physical coordination also good. 'Expressive', 'vocal', 'keen', 'interested', 'able to organize her work'. Receives 'constant correction' for handwriting. Records criticize home for teaching writing in capital letters.	Mrs Barnes 'couldn't fault' teacher, feels Reception is 'home from home' for Elizabeth. Thought Elizabeth was 'a bit boisterous' and 'inclined to giggling and silliness' at school but 'not disruptive'. She understood that Elizabeth 'did what was asked of her'.	No data available from peers, but probably some disparity between the ways teacher and peers viewed Elizabeth (see below).
Teacher also views Elizabeth as 'quarrelsome', 'disruptive' with peers, especially boys, often 'morose' and 'sulky' in response to her.	Mrs Barnes sees herself as 'strict' and 'watchful', concerned for Elizabeth's behaviour and safety from the earliest age. Father more relaxed, believes 'she will be okay' and mediates to reduce friction between mother and daughter.	
Many negative views in teacher records moderated in discussion with her mother.		
Year 1: Mrs Tucker		
Class position: Ma, 3/4 the way down. Eng 1/2 way down. Enjoys number work, good powers of observation in science, expresses herself clearly and precisely, presents detailed art work, articulate and enthusiastic.	Mrs Barnes is concerned about Elizabeth's behaviour and supportive of Mrs Tucker's curbs on it.	Elizabeth enjoyed the 'noisy table' she sits at, likes to associate with those who are 'funny' and chooses friends on the basis of 'having fun'.
Teacher also sees Elizabeth as boisterous, mischievous, argumentative with peers, easily distracted. Progress 'slow'. The attraction of 'naughty boys' is seen as particularly problematic.	Mrs Barnes feels that this year was difficult for Elizabeth because of the concentration on work and curbs on 'playing about'. She supports work being sent home for Elizabeth to finish. Mother describes her as 'a joker'.	Sociable, and highly interactive, popular among girls and boys, seen as 'bossy', noisy, but nice to play with. Many see her as someone who likes them, will play with them and come to their house.
Her behaviour is accorded a low profile in the classroom, though criticized frequently in her report.		

behaviour and safety from the earliest age. She was particularly sensitive to the ways in which her daughter behaved in school. At home, in interview, she gave her views on parental responsibilities in this respect:

> It's the school's responsibility to *teach* the children, but as for behavioural – I mean, that still belongs to the parent. What a child is taught *before* it goes to school shows up when it's *at* school. I say if the parents let the child run riot before they go to school and don't show any discipline whatsoever, how can they expect that child to behave itself when it goes to school? (Eleanor Barnes, parent interview with Ann Filer, July 1994, Year 5)

Other expectations held by Elizabeth's mother related to Elizabeth's identity as a girl and a wish that she was 'more dainty' and, in the opinion of her Year 2 teacher, a wish that she could

Matrix 4.2   *Elizabeth's assessment experience in Years 2 and 3: a summary matrix*

TEACHER RELATIONSHIPS AND ASSESSMENTS	FAMILY RELATIONSHIPS AND INTERPRETATIONS	PEER-GROUP RELATIONSHIPS AND INTERPRETATIONS
Year 2: Mrs Major		
Class position: Ma, in third quartile. Eng, about halfway down. SATs results: Ma, L1; Eng, L2; Sci, L2. 'Could have reached L2 in Ma with more class work.' Detailed, precise and 'developing a flair' for art, mature in speech, interested, rhythmic, supple, imaginative.	Mrs Barnes sees this as 'not a good year' for her daughter and collaborates with Mrs Major to curb involvement with disruptive boys.	More volatile, tense relationships and disputes among children generally this year.
Publicly described as 'naughty' and 'dreadfully unfriendly', but also seen as 'very adult' and 'sensible with adults', 'exciting' for her peers and 'appreciates a joke'.	Head teacher takes the class for a term. Elizabeth is told publicly that she is 'not a nice girl'. Mrs Barnes is called in about Elizabeth's behaviour, is upset by head's attitude, embarrassed and angry with Elizabeth. At home she slaps her and is determined to 'stick with it' in battling to curb Elizabeth.	Elizabeth's behaviour is not seen as problematic by peers, though some views of her as 'naughty' and 'silly' may be a reflection of the high profile given to classroom behaviour this year.
Association with 'difficult' boys strongly disapproved of, attributed to her mother's expectations for a neat, quiet child. Mother advised to let her have more social life. New reporting style reduces comments on behaviour. Behaviour given high classroom profile and discussed frequently with mother.	Y2 represents maximum tension between Elizabeth and adults in her life.	Elizabeth appears to suffer some loss of popularity compared with other years, but continues to be well regarded by peers. Competent in the peer culture, she is 'nice to sit by', 'playful', 'sometimes silly', 'naughty'.
Year 3: Ms Luke		
Class position unchanged.	Mrs Barnes feels that Elizabeth has 'settled and improved' this year.	Elizabeth sees herself as someone teachers like chatting to. Feels she is doing 'okay', likes art, singing and writing stories. Sums are 'easy'.
Time on tasks and content are highly structured and controlled in this class and Ms Luke says Elizabeth 'always involved' and finishes her work.	Mrs Barnes regards Ms Luke as a 'strong, no nonsense' teacher who is good for Elizabeth. Mother thinks Elizabeth found her teacher a bit daunting at first but likes her.	Observations show Elizabeth's classroom relationships are unchanged. She organizes, bosses, scolds and argues with peers.
Teacher descriptions of Elizabeth now focus primarily on her social *skills*. Ms Luke sees her as 'humorous', she sees a joke that other children miss, with 'well-developed social skills', 'always smiling and involved', also 'loud'. Ms Luke does not view Elizabeth's relationships as problematic.	She continues to be supportive of Elizabeth's struggle with maths and 'talks things through with her' at home.	Continues to choose companions on basis of friendliness, play and jokes.
Home life is no longer subject to discussion or conjecture and is not considered problematic.		

have 'a neat, quiet child'. Certainly Eleanor Barnes held gendered expectations regarding the learning styles of girls and boys. Though, of course, she certainly wished for Elizabeth to do well at school, she revealed in many of her conversations in interview an expectation for a physical and intellectual passivity in girls that Elizabeth did not conform to. For instance:

Matrix 4.3   *Elizabeth's assessment experience in Years 4 and 5: a summary matrix*

TEACHER RELATIONSHIPS AND ASSESSMENTS	FAMILY RELATIONSHIPS AND INTERPRETATIONS	PEER-GROUP RELATIONSHIPS AND INTERPRETATIONS
Year 4: Mrs Robinson		
Class position: Unchanged. Mrs Robinson describes her as lively, spontaneous; 'works effectively with others', 'concentrates', work is completed, a good and effective listener, active in discussion, effective in PE teams. No problems. Finishes work and also 'has a laugh'.	Mrs Barnes continues to closely monitor Elizabeth's behaviour, both through close observation and questioning of Elizabeth and through discussions with Mrs Robinson.	Elizabeth worries about maths, and about her academic identity vis-à-vis peers and being on low maths book. She wishes she could do PE all the time.
Mrs Robinson is a maths specialist and identifies Elizabeth's difficulty with maths as a lack of understanding rather than lack of application.	Mrs Barnes has ongoing discussions about Elizabeth's maths with teacher and helps her at home.	Friends like to work with Elizabeth because she is 'funny' and 'clever' and she will help.
Mrs Robinson says Elizabeth's mother comes into classroom, organizes her books for her and is reluctant to leave. She reassures Mrs Barnes that she had a daughter the same and that it was no problem.	If Elizabeth gets a 'warning' within school assertive discipline scheme, she gets punished at home.	
Year 5: Ms Luke		
Class position: Ma, about two-thirds down class. Eng, about halfway down. Sci, about two-thirds way down.	Elizabeth is one of the earliest in the class to physically mature. Her mother would like her to be 'more dainty' but accepts that that is not Elizabeth's style. She feels children grow up too soon. Her father thinks she needs more freedom.	Seen as 'definitely a leader' by peers, as 'bossy' and 'talks a lot in class' and 'gets what she wants'. She claims to dislike boys but often chats and jokes with them.
Again much classwork is highly structured in content and pacing by Ms Luke and Elizabeth 'completes most things on time' and is 'increasingly confident in maths'. Continues 'expressive and fluent' in reading.	Monitoring of classroom behaviour by Mrs Barnes and discussion with teacher continues. Mother is supportive of national tests, feels they are informative regarding strengths and weaknesses.	A splintering of a large friendship group occurs. Some academically 'more serious' and 'responsible' girls with high teacher as well as peer status break from Elizabeth's group who 'like a laugh'.
Ms Luke says she lacks confidence if she doesn't know what she's doing.		
Ms Luke says Elizabeth 'needs her friends' and doesn't want to look foolish in their eyes. She also sees her as 'outspoken' to peers, can be 'hurtful' and 'loud'.	Elizabeth does not read her reports but they are relayed to her by her parents.	

> I mean, in some ways I think she should have been a boy because she's got so much *energy*, and she just wants to know about *everything* – How does this work? Why does it work like that? What do you do with this? – I mean, probably that is *her*. That is her personality. She wants to know everything and she wants to know what everybody else is doing. (Eleanor Barnes, parent interview with Ann Filer, July 1995, Year 6)

Several key factors therefore shaped Eleanor Barnes' response to the assessments that began to emerge from school and, in turn, to affect her ongoing relationship with Elizabeth. These factors were concerned with her high expectation for good behaviour, perhaps to be reflected in a more

Matrix 4.4 *Elizabeth's assessment experience in Year 6: a summary matrix*

TEACHER RELATIONSHIPS AND ASSESSMENTS	FAMILY RELATIONSHIPS AND INTERPRETATIONS	PEER-GROUP RELATIONSHIPS AND INTERPRETATIONS
Year 6: Mrs Hutton Class position over year: just above average. TA: Ma, L3. Eng, L4. Sci, L4. SATs: Ma, L3 (about one-third the way down the class). Eng L4 (average for class). Sci, L5 (in top 5). Elizabeth is 'capable but hard to motivate' and 'needs channelling'. Mrs Hutton sees her as 'lively', 'cheerful', 'strong willed' and also 'rude'. She reprimands her often for muttered comments and complaints. She is 'loyal to friends', will 'stick up for herself', is concerned for her academic identity vis-à-vis peers and being made fun of. Like the Reception teacher, Mrs Hutton minimizes classroom conflicts with Elizabeth in reporting to parents.	Mrs Barnes feels Elizabeth is too honest to be devious. Mrs Barnes says Elizabeth knows she always finds out if her 'name gets on the board' and will go in to see Mrs Hutton. Mrs Barnes is told by Mrs Hutton that Elizabeth spends too much time perfecting illustrations. Mrs Barnes tells her 'That's not what they want. Move on. Speed up.' Practice given at home for national testing in maths. Elizabeth's anxiety high before the maths test. Mrs Barnes thinks she may be 'too demanding, too protective'.	Elizabeth continues to choose friends for 'funniness' and 'a laugh', 'messing around', but also for 'getting help' and 'good ideas'. Elizabeth thinks she is 'only good at story writing, technology and drawing'. She says 'Mrs Hutton thinks I'm rubbish at everything'. Peers like to work with her because she helps, she 'likes to make things perfect', is 'good at technology', 'artistic' and cooperative. She is also described as flirtatious with boys, cheeky with teachers, 'more confident than other girls', someone who 'gets batey', 'tough', 'a leader', 'bold' and confident.

'girl-like' identity, and a tendency to feel directly responsible for, and to closely supervise, Elizabeth's behaviour at school. We shall see through the chapter some ways in which these factors were brought into play and affected mother–daughter relationships.

In similar ways, of course, teachers' varying expectations for pupils' behaviour, and for girls, also shaped their relationships with Elizabeth. As suggested in Barbara Joy's records above, gendered expectations for appropriate behaviour for a girl negatively affected her relationship with Elizabeth. Indeed, through Elizabeth's early years of schooling, her attraction towards some of the 'naughty boys' in the class was regarded as particularly inappropriate and a cause of disruption. This observation came from Elizabeth's Year 1 report to parents.

> Elizabeth is a capable little girl who can work well, however she tends to be boisterous and argumentative with her peers, especially the boys. She is keen and enthusiastic but unfortunately her tendency to play about and to be disruptive means she has to be nagged/bribed to complete tasks. (Marie Tucker, report to parents, Year 1)

However, teacher and pupil purposes in classrooms are often in conflict and it was the case that Elizabeth and her peers perceived their relationships somewhat differently from their early years' teachers. Certainly Elizabeth was often observed to be involved with others in a good deal of 'off task' play, chat, teasing and argumentative interaction. Here Becky is being asked about working on what children called 'the noisy table' (see Chapter 6).

AF   What is it like working in that group?
Becky   Well, Jane and Elizabeth, they keep bossing me about when I'm doing my colouring, and Simon. And they keep gossiping when I'm trying to do my work and I don't like them gossiping with me. Ricky and Katie don't gossip with me. Simon, Elizabeth and Jane and Nathan calls me names.

(Individual pupil interviews, summer 1990, Y1)

Despite the arguments and 'bossiness', Elizabeth was generally perceived by her peers to be lively, fun and a good friend. Sociometric interviews designed to gather information relating to who children would choose to work with across a range of classroom activities indicated Elizabeth's classroom popularity to be well above the average in the class. It also indicated that she was the most popular of the girls because, of course, she was nominated by boys as well as girls. Some reasons for liking to work with Elizabeth included:

> Because she's my friend and she likes me.
> 'Cos she's nice and plays with me in the playground.
> (Sam)

> Because I like the dresses she wears.
> 'Cos she plays with me in the playground.
> (Katie)

> Because she likes coming over my house all the time.
> Because she likes me.
> (Stuart)

> (Sociometric interviews with individual children, January 1990, Year 1)

In Elizabeth's stated preferences for companions in interview, she reciprocated other children's choices with regard to playing together and liking. However, in addition, fun, laughter and general enjoyment of classroom life were important to Elizabeth. Such priorities, evidenced in her classroom preferences, were likely to win popularity with peers, though to be less appreciated by teachers. For example, Sam and Adrian, two particular friends cited here by Elizabeth, was the 'mix' that, as we have seen above, was 'not encouraged' by her Reception teacher:

> (Sam) 'Cos I like him very much and have lots of fun with him.
> (Katie) 'Cos she's funny and she plays with me as well. She keeps laughing and playing jokes.
> (Adrian) 'Cos he's funny. He tells me lots of things. 'Cos Adrian's brilliant.
> (Elizabeth, sociometric interviews with individual children, January 1990, Year 1)

As readers will begin to appreciate, Elizabeth was vulnerable to a good deal of criticism and correction from teachers though her early years at Albert Park. In multiple ways, but most particularly in her relationships with teachers and peers, she contravened teacher expectations for pupils, especially for *girl* pupils. Membership of the peer group is important for children for the solidarity it offers in countering their vulnerability in classroom settings, as well as for the enjoyment it offers. However, pupil 'interests-at-hand' (Pollard, 1985; see Figure 5.1) in this are often in tension with those of teachers and their requirements for order, control and the enjoyment of *their* work. Such tensions go a long way towards explaining the disparity between teacher and children's perceptions of Elizabeth in relation to her peers. Some of the disparity between teacher and peer perceptions of Elizabeth's relationships can also be accounted for in their differing gendered expectations and interpretations of her identity as a girl. These issues are further discussed below in relation to 'What is being assessed?'

In this section we have considered 'Who is being assessed?'; issues relating to Elizabeth's identity and important relationships through her early years of schooling. As we go on to consider some of her later teachers' perceptions of her identity and relationships, issues connected with the question of 'Who is assessing?' come to the fore.

4.3   WHO WAS ASSESSING ELIZABETH?

As we can see in those early assessments of Elizabeth, in addition to judgements relating to pupils' academic attainments and progress, teachers also form judgements concerning a range of attitudinal, psychological, motor, motivational and social factors considered to affect that attainment and progress. Indeed, the content of this kind of 'social diagnosis' (Filer, 2000) will frequently extend beyond the classroom to include aspects of home and indeed the wider community (see also Chapters 3 and 6). Inevitably, some of these wider contexts and their effects will be evaluated on the basis of incomplete factual, social or cultural knowledge on the part of teachers. Clearly, the greater difficulty a pupil is considered to be experiencing in relation to the social or academic expectations of school, the more of the pupil's physical, sociocultural and emotional identity will be perceived to be legitimate areas of enquiry and the more formalized will be the assessment process surrounding such enquiry. However, as we showed in relation to the studies of Greenside pupils in Chapter 3, teachers experience and interpret pupils' behaviour differently. In part this is a consequence of individual pupils responding differently to the curricular and social contexts that different teachers create. Similarly, what physical, socio-cultural or emotional factors are considered to be problematic and whether 'remedies' will be explored will vary from teacher to teacher, and often from school to school. Thus the issues in 'Who is assessing?' relate to the professional and sociocultural sources of teachers' perceptions and expectations, as well as to their day-to-day interests-at-hand in classrooms. We discuss such issues concerned with the origins and background to teachers' pedagogies and their affects on classroom assessments in Chapters 5 and 6. However, here we can briefly consider some further differences among Elizabeth's teachers with regard to aspects of her identity they assessed as problematic, to be monitored, curbed or remedied.

As we have described, through her early school years Elizabeth's relationships with her peers, and particularly with the 'naughty boys' (see Chapter 6), was considered most problematic and a cause of lack of concentration and progress and disruptive to the class generally. Her home life was included in the formal diagnosis of the perceived problem and shaped discussions with her mother about the quality of her parenting and suggested remedies. When asked in interview about Elizabeth's progress, her Year 2 teacher told about such discussions with Eleanor Barnes:

> She is quite a bright little girl. In truth, I think she is frustrated by her home background and Mum's under the neuro surgeon at the hospital. I do know that. She definitely sees a specialist about something. She has terrific headaches and whatever, but I don't know. So Elizabeth has a lot of confinement at home. Mum doesn't like having other children (to play). . . . But Mum said 'Well, is she going to grow up to be a *boy*? You know she just only wants to play with the boys.' I said (to Eleanor Barnes) 'Well, to my way of thinking, the boys provide that kind of activity and exciting play that she craves, that she doesn't have at home'. (Peggy Major , teacher interview with Ann Filer, July 1991, Year 2)

Peggy also described how she had been encouraging Eleanor to expand Elizabeth's social life, by enrolling her in the Brownies for instance.

It can be seen from the matrices, however, that although Elizabeth's peer relationships, the way she was viewed by peers and her style of interaction with them, remained virtually unchanged, that same behaviour was not regarded as especially problematic by her subsequent teachers. In Years 3, 4 and 5, her teachers were more likely to identify any lack of application as stemming from lack of understanding and lack of confidence on Elizabeth's part than from social or relationship problems. This change of diagnosis meant, of course, that in those later years her home life and relationship with her mother was no longer subject to scrutiny and conjecture. The great reduction of these kinds of social assessments in school documentation can, of course, be accounted for by pressure to remove them from recording and reporting. Records, often in the form of ticked boxes, based on 'evidence' and carefully worded reports to parents were now replacing the 'frequently generalised laconic statements' (Alexander *et al.*, 1992) that parents had traditionally received (see e.g., Elizabeth's reports in Figure 12.1). However, as we discussed in Chapter 3, research findings show that, though they may no longer record them formally, such 'whole child' and often intuitive forms of assessment have not disappeared from teachers' classroom assessment practices (see also Chapter 5). Of course, our studies show that neither had they disappeared from Albert Park or Greenside School. Rather it was the case that Elizabeth's teachers perceived and interpreted her classroom behaviour in ways that were different from her early years teachers. In interviews with Ann Filer, for example, teachers no longer made gendered observations regarding Elizabeth's behaviour and relationships. Also Jenny Luke, Elizabeth's Year 3 and Year 5 teacher, experienced it differently. In Jenny's class, as in many classes at Albert Park School, tasks were highly 'routinized' (Pollard, 1985) and structured. In addition, however, they were also paced on a whole class basis, with regular reminders that children should be 'finishing' and 'moving on'. Different teacher approaches to the organization of tasks do, of course, have a range of impacts on children's learning and their strategies for approaching or avoiding tasks (see Chapters 6 and 10). Nevertheless, from Year 3 Elizabeth began to get tasks finished on time and, as we have seen, any lack of progress or application was attributed to different causes.

In Year 6, Elizabeth's social relationships were again a cause of concern, though not her peer relationships. There were frequent conflictual exchanges between Pat Hutton, the Year 6 teacher, and Elizabeth. Pat identified this as a problem in Elizabeth's relationships with adults generally around the school, with 'dinner ladies' for example. She guessed that this might have been 'because of her age', being the first of the girls to begin to mature physically. Pat Hutton found Elizabeth capable but hard to motivate, slow working and in need of 'channelling'.

As we discussed in Chapter 3, primary school teachers do have a wide knowledge of their pupils. They observe their pupils in a range of social as well as academic settings and activities. They see them interacting with peers and other adults, they usually know their families, and often siblings, perhaps over a number of years. They are frequently privy to personal knowledge regarding their pupils' family circumstances and particular health, social or economic difficulties. Inevitably teachers use such 'whole child' knowledge as they have in attempts to diagnose, intervene or 'make allowances' in the process of forming judgements about their pupils' progress, attainments and needs. However, like the careers of Greenside children summarized in Chapter 3, Elizabeth's longitudinal data also problematizes what is involved in a teacher 'knowing' a child. In posing the question of 'Who is assessing?' therefore, we begin to be concerned with *teachers* as individuals. Thus in Chapters 5 and 6 we explore further the professional and biographical experiences which shape teachers' pedagogies and the assessment contexts they create in individual ways.

4.4   HOW WERE ASSESSMENTS OF ELIZABETH INTERPRETED AND MEDIATED?

Teacher control of assessments

Issues concerned with interpretation and mediation relate to ways in which teachers' original assessments are often subject to transformative processes before they recursively affect pupils' self-perceptions and relationships. Beyond the usual requirements upon them to record and report curricular attainment, teachers will exercise control over, and mediate, a range of judgements that may or may not reach pupils, their peers, parents and other professionals. For example, some of the earliest teacher records relating to Elizabeth noted:

> Elizabeth didn't attend our playschool (Albert Road nursery class) and she is, in fact, still going through the settling in period. Elizabeth can be disruptive during story and discussion time and she is loud during class activity time. She never looks particularly happy unless she is doing something she shouldn't. Elizabeth doesn't mix well with the girls in the class and disrupts them at any given opportunity. (Barbara Joy, teacher records, November 1988, Reception)

Barbara Joy's records for that year express many similarly negative opinions of Elizabeth. However, perhaps having given expression to some frustration in the context of school records, it seems that Barbara considerably moderated her response in discussion with Elizabeth's parents. Parents did not receive written reports in the Reception year, however, Eleanor Barnes' recall of Barbara Joy's assessment of Elizabeth was somewhat at variance with teacher records at the time:

> She settled in very well and did everything that was asked of her. I can remember her teacher saying to me that she was a bit boisterous, not disruptive but if there was any giggling or silliness going on, Elizabeth was amongst them. (Eleanor Barnes, parent diary, autumn 1993, recalling Reception)

Moreover, this is unlikely to be a case of forgetfulness on Eleanor's part or of her putting a retrospective gloss on events in responding to a researcher's question. Eleanor was never reluctant to recall and discuss at length the ups and downs of her daughter's relationships with teachers.

In Years 1 and 2, on the other hand, teachers gave prominence to Elizabeth's classroom behaviour in reporting and discussion with her parents. However, the two teachers were very different with respect to the public prominence they gave that behaviour in the classroom, before an audience of peers (and before Filer as researcher). It was probably a reflection of the Year 1 teacher's reputation for being good with 'the problems' (see Chapter 6) that Elizabeth's behaviour and her behaviour as a *girl* were accorded a low profile in that classroom. However, in Year 2, teacher definitions of Elizabeth's academic as well as her social identity became very obvious to peers, and to her parents, on a day-to-day basis. For instance, Peggy Major was more verbal than Marie Tucker in identifying miscreants in the classroom. Public criticism of Elizabeth, before her peers, by her teacher and the head teacher that year identified her as variously 'naughty', 'dreadfully unfriendly' and 'not a nice girl'. In addition, highly visible systems of rewards and encouragements identified the best and the slowest, more distractable pupils that year. For instance, a 'crown' to wear home and a very large star pinned on the chest identified 'best worker' for the day. At the other end of the scale, Elizabeth and some other children were issued with 'programme books' in which they had their tasks for the day set out. They worked for 'stars' in the book (not on their chest) as tasks were accomplished and unfinished work had to be taken home.

The following observation was made early in the autumn term of Year 2, shortly after the reward systems had been introduced. In it, the meaning attaching to the 'programme book' is being batted around among the children. First Elizabeth makes a failed attempt to identify it as a status symbol. Katie, her friend with whom she has just had cross words, uses it to put Elizabeth down, identifying it as for people who are not 'good', unlike her. Peter, towards whom Elizabeth has just been helpful and friendly, appears to be attempting to save Elizabeth's face by identifying it as a precautionary measure.

> *Elizabeth starts work on a maths card. Peter comes to her side for a brief conversation before returning to his seat opposite her.*

Elizabeth   (To Peter) Do you need any help?
Elizabeth has a brief inaudible conversation with Peter before returning to her work. Three minutes later she announces:
Elizabeth   I'll tidy up the table. I hate a mess.
She busies herself, moving Katie's box of shapes and straightening the pencil tray. Katie, irritated, grabs the box of shapes that she has been using and puts it back where it was.
Elizabeth   (Scolding Katie) Put it over on your own side then.
Elizabeth removes another tray from the table, puts it under the table, then returns it to the maths corner. She returns to her work briefly before telling Becky:
Elizabeth   I can't get on with this, and I can't get on with you talking.
Elizabeth stands an exercise book – her 'programme book' – on end on the table, as if creating a barrier between herself and the others. Katie peers at the book to see what it is. Elizabeth tells her:
Elizabeth   It's a programme book. You haven't even got one.
Katie   I haven't got a programme book because I've been good.
Peter   You have a programme book just in case.
Elizabeth   (To Peter) Yeah, I'm trying to get on with my work but Becky's talking all the time.
This is followed by some chat and jokes with Peter about screwing ears off so she can't hear and sticking pencils in ears.
Elizabeth chats, plays, teases and argues with other children on the table in similar vein for the next twenty minutes. Then Peggy Major, who has been working with other groups, comes over to the table.
Peggy Major   Have you finished that page Elizabeth?
Elizabeth   No.
Peggy Major   Well you won't get a star today then, will you?

(Ann Filer, fieldnotes, October 1990, Year 2)

In many ways, therefore, Year 2 was not a good year for Elizabeth. However, as we described in Chapter 3, findings from our longitudinal data from both schools show that as cohorts moved through successive classroom contexts, aspects of teacher-created environments affected different children in different ways. In Chapter 10, for instance, we can see that for Peter (above) the change from Marie's Year 1 class to Peggy's Year 2 class had a very powerful and *positive* affect on his classroom language and on his confidence.

Parental mediation and interpretation of assessments

We referred above to teachers' reward and motivational systems but, of course, parents are also involved in rewarding, in encouraging or discouraging behaviours and in attributing success and failure. Therefore children's socialization into school and their classroom strategies and motivation will be shaped by family culture, relationships and expectations, as well as those of the school and individual teachers (see *The Social World of Children's Learning* and *The Social World of Pupil Career*). Evaluations will further be made by parents of teachers' and schools' assessment practices in decisions to support, ignore, contest or offer alternative interpretations to the child.

In the case of Eleanor Barnes, support for the teacher's opinion was such that differences in teacher reporting tended to be interpreted by her as reflecting changes in Elizabeth herself, or at least in her objective behaviour. Perhaps because of her relative isolation from other parents she tended not to show the same levels of judicious scepticism that many parents were prepared to bring to the pronouncements made on their children's character. In relation to their own child, most parents were aware that some teachers were likely to 'get the best out of her' where others were less successful. In other words, there was a reciprocal assessment of individual teachers in relationship with their child, in interpreting and mediating teacher reports. However, for Eleanor Barnes, the high profile given to Elizabeth's behaviour in Year 2 was interpreted as reflecting an objective change in Elizabeth's behaviour, rather than a response to Elizabeth by a particular teacher. This interpretation of the situation certainly had repercussions for her relationship with her daughter as her concerns rose:

> and of course, particularly that year (Year 2) was a terrible time. I was in there every five minutes. I mean, it was embarrassing because people thinking – well I shouldn't really worry about what people think, but you can't help it when you're the same mum being called into the classroom. But it was just silliness and giggling and things like that ... and well, the times when we'd got home and we sat there and *talked*, I mean, I must admit, one time I even slapped her because I was so cross. I slapped her on the back of the legs. I felt awful because I was thinking I shouldn't have to be doing this. But either she didn't want to know or she didn't care. Anyway, I thought, well, I'm not having that sort of attitude so I stuck with it and I thought – you're not going to get the better of me, young lady. (Eleanor Barnes recalling Year 2, parent interview with Ann Filer, July 1994)

Peer mediation of assessments

The impact of the academic and social assessments which teachers make will also be mediated by those of peers who will provide alternative sources of identity. Indeed, as we have seen, the ways in which Elizabeth's peers and teachers interpreted her classroom relationships was often at variance. Elizabeth was certainly often observed to be argumentative, scolding and distracting with peers, yet this behaviour, seen by her early years teachers as problematic with regard to peer relationships, was not altogether viewed as such by peers. Typical peer views of Elizabeth in Year 2 were, as we have described, that 'she is nice to sit by' and 'playful' (Year 2). Nevertheless, probably as a result of the high profile accorded to her classroom behaviour, analysis of sociometric interviews did suggest a slight loss of popularity for Elizabeth compared with other years. Also some peers did identify Elizabeth as 'naughty' and 'silly' that year.

In Chapters 11 and 12, we elaborate in more detail the multidimensional and dynamic processes involved in the interpretation and mediation of classroom assessment. In the following section, however, we see how some of this dynamic worked out in relation to Elizabeth's academic as well as her social identity, and outcomes. There we also discuss peer mediation more fully in relation to the question of 'What is being assessed? to which it also has particular relevance.

4.5   WHAT IS BEING ASSESSED?

In answering the question 'What is being assessed? we consider ways in which Elizabeth's responses to classroom tasks drew on a wider field of action than that posed by teacher expectations. Many of Elizabeth's classroom responses to tasks took place simultaneously with her need to maintain important friendship relationships and her sense of self among peers. However, this well-understood dynamic of classroom life can have a positive as well as a negative influence on pupils' responses. That is to say that some responses, embedded in the values of the peer culture, may accord with teacher expectations for behaviour and tasks and enhance assessment outcome. At other times they can conflict with them and detract from assessment outcomes.

For instance, peer admiration of Elizabeth's art work and presentation skills conflicted with teacher concerns that she spent too much time perfecting illustrations of her work. However, for Elizabeth as for other schoolchildren carving out an acceptable identity involves displaying competencies in skills that are valued in the peer culture (Woods, 1983; Pollard, 1985). On the one hand, therefore, her mother was supporting teacher urgings with 'That's not what they want. You've got to move on, speed up.' On the other hand, her peers' obvious admiration for her art work and for the fact that 'she likes to make things perfect' were a vital source of status and affirmation for an aspect of her identity which was important to her.

Similarly her boisterous associations with 'naughty boys' in early years was a source of much conflict for Elizabeth with her early teachers and with her mother. As described in Chapter 3, however, friendship support and approval are necessary to pupils in a vulnerable classroom situation. They were also likely to have provided a powerful counter incentive in the face of teacher and mother's attempts to modify her identity as a girl. Peers did not describe or react to her behaviour in gendered terms. In those early years her behaviour was simply identified as 'playful' and 'funny'. Certainly in later years, peers' descriptions of her as 'tough', 'a leader', 'cheeky', 'someone who gets batey' and 'more confident than other girls' were signals of admiration and respect for her as a *girl*. This was so among girls and boys and, as such, an important source of power and status in the peer group. That peer relationships were a strong factor in shaping her classroom responses was recognized by teachers. Her Year 6 teacher, for instance, saw her as 'loyal and supportive of friends' but 'hard to motivate by teachers'.

However, as suggested above, demands upon Elizabeth in the maintenance of peer relationships could also coincide with teacher expectations and requirements for tasks. In later years, for instance, her struggle with areas of the curriculum in which she was weaker, such as mathematics, was seen by one teacher as a concern for her academic image in the eyes of her peers. Peers saw her as generally clever and helpful to them and mathematics was an area that represented a particular threat to that image. In Chapter 8 the social contexts of children's responses in their Year 3 'news' sessions is examined. There it can be seen that Elizabeth's awareness of peers as an audience for her 'news' coincided with her teacher's expectations for 'speaking and listening' skills. Whilst Elizabeth, of all the children, engaged most directly, warmly and entertainingly with her peers in those sessions, this was not in response to any teacher instruction. Rather attention to her peers and concern for their responses were enduring contexts which, in this, happened to powerfully and positively influence assessments of her classroom language and communication skills.

Thus we can begin to appreciate that a key issue involved in the question 'What is being assessed?' concerns the social and cultural contexts within which pupils' assessed responses are located.

4.6   HOW DID ASSESSMENT FUNCTION IN ELIZABETH'S LIFE?

In considering the functions of assessment in Elizabeth's schooling, it might first be useful to consider the nature of assessment outcomes for Elizabeth through successive classroom contexts. Through the above synopsis of her career we have expressed outcomes in terms of her evolving identity and self-esteem as a pupil and as a girl, her evolving classroom status and relationships among teachers, peers and within the family and her evolving approaches to academic tasks. All of these social or behavioural outcomes accompanied, and were in dynamic relationship with, assessment outcomes concerning attainment and progress levels, etc. These in turn, of course, culminated in particular 'high stakes' SAT and Teacher Assessment scores at the end of Key Stage 2 (see Matrix 4.4 on p. 41).

Bearing in mind then the interrelation between social and academic outcomes, what can we say about the way assessment functioned in Elizabeth's life? As we have described in Chapter 3, in addition to its ostensible role in supporting learning and monitoring outcomes, classroom assessment is also used as a means of socializing children into school life, especially in the early years (Torrance and Pryor, 1998). We can see this early socializing process in Elizabeth's career whereby, as well as being concerned with her academic progress, teacher assessments and parental support for them were highly concerned with monitoring and supporting her adaptation to school expectations. Such socializing processes are of course also closely linked to issues of control and the maintenance of a classroom environment in which teachers can teach and pupils can learn. Thus the socializing and control functions of assessment in Elizabeth's case would have been concerned with her teachers' interests-at-hand and with other children's learning as much as with Elizabeth's development as a pupil. As we have seen though, assessment of Elizabeth's behaviour and relationships went beyond straightforward conceptions of her as a *pupil*. Socialization into appropriate pupil behaviour included attempts by teachers and her mother to socialize her as a *girl pupil*. Elizabeth's case makes explicit some of the gendered norms and values that can remain implicit in assessments of pupils' behaviour unless a pupil persistently contravenes them. One of the functions of assessment in Elizabeth's life, therefore, was in providing a form of communication through which gender expectations were shared and communicated among Elizabeth's teachers, parents and her peers. Whilst implicit norms relating to gender were made explicit here, other norms and values relating to culture and ethnicity of pupils similarly remain implicit until challenged. For example, Adams (1997), writing within the US context, presents the case study of a white adolescent girl, Sharon, who contravened gender and racial norms. Sharon's toughness and powerful identification with black gang culture gave rise to sustained criticism, in approaches to her mother and before her peers, as teachers tried to re-socialize her into an appropriate pupil identity. As Adams puts it:

> Embedded in the pervasive rhetoric of schooling is the assumption that schools are apolitical sites where identity-less students gather, absorb the same information, and share the same opportunities to succeed. (Adams 1997: 153)

Reviewing again the question of 'Who is being assessed?' we might consider that Elizabeth's resources and potential with regard to her physical and healthy attractiveness and liveliness and her linguistic, physical and artistic skills were characteristics and competencies that were likely to have been highly valued within the peer group. Indeed our data indicates that that many of them were. It is likely also that these resources would, for her peers, considerably outweigh some of the more contentious characteristics which accompanied them and which tended to dominate the perceptions of her early teachers. However, Elizabeth's case study also reveals the ambivalence nearly all her teachers felt regarding her social identity. For instance, of all her teachers, her Year 2 teacher made the most overt and strenuous attempt to curb Elizabeth's social behaviour as a pupil. Whilst, as a teacher, strenuously socializing Elizabeth into the pupil role, Peggy Major as an *adult* appreciated Elizabeth's *adult* behaviour and ability to appreciate a joke. She recognized that Elizabeth was attractive to her peers, that she was exciting and funny. On the one hand, her liveliness, boldness, strong will, lack of conformity and her well-developed sense of humour made for an extremely vital and attractive *social* identity. On the other hand, for her teachers and mother, they also stood in the way of an acceptable *pupil* identity, as well, is some respects, as an appropriate identity for a pupil who was also a girl. At this point we will leave readers to ponder the nature of schooling in general that these contradictions should exist, and to consider also the role of school assessments, of all kinds, in mediating them.

4.7   WHAT SOCIAL FACTORS AFFECTED ASSESSMENT PRACTICES AND OUTCOMES FOR ELIZABETH? – A THEORETICAL MODEL

The model in Figure 4.1 bears a direct relationship to the 'Questions concerning social influences on assessment' which were posed in Chapter 1 and summarized in Figure 1.1. It also bears a direct relationship to the text of this chapter which has explored the issues embedded in the questions, and especially in the question of 'Who is being assessed?' The model is an expression of recursive cycles in which identity, teacher practices, peer and family cultures and the interpretations and mediations of teachers, family and peers feed into, reinforce and condition each other. Importantly, of course, the micro processes of pupil and teacher identities, practices and interpretations are embedded in macro socio-historical and political contexts which shape the policies of schools and the perceptions and expectations of teachers and families.

As in a model of a similar structure developed for *The Social World of Children's Learning* and *The Social World of Pupil Career*, the recursive cycles represent the analytic insights generated through longitudinal tracking of pupils' identity, learning and careers as pupils. Here the model can be seen as an abstraction of the details of Elizabeth's experience over the seven years. As with the original model, it can be seen in terms of a major cycle through each year or as informing innumerable cycles through which assessment processes and outcomes influenced Elizabeth's identity and relationships. Whatever the time frame, whether that of major or minor cycles, the factors in play remain the same.

4.8   CONCLUSION

In this chapter we have explored further issues relating to our basic 'Questions concerning social influences on assessment' through data relating to Elizabeth and an analysis of some assessment processes that shaped important outcomes for her as a pupil. At the same time, through this case study, we have been able to present some substantive data and analysis to illustrate our theoretical approaches to the question of 'Who is being assessed?' The issues raised in addressing the questions have enabled us to present a model (Figure 4.1) of assessment in a social context. The case-study data and analysis here also serve to further illustrate an issue raised in Chapter 3, where we problematized what might be involved in a teacher 'knowing' a child. More detailed accounts of some of the pedagogic, peer group and classroom assessment contexts referred to in Elizabeth's case study are to be found in Chapters 6, 8 and 10.

Subsequent pairs of chapters in this book will follow a similar pattern of a theoretical chapter followed by a substantive chapter, informed by case studies of teachers, pupils and families. These chapters will enable us to illustrate wider teacher, peer group and family perspectives relating to the model than those of one pupil; the 'who' that has been the focus of this chapter. They will include teacher perspectives on factors shaping their professional practice and perspectives on the sociocultural sources of children's classroom responses and teacher judgements. In connection with the social, as well as academic processes that classroom assessment accomplishes, we look at the role of classroom language and the framing of educational knowledge in shaping pupil responses and learning. We complete our elaboration of the model

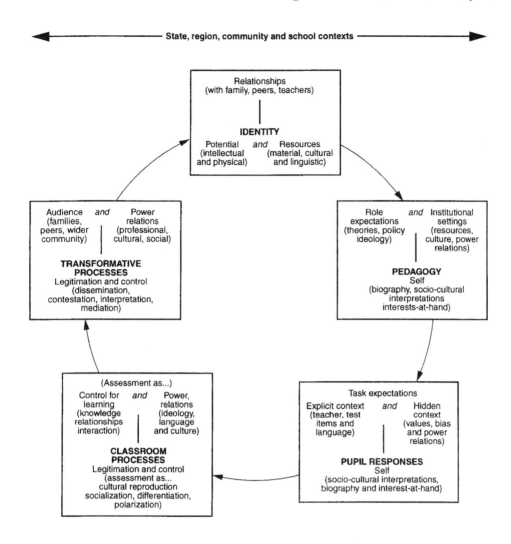

Figure 4.1   *A model of assessment in a social context*

with a consideration of assessment as a multidimensional process in which teachers, parents and pupils are both 'audiences' and actors. That is, they are both assessors and assessed in the mediation and interpretation of classroom assessments.

As with the case-study issues set out in this chapter, so the 'questions' in the model are inextricably interrelated. For instance, we noted in Chapter 3 that we could not address issues of pupil identity without considering ways in which different pupils' identities were experienced and interpreted by particular teachers. Thus each pair of chapters will provide further comparative contexts for considering the model as a whole and for further illuminating each case-study chapter. The data in the chapters relate predominately to Albert Park School. However, we also draw on data relating to Greenside School and on the analysis and findings from the *Identity and Learning Programme* as a whole. Thus, whilst theoretically extending our earlier studies, the following chapters also invite comparisons with the classroom, school and community contexts of a socio-economically different suburb of Easthampton.

Part Three

Elaborating

Chapter 5

Who is Assessing? – An Introduction

5.1   INTRODUCTION

Through previous chapters we have problematized what is involved for a teacher in 'knowing' a child. Drawing on our longitudinal case studies we showed how, for assessment purposes, the 'whole child' is the 'child in context'. Therefore, we argued, a reciprocal understanding is needed of the distinctive nature of teachers' individual practices and their perceptions of pupils, combined with the differentiated nature of pupils' responses within a given classroom context. Thus in relation to our 'Questions concerning social influences on assessment', 'Who is being assessed?' needs to be followed by addressing the question; 'Who is assessing?' In the following pair of chapters, therefore, we extend our analysis of the social contexts of classroom assessment set out in Figure 4.1 with a focus on 'pedagogy'.

Our account of pedagogy in this chapter shows ways in which 'teacher identity' is constructed through a synthesis of the internal and personal concerns of the individual with the external influences of culture and expectations of appropriate groups within the wider society. We model this 'internal–external dialect' (Jenkins, 1996: 171) using the concept of 'coping strategies' which attempts to analyse the relationship between macro socio-political analysis and micro perspectives of individual teachers and school settings. We illustrate that process with research findings regarding the personal and the contextually specific ways in which teachers integrate national assessment requirements into their existing practices and manage the contradictions and constraints involved.

Thus this chapter builds on and complements our analysis of 'identity' in relation to pupils presented in previous chapters. It is also intended to sensitize readers to our theoretical modelling of 'pedagogy' prior to engagement with the case study in Chapter 6. That second of this pair of chapters illustrates the personal and highly contextual nature of a Year 1 teacher's practice at Albert Park School. This chapter also provides a background to that study, enabling readers to contextualize the teacher's perceptions and experiences within the wider framework of contemporary and ongoing experience in English primary schools.

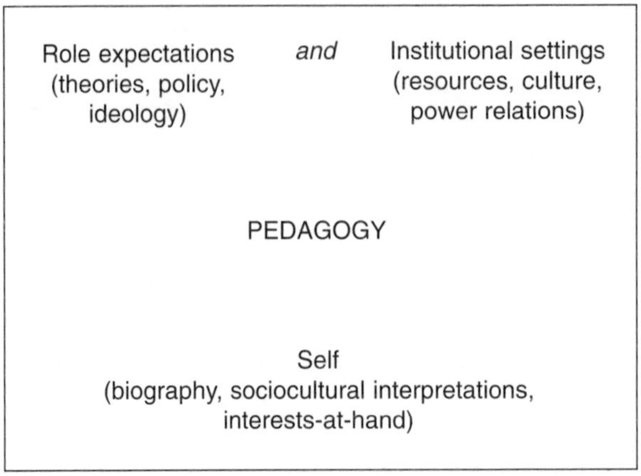

Figure 5.1   *Role expectations, institutional settings and 'self': three factors in pedagogy*

5.2   TEACHERS AND COPING STRATEGIES

In Chapters 3 and 4 we explored issues of 'pupil identity'. We argued that accounts of 'identity' have to synthesize the internal and personal concerns of individuals with the external influences of cultures and the expectations of appropriate groups and the wider society. In this chapter we take a similar approach in exploring issues of 'teacher identity' and focus on the three groups of factors that we see contributing to teachers' individual pedagogies. These internal concerns and external influences, shown here in Figure 5.1, are those of 'role expectations', 'institutional settings' and 'self'.

In exploring the relationship between these factors we are able to appreciate individual pedagogies as expressions of teachers' unique experiences and perceptions, as well as of pressures and constraints shared with others at different levels of school, local and national context. In attempting to understand ways in which these factors play out in teachers' lives and work, we have employed the concept of 'coping strategies'.

The development of the concept of coping strategies can be traced through Woods (1977), Hargreaves (1978), Pollard (1982, 1985) and Filer (1993a, 1993b). Coping strategies represent the creative response of teachers in managing and reconciling contradictory educational goals, the proliferation of educational ideologies and the constraints of local and school provision. They constitute the broad base of classroom policy which teachers construct and which subsumes and informs moment-to-moment decisions and actions. They represent an attempt by sociologists to analyse the relationship between macro-historical and socio-political analysis of society and micro perspectives of social and academic demands upon individual teachers in classrooms and schools.

Relating 'coping strategies' to the model in Figure 5.1, therefore, *role expectations* concern those wider, macro perspectives of educational goals, ideologies and professional values which shape policy initiatives and professional and public opinion on education. By definition, there-fore, *role expectations* will embody contradictory historico-political and sociocultural perspectives on how teaching should be conducted and how learning takes place.

These wider expectations will also be mediated by *institutional bias* in the form of teacher and peer cultures, those who hold positions of power in the school, particularly head teachers, and the nature of the school's intake of pupils.

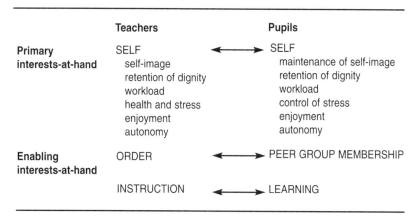

Figure 5.2   *Primary and enabling interests of teachers and children.* (Reproduced from Pollard, 1985, *The Social World of the Primary School*, p. 156, Holt, Rinehart and Winston)

Factors concerned with the 'self' in Figure 5.1 are those aspects of biography, the sociocultural backgrounds of teachers and their individual perspectives developed in relation to school. They represent aspects of 'self' that individuals bring to the school situation and which must, to some degree, be integrated into classroom actions in order to maintain 'self image'. An important aspect of *self* is concerned with 'interests-at-hand', an aspect of coping strategies developed through *The Social World of the Primary School*. 'Interests-at-hand' reflect teachers' more immediate and personal concerns in coping with their pupils and with the realities of classroom life. They reflect teachers' concerns with dignity at work, with managing workloads, health and stress and with job satisfaction and enjoyment in work. In Figure 5.2 we present a model of 'interests-at-hand', suggesting areas of shared and opposing teacher and pupil interests; mutual accommodation to these providing a basis for the 'working consensus' (Pollard, 1985) in classrooms. Pupil-coping strategies and ways in which they 'mesh' with teachers in this way are further explored in relation to the case study of one teacher's practice in the following chapter.

In terms of symbolic interactionism, coping strategies are lines of action, for pupils as well as for teachers, which have their origins in *meanings* concerning what an individual wants, 'what is required, goals, and the possibility of achieving them' (Blumer, 1969).

Below we explore further the three factors of pedagogy presented in Figure 5.1 concerned with 'role expectations', 'institutional settings' and 'self' and illustrate them in turn with research findings, our own and those of others. In this we show the personal and contextualized ways in which teachers continue to respond to national assessment requirements and integrate them into their own practice. As suggested above, an important aspect of such processes concerns the management of contradictory expectations, workload and constraints and the maintenance of a measure of personal autonomy, integrity and sense of 'self'.

Role expectations, contradictions and change

A consideration of role expectations and the structural, material and ideological constraints that shape pedagogic practices highlights the subservient position of schools and teachers within state policy frameworks. As we have suggested, such an analysis would consider the proliferation of contradictory theories and ideologies surrounding teaching and the existence of particular conceptions and concerns which dominate the mindset of much of the public and media. The analysis also recognizes that such pressures and constraints penetrate, and are mediated, through multiple levels of educational provision until they have their effect in classroom contexts. We thus have particular curricula requirements, recommended pedagogies, prescribed forms of assessments, delineated resource frameworks and management and accountability systems to which both teachers and pupils must respond. Through an analysis of some of the 'role expectation' in play through recent tumultuous changes in primary practice, we can address the question of what it is that teachers have had to cope with. We can begin by considering some role expectations underpinning national assessment requirements and ways in which these conflict with existing and well-established role expectations held by many primary school teachers in England.

We can begin to appreciate some of the contradictions surrounding recent primary school changes by placing them in the context of wider UK and international pressures for change. Such a comparison also locates the tensions and oppositional stances that many primary school teachers continue to express, within a broader context and perspective. In *Assessment: Social Practice and Social Product* Filer (2000) describes ways in which assessment has become one of the most significant areas of interest in educational policy development worldwide. There is a growing awareness of the limitations on teaching and learning of some traditional forms of assessment and this awareness together with international economic and employment trends has engendered much interest in new forms of assessment. The learning needs of post-industrial societies is being conceptualized in new ways, creating demands for transferable skills such as those of communication, information retrieval, problem solving and critical analysis. As a result there is a fast-growing interest, especially in the USA, in more formative, holistic and contextualized forms of assessment in schools, often described as authentic or competence-based assessments.

However, in UK primary schools the trend in assessment practices since the late 1980s has been in the opposite direction from the international pressures and trends described above. For the youngest children in our educational system, that is, new forms of national assessment have entailed requirements to move *away* from the sort of 'whole child' individualistic approach which has traditionally been associated with teachers' assessments of young children in UK primary schools. Since the late 1980s, government agencies for curriculum change have criticized such approaches as 'intuitive' and 'subjective' and the move has been *towards* formal tests, perceived objectivity and accountability whereby pupils can be graded, school performances ranked, targets set and 'standards' raised. Therefore recent primary school changes represent something of an interesting paradox in that they have been taking place just as international economic and educational imperatives are propelling secondary and higher education towards assessments geared to, and responsive to, individual students in *more* holistic ways (Filer, 2000).

It is useful at this point to examine more closely some aspects of current primary assessment practice in the UK. This is because the tensions and contradictions between 'holistic' assessment practices and requirements for 'evidence' and 'comparability' heighten awareness of some of the contradictory role expectations that teachers have to cope with.

Following the Education Reform Act and the introduction of the National Curriculum in 1989, a study of early adaptations to change suggested that teachers were incorporating new requirements for teacher assessment into their practices in a variety of ways. Gipps *et al.* (1995) describe three broad approaches to teacher assessment identified by teachers as characteristic of their practices in the early years of national assessment. Following that Gipps *et al.* analysis, which we present below, we go on to describe more recent research in the same field. That more recent research indicates that, with increased pressure towards formality and transparency, the Gipps *et al.* analysis no longer applies. That is to say, the sense of ideological or professional 'choice' that is apparent among the teachers Gipps *et al.* interviewed had disappeared a few years later. Nevertheless, it is worth setting out something of teachers' early expressions and interpretations of their practices, as they serve to clarify what the issues are for teachers. Most particularly, they express some of the tensions between pre-existing, child-centred approaches to assessment and new requirements for formal procedures and evidence.

The assessment approaches identified by Gipps *et al.* were described by them in terms of teachers who were 'intuitives', 'evidence gatherers' or 'systematic planners'. 'Intuitives' relied on memory of what pupils could do together with a kind of gut reaction in assessing. For 'intuitives', assessment was built on a close all-round knowledge of pupils and could only be done by their teacher. 'Intuitives' had made the fewest changes in integrating teacher assessment into their practices. Perspectives of 'intuitives' included such statements as:

> I don't think I can discount what I know about a child from its attainment.
>
> You have to take account of contextual issues because that's what being a professional is.
>
> It's so unfair – one of the August birthdays is quite a bright little boy. He just hasn't got there yet. So I feel like giving him a little more leeway.
>
> (Gipps *et al.*, 1995: 37)

'Evidence gatherers', on the other hand, collected evidence, sometimes enormous amounts, which they periodically went through to assign levels. They did not rely on memory. Perspectives of 'evidence gatherers' included such statements as:

> I would never rely all on my memory. You must have it backed up with evidence. You've got to keep your notes as evidence.
>
> I don't really plan a task to cover assessment. I plan first what I want to do and then see how it can be fitted into assessment.
>
> (Gipps *et al.*, 1995: 40)

'Systematic planners' planned specifically for teacher assessment with particular nationally prescribed criteria in mind. They used multiple techniques for assessment. Some 'systematic planners' gave daily concentrated time to assessment, some integrated it into normal classroom tasks. Perspectives of systematic planners include such statements as:

> I don't think memory is accurate enough. I think that's when you assume things about children.
>
> I need to know that at a particular time of day, I am actually going to be assessing one thing. You've got to be structured, you've got to know what you're looking for.
>
> (Gipps *et al.*, 1995: 42–3)

In the above, therefore, there are some fairly clear contradictions among teachers concerning the nature of assessment practice and what constitutes professional practice. Professionalism means taking account of contextual issues or it is ignoring them and focusing only on 'evidence'. Teachers should use their knowledge of a child; 'give a little more leeway' or they should 'know what they are looking for' and not rely on memory or assume things about a child. The tension across these approaches is, therefore, between assessment viewed as a *process*, which, like the 'authentic' approaches described above, is geared to individual children in continuous and holistic ways, and assessment viewed as *products* as 'objective' and, it is hoped, comparable because of attempts to eliminate a teacher's subjective judgement.

However, reporting three years after the above (Gipps *et al.*) analysis, Torrance and Pryor (1998) describe how the public face of assessment and expectations of teachers had shifted towards a greater formality. Teachers had experienced increased pressure to produce 'evidence' coming from external moderation and local and national systems of inspection. In all respects, a general expectation of excessive formality had been communicated to schools. Thus Torrance and Pryor did not find the above distinct 'types' of teachers and the sense of professional 'choice' they convey. Rather the 'types' tended to overlap so that conflicting attitudes and practices occurred within the same people (Torrance and Pryor, 1998: 23). Osborn's (1996a) reporting of the *Primary Assessment, Curriculum and Experience* (PACE) study of 48 schools in eight LEAs accords with both above findings. Osborn describes an initial phase after the introduction of the National Curriculum, in which teachers felt that they would be able to incorporate change into their existing patterns of working. However, this was followed by a period of stress when teachers were under pressure to change their methods or to fight harder to resist. Like Torrance and Pryor, PACE found that under these conditions of stress, though teachers had had to change their methods, they did not abandon their traditional role expectations. Excepting some new teachers, trained since the 1988 Education Reform Act, professional primary practice remains synonymous with traditional practice and knowledge of the 'whole child'.

However, just as Torrance and Pryor (above) found individual teachers with conflicting attitudes and practices, so PACE found that teachers in their studies revealed some ambivalence in their attitudes. So, for instance, notwithstanding their continued assertion of traditional definitions of teacher professionalism, for many of those same teachers, the new assessment skills they were developing were also an important aspect of their professionalism (Osborn, 1996a: 48–9).

As we described above, however, an important aspect of coping in classrooms is concerned with the maintenance of integrity and a sense of autonomy and 'self' by teachers. Below we review research which shows some different ways in which teachers have struggled to reconcile the contradictions within their practice and within their expression of professional identity. First, though, we consider the second of our three aspects of pedagogy; that concerned with 'institutional settings'.

Institutional settings, power, mediation and autonomy

The PACE project cited above uses the concept of mediation to represent the series of transformations that inevitably take place in the process of translating policy directives into classroom practice (Pollard *et al.*, 1994: 25). The social context of assessment at the macro level, to which teachers must respond, is also mediated by that of the school setting in which they find themselves. *The Social World of the Primary School* describes ways in which those with the greatest authority, usually the head teacher, work through the micro politics of the school to negotiate an 'institutional bias'. For instance, the next chapter explores through the case study of one teacher's practice the power and influence of the head teacher at Albert Park School. There we see diverse ways in which the head teacher mediated LEA initiatives and expectations and the influence of 'institutional bias' on different areas of classroom practice. In similar ways, though with less autonomy in this case, head teachers are responsible for implementing national assessment and mediate ways in which it is conducted in schools. In addition, however, they also act to mediate and to protect staff from some of the potentially stressful effects flowing from official directives and advice (Broadfoot and Pollard, 1996; Torrance and Pryor, 1998).

Of course, head teachers do not have complete power as teachers also make a contribution to the social order in schools. Their contribution may be simply to accept or reinforce the institutional bias or it may be to bypass, subvert or challenge it (Pollard, 1985: 133–42). Certainly in the past teacher autonomy has been a source of power in resisting institutional bias. However, since the Education Reform Act, the National Curriculum mediated through the school setting has meant that teachers have experienced a major loss of autonomy. They are, for instance, increasingly controlled by school-based planning and programmes of work and by the concomitant need for a close collaboration with colleagues (Osborn, 1996a: 49, citing Hargreaves, 1994). This trend towards a collaborative professionalism has persisted since 1990, suggesting a definite shift and an important dimension of the changing role expectations of primary teachers (Osborn, 1996a: 47). However, whilst, as Osborn reports, peer collaboration has become a significant focus of teachers' work and a major support in coping with change, it does signal a further reduction of the autonomy of primary teachers in their classrooms.

Parents are also a threat to autonomy and like head teachers and colleagues represent 'significant others' for teachers in shaping their classroom strategies. As Pollard (1985) points out, for teachers, being considered to be a good teacher significantly influences classroom autonomy. In Chapter 6, for example, we see the importance to that teacher of maintaining that reputation through her struggles with change. Also, in Chapter 11, we see examples of ways in which parents evaluate teachers' judgements of their child's capabilities, teacher provision of appropriately challenging work or teacher support for their children's progression. These assessments made by parents of their child and teacher together formed a basis for decisions to accept or challenge the day-to-day judgements teachers made of their children. This, of course, also provides a sidelight on our problematizing of what is involved in a teacher 'knowing' a child. For, as we found through our longitudinal case studies in both schools, nearly every parent evaluated their child's progress *in the context of a particular teacher's class*. Parents and their children were both aware that different teachers interpreted and *valued* pupils' individual identities differently.

In conclusion then, the effects of 'institutional bias' will play out differently within different school and local contexts, with different headteachers and among different teachers. As the PACE study found, even within the same school, teachers of similar experience varied according to the extent to which they felt able to mediate the effects of change. Among teachers, an individual's confidence and self-esteem seemed to be the factor most likely to affect their sense of agency in mediation processes (Osborn, 1996a: 51).

Integrity and maintaining a sense of 'self'

However, the above analysis of mediation and change cannot tell us what 'coping' will actually mean to any particular individual. To understand that we need to know much more about that teacher. In particular, we need to understand the subjective interpretations which each individual makes of the contexts in which they find themselves. For symbolic interactionists, the key factor here is that of 'self'. How does each person think about themselves? What is their sense of identity? How do they see themselves in the context of their social group? Interviews, discussion and the study of biographies are essential ways of trying to understand such issues and these methods lie at the core of the longitudinal ethnographies of pupils and the teacher case studies examined through the *Identity and Learning Programme*. As described above, an example of just such an analysis in relation to one teacher's reflections on her biography, values and practice, as well as on her pupils and the school setting, is to be found in Chapter 6.

Recent research makes it clear, therefore, that national assessment requirements have given rise to contradictions and internal inconsistencies within teachers' practices, identities and concepts of professionalism. Moreover, these contradictions and inconsistencies have represented a serious challenge to teachers' sense of integrity and 'self" because they challenge what has been important to them in the past and continues to be important to them. Teachers make a heavy investment of 'self' in their work and in maintaining personal integrity. The PACE study, like *The Social World of the Primary School*, found that teachers drew on their personal and career biographies and the influence of gender, social class and social context, their own and that of their pupils, in forming their values and beliefs about teaching. Thus the personal and professional is 'fused' in their sense of professional identity (Pollard, 1985; Nias, 1989; Osborn, 1996b: 61).

Both PACE and Torrance and Pryor suggest that individuals, in different ways, do maintain their beliefs, integrity and personal and professional identities in the face of change. However, Torrance and Pryor found intense anxiety among some teachers as their long-standing professional practice and strongly held beliefs were disparaged and as they found themselves acting in ways that were antithetical to their values and theories of teaching and learning. As described above, their practices remained rooted in a child-centred model of schooling. Reconciling this with a role expectation in which they were accountable for measuring and categorizing children and data gathering for external consumption was difficult (1988: 23). Many of these teachers appeared to manage their contradictory assessment roles through a kind of splitting of their public and private identities. Thus they appeared to maintain a personal and separate sense of integrity through locating their practices within two distinct discourses. On the other hand, the PACE project found many teachers adopting successful coping strategies to mediate change, internalizing the changes in *selective* ways, to ensure that their practice remained consistent with their beliefs and values. These teachers managed to maintain a sense of ownership and control over their work (Osborn, 1996a: 51). However, this was not achieved without a struggle, nor without cost. Many teachers expressed the view that these struggles could not be sustained long term. They were experiencing stress or burn-out; considering early retirement or change of career (1996b: 61). Thus, through a study of changing role expectations, mediations through local settings and through teachers' struggles to shape and maintain their identities, we can begin to appreciate what 'coping' might mean for any particular individual. We can also appreciate the complex origins of teachers' individual classroom practices and their inevitably distinctive natures.

5.3   CONCLUSION

This chapter has addressed the question of 'Who is assessing?' with a focus on 'Pedagogy' as depicted in Figure 4.1. Through previous chapters we explored 'pupil identity' and asserted that a more complete understanding of the 'whole child', for assessment purposes, could be arrived at through an understanding of the 'child in context'. Thus, in this chapter we have taken a reciprocal approach to understanding 'teacher identity' and the personal and contextual aspects of individual teachers' practices.

In theoretically modelling 'pedagogy' we have used the concept of 'coping strategies'. In this way social influences on teachers' practices can be seen as a mediation of external role expectations. This occurs through local and institutional settings and through the biographies, sociocultural perspectives and interests-at-hand of individual teachers. We illustrate this synthesis of internal–external concerns with research findings regarding ways in which teachers reconcile national and school-level requirements with the need to maintain personal integrity and a sense of 'self' in the classroom.

The following chapter is the second of the pair concerned with the question of 'Who is assessing?' and it is set in the first year of the longitudinal study of the pupil cohort at Albert Park School and thus draws on Filer's PhD (1993c). It presents a case study of the professional, social and personal influences on the practice of one teacher and her concerns with integrating the National Curriculum and new assessment procedures into her practice. It brings together our concerns with the 'child in context' in analysing the reciprocal strategies of pupils in coping with the day-to-day routines of classroom tasks. It also analyses the differentiating affects of the 'meshing' of pupil and teacher coping strategies upon social and academic assessments relating to different groups of pupils. It goes on to show the teacher's experience and interpretations of pupils' academic and social identities not as neutral forms of diagnostic or formative assessments which attach to individual pupils but as inseparable from the teacher-created context that gave rise to them.

Chapter 6

Who is Assessing? – A Case Study of Marie Tucker's Practice

Ann Filer

6.1   INTRODUCTION

This is the second of a pair of chapters concerned with the question 'Who is assessing?' and addressing issues of 'pedagogy' in relation to the model of 'assessment in a social context' (Figure 4.1). In the previous chapter Pollard and I outlined for readers ways in which we have conceptualized 'pedagogy' through the *Identity and Learning Programme*. We used the concept of 'coping strategies' to model ways in which policy change and role expectations are mediated through local and institutional settings and through teachers' own sense of self derived from their biographies and interests-at-hand.

In this chapter I present a case-study analysis to illustrate the issues raised. I describe some of the professional and social influences shaping the classroom practice of Marie Tucker, the Year 1 teacher at Albert Park School who also featured in Elizabeth's case study. I present something of Marie's perspective on the origins of her well-established practice and her perception of the threats to its integrity as she copes with the new demands of national assessment procedures. I show the coping strategies of different groups of pupils, as they 'mesh' (Pollard, 1983) with those of the teacher, bringing about a differentiating effect on the progress of different groups of pupils. Mathematics National Curriculum attainments and the 'social diagnostic' assessments made by Marie Tucker are shown to contain elements of the teacher-organized context in which they were produced.

The important consideration of 'Where and when is the assessment taking place?' has been set out in Chapter 2. At the point of the commencement of my PhD research at Albert Park School in 1989 some key changes were being most profoundly felt by Marie Tucker as a Year 1 teacher in the first wave of new National Curriculum and assessment provision. The analysis here illustrates the continuing value of 'coping strategies' as a conceptual tool for understanding the ways in which change is mediated in individual situations to give rise to classroom contexts which are inevitably idiosyncratic in their structures and effects. Some brief details of the school setting, neighbourhood and pupil intake of Albert Park School, which also mediated her practice, are also to be found in Chapter 2. However, in this chapter Marie recounts in greater detail her perceptions and experience of Albert Park as someone who lives and works in the area as she describes how the school and neighbourhood settings inform and mediate her practice.

6.2   MARIE TUCKER'S COPING STRATEGIES AND THEIR ORIGINS

Classroom organization

I begin this account of Marie's practice with a description of her classroom organization as I observed it during my first year of study in Albert Park School. This description will better enable readers to appreciate some of the implications of her biography and of institutional factors in supporting it. In the course of my weekly visits over the year, I could see that some changes brought about by the introduction of the National Curriculum were beginning to be integrated into her practice. Though a calm atmosphere prevailed in the classroom, new assessment requirements were beginning to be seen by Marie, as by so many teachers at that time, as a threat to the integrity of her practice.

Classroom tasks for the Year 1 pupils under study were, in almost every case, formally structured by Marie. Where mathematics and language were concerned, this structure consisted largely of progression through work cards with one piece of writing a week on some aspect of the current topic (Filer, 1993a). All children wrote on the same subject with a word bank of some six to eight words provided by Marie. They also wrote 'news' once a week. Most pupil time in the classroom was spent sitting at designated tables or, as a whole class, on the carpet for teacher-led discussion or other teaching activity. When children completed their designated tasks they had a choice of games, puzzles and construction sets which could be played with on the carpet. However, as I describe later, less than half of the children routinely managed to complete their work. With the introduction of the National Curriculum much of the free choice and spontaneous play with this equipment was being replaced by structured group work in, for example, technology and science. There were other strictures on 'free play' in the class that were aspects of Marie's pedagogy and not attributable to National Curriculum changes. For instance, there was no home, shop or other suchlike activity centre in the classroom, neither were there any free-writing or drawing facilities. Sand and water were only available for specific mathematics activities. Paint and other art materials were only available for specific, directed and supervised activities. Marie spent most of her time based at the end of one of the children's tables from where she would simultaneously closely supervise particular children, hear readers and attend to queuing children, marking and assigning tasks on an individual basis.

The school house point system was used consistently and to effect by Marie and I was alerted to the importance of house points to children through interviews with them and observations. Generally, house points were not used in the class for the control of social behaviour. As is described below, behaviour problems were managed through strategies concerned with the routine organization of tasks, pupil groupings and teacher surveillance. Rather, house points were used in motivating pupils to concentrate and stay on task and to encourage speed and efficiency in the classroom. Children typically received house points for work that showed improvement, for quick working and for trying hard. Though some pupils inevitably had reputations for getting many house points, all were able to collect them with some regularity. House points were also used to encourage speed in tidying up, each child on the 'first table to be ready' gaining points. As described below, groups were differentiated by achievement, high-achieving tables in this class also being also marked by organizational skills and 'independence' from the teacher. Grouped together in this way, highest achievers also scooped most house points at tidying up times. Thus house points not only served the functions of promoting speed, efficiency and concentration on tasks; along with seating arrangements, the grading of tasks and the numbering of exercise books, house points also provided a highly public measurement of children's places in the teacher-defined hierarchy of the classroom.

Background to Marie's coping strategies – biography, culture and the school setting

Marie began her teaching career in 1966 and maintained a theory of education prevalent at the time of her training which can best be conceptualized as a 'traditional', 'three Rs' approach to teaching and learning. The following extract from a tape-recorded, semi-structured interview were her volunteered opinions concerning her role as teacher and the needs of the children she teaches.

> I happen to think, you know, okay, I am nearly forty-five and I've been teaching for a long time, but you know, it seems to me that at middle infant stage, and speaking as a parent, and I'm sure I speak for a lot of parents in my class, what I want to see these children do, leaving me – I would like to think they were happy. I would like to think they were reasonably well adjusted socially, that they were beginning to be fluent readers, that they were on the way to becoming numerate and that they were on their way, (with) language, generally, (to be able to) express themselves and so on. I feel very much, yes, well, obviously they've got to be aware of the science and technology, but I think quite honestly at the age of five and six, unless you have got that basis, unless they are reasonably literate you've got no foundations on which to build. (Marie Tucker, teacher interview, Year 1, 1990)

As described in Chapter 5, teachers also have to operate within the constraints and opportunities of the particular classroom and school context in which they find themselves. Marie, who also lived in Albert Park, described the pupil population of the school as 'middle of the road' in terms of social class. The school did not have any cases of real need or neglect, she said, and neither did it have more than two or three children from professional backgrounds. She pointed out that at a time of rising unemployment nationally, few fathers were unemployed (though by the end of my PhD study, three years later, four children in the class of twenty-six had a father or both parents unemployed). In describing the constraints she felt with respect to the pupils and the neighbourhood, she drew on her own experience and that of a teaching colleague to 'place' the children in terms of their social background and its consequences for learning:

> To some extent you do (feel constraints). If you were teaching in somewhere like Oak Hill (an extremely affluent part of Easthampton adjacent to Greenside) where, one assumes, the majority of your children would be more articulate and probably more put under pressure and generally (having) a wider experience. Then probably one could go into things in perhaps greater depth and in a wider way. I'm drawing now on experiences I had when I taught in a private school in Italy. You were able to spend far more time teaching, rather than coping with social problems. At the other end of the scale it's interesting to talk to Janice, the girl in the nursery. She taught in an inner city nursery school in Seaport, and hearing her talk about the different types of children and the differences between the parents in the two schools, it's just like another world. ... In that sort of area even more of your time is going to be devoted to social problems. So yes, it depends on the sort of material you've got to work with really. (Marie Tucker, teacher interview, Year 1, 1990)

Thus Marie brought to the classroom a view of teaching which was justified in terms of her personal experience as a teacher and as a parent. As illustrated in Figure 5.1, these aspects of 'self' were embedded in her particular sociocultural perspectives on the families of Albert Park, on her perceptions of the needs of their children and the expectations of their parents.

Background to Marie's coping strategies – the head teacher and institutional bias

The head teacher was another institutional factor which shaped Marie's practice. Although they had different perspectives on the head's approach, in different ways Marie and other teachers had difficulty in implementing her demands. This was, one teacher told me, mainly on account of the contradictions inherent in them. Teachers in the school were regularly instructed to implement new initiatives emanating from LEA advisers, yet at the same time they knew that they had to respond primarily to the head teacher's true leanings, which were rather more traditional in nature. A structured 'three Rs' approach and 'presentation' were what she was 'really hot on' and what she insisted on and checked up on in classrooms. She insisted that only good and well-presented work went home and nothing else must leave the school. Although Marie in some respects shared the head teacher's perspectives, many of the more formal aspects of her classroom routine she attributed to the head's demands. Like most other teachers she complained about having to hear children read each day as she could not do that job properly and discuss work with children in the queue at the same time. She was also critical of the phonic work cards which the head insisted had to be used on the grounds that they were 'antiquated' in content and of little value in learning. She was, however, critical of 'change for change's sake' and, given the perception of a lack of commitment to many changes on the part of the head teacher, she, like other teachers, was able to marginalize new initiatives or integrate them into her practices as she saw fit. Indeed, the head teacher herself mediated and subverted the expectations and resources of the LEA. For instance, the allocation of 'real books' had been put in the library for children, supervised by parents, to borrow for home reading in addition to the structured reading scheme books. A teacher told me that was because the head teacher did not believe in the value of the 'real books' approach to teaching reading. Thus, like many other teachers at Albert Park, Marie was of the opinion that the head 'likes to be seen to be doing' and with this knowledge she had been able to cope with new initiatives in the school, as she told me:

> I mean I think it's like anything else. You don't encompass it wholeheartedly. There are certain parts of it which you think, yes, that would work for me. One doesn't have to be inflexible, but by the same token I don't think one, you know, throws out all your tried and tested ways. Quite honestly, you know that in another six months it's all going to be different and something else is going to be (the thing to do). Says she, sounding very cynical. (Marie Tucker, teacher interview, Year 1, 1990)

Some new initiatives in the process of being introduced into classrooms at that time included the teaching of 'cursive script' and 'bubble time', which was time devoted to individual pupils to discuss work and assess progress. Cursive script had to be introduced by all teachers because, of course, there were no 'half measures' available in that. Further, notwithstanding her comments above, Marie also continued to struggle with the implications of 'bubble time' because, at this point, national assessment requirements were beginning to replace the autonomy of head teachers and teachers. Marie was feeling greater pressure to integrate this and other assessment-related initiatives into her practice.

Thus, in addition to coping with the particular situational constraint and expectations described above, Marie also had to devise strategies to cope with role expectations derived from contradictory and conflicting educational theories, ideologies and policies. These role expectations, mediated at government, local and institutional levels, were further interpreted and mediated by Marie enabling her to maintain a level of personal integrity and autonomy in her classroom.

The final aspect of pedagogy that Pollard and I identified on the model in Figure 5.1 relates to those aspects of 'self' concerned with the maintenance of interests-at-hand (Pollard, 1985) in the classroom. In the following section I examine the key elements of this which are concerned with self-image, enjoyment of work and order and instruction on a day-to-day basis.

Background to Marie's coping strategies – control and learning

In *The Social World of the Primary School* 'order and instruction' in the classroom are described as 'enabling' for the teacher in that they facilitate enjoyment, the maintenance of self-image and the management of health, stress and the workload. Without order and control in the classroom teachers are unable to defend themselves against criticism or achieve some autonomy and independence in the classroom.

In addition to an emphasis on structured routines, an emphasis on 'control' was also an aspect of Marie's teaching that made an early impression on me. On my first morning in Marie's classroom, whilst the children were sitting on the carpet after registration, she spelt out to me, above the heads of the children, that she had been given 'the p-r-o-b-l-e-m-s' because she was considered to be 'good with them'. Although Marie took a lot of care to explain to me the behaviour of these children and the problems they posed for her, her attitude towards them was generally one of acceptance. She had a firm, patient and quiet way of dealing with misbehaviour to which children responded without demur. However the group of about six boys (the p-r-o-b-l-e-m-s), generally recognized by other children as 'naughty', missed few opportunities to balance their own interests with those of keeping out of trouble with the teacher. Hence Marie's concern, expressed from time to time, for 'keeping a watchful eye' on some children. In this extract from a recorded interview she was explaining her objections to recent educational changes in the light of this need. 'Bubble time', described above, is the time devoted to one child for discussion and assessment.

> And, um, I am unhappy about things like 'bubble time' and the assessments under the National Curriculum and so on, because in spite of being reassured, you know, about the situation, I mean, I can't. I tried doing bubble time in my class and I can't. The only way I can do bubble time is to do it at dinner time. You know, you take ten minutes and you kind of withdraw for ten minutes with one child and I mean, the Bobbys and the Thomases, they only need two seconds and they know your eagle eye is not upon them and they're sort of flicking crayons and jumping on the table and generally sort of kicking each other's 'privates' as they call it. (Marie Tucker, teacher interview, Year 1, 1990)

Thus, apart from being easily distracted and losing concentration, and these were greater problems for some than others, Marie was currently coping with these boys, they were kept pretty well 'on task' for most of the time. Marie's vigilance meant that, for most of the time, other children were not disturbed by the group. Their academic abilities and rates of progress were varied and spanned those of the rest of the class, almost to the extremes. Although she took care to explain to me the difficulties these boys presented her with, she also at the same time gave full credit to the intelligence of three of them and commented on good progress or more socially favourable aspects of two others. Thus, clearly, for Marie good control of those children considered to be 'problems' was a very important aspect of her self-image as a teacher and one which was rewarded and reinforced through the beneficial consequences for those children, for the rest of the class and through her standing in the school.

Marie's coping strategies can be construed as a means of maintaining both her self-image and her image in the eyes of those significant others in her life to whom she made reference. Thus, as 'pupil identity' was construed in Chapter 3, so we can similarly construe Marie's continued maintenance of her identity as a teacher. That is, we can see it in terms of a synthesis of the internal and personal concerns of the individual and the external influences of culture and expectations of appropriate social groups and the wider society. In Jenkins (1996) terms, that maintenance of identity can be described as an internal–external dialect of identification (Jenkins, 1996: 71). In this way, through a consideration of role expectations, interpreted and mediated through institutional and personal considerations (Figure 5.1), we can appreciate the inevitable distinctiveness of contexts in which children are assessed. Below I examine differentiated National Curriculum outcomes for pupils in the class and show how they have their origins in Marie's particular ways of coping. First, however, I show how Marie's coping strategies also gave rise to particular social assessments of her pupils.

6.3   ROUTINE, CONTROL AND SOCIAL ASSESSMENT

Accounting for success and failure

As discussed in Chapters 3 and 4, in addition to judgements relating to pupils' academic attainments and progress, teachers also form judgements concerning a range of attitudinal, psychological, motor, motivational and social factors considered to affect that attainment and progress. As we saw in the case of Elizabeth, the content of this kind of social diagnosis will frequently extend beyond the classroom to include aspects of home and indeed the wider community. As we also saw in relation to Elizabeth's career through successive classroom contexts, the greater the difficulty a pupil is considered to be experiencing in relation to the social or academic expectations of the school, the more of the pupil's physical, sociocultural and emotional identity will be considered to be legitimate areas of enquiry. However, as has been shown both in relation to the studies of Greenside pupils in Chapter 3 and in Elizabeth's case study in Chapter 4, teachers can experience and interpret the behaviour of individual pupils differently. In part this is a consequence of individual pupils responding differently to the curricular and social contexts that different teachers create. Similarly, the physical, sociocultural or emotional factors that are considered to be problematic will vary from teacher to teacher. Thus, an important aspect in considering 'Who is assessing?' is to explore the origins and backgrounds of the social assessments teachers make of pupils and the particular classroom contexts that give rise to them. As Pollard and I argue in Chapter 3 all of our findings from the *Identity and Learning Programme* lead us to problematize what is involved in a teacher 'knowing' a child. There we pointed out that the 'whole child' as a subject for assessment has to be the child *in context*. Thus, as Leiter (1974) concluded:

> Social types are not just a mere overlay on the setting by the teacher, rather they are an inseparable part of the setting. (Leiter, 1974: 123)

This is an area of key importance in classroom assessment processes and outcomes. These social assessments of pupils are not the neutral nor always beneficial forms of diagnostic 'knowledge' that teachers often present in accounts of 'whole child' assessment practices (see Chapter 3.3). As a key finding of the *Identity and Learning Programme* and as Pollard and I have illustrated in our case-study accounts in Chapters 3 and 4, they have an important role in shaping classroom and home relationships and individual children's approaches to learning. Thus, as with all descriptions of Marie's practice here, what follows is not presented as a criticism of Marie's practice but as an illustration of processes that in one form or another are common to all pedagogies.

Below, I examine some of the origins and outcomes of the way in which one teacher, Marie, accounts for the success and failure for pupils in her class. I show how the particular kinds of judgements which Marie made of pupils were related to pupil behaviour which, on the one hand, rewarded her sense of self and of coping or, on the other hand, contributed to her feelings of frustration and failure. The ways in which she differentiated pupils along these lines were also reflected in her groupings of pupils and, in turn, in the academic outcomes for pupils. First, therefore, it is necessary to describe the ways in which pupils were grouped in Marie's classroom.

Coping, control and groupings

For most tasks Marie's pupils had fixed positions, allocated by Marie, around five tables in the classroom. Descriptions of the five tables given to me by the children in interviews can best be summed up as the 'good' table, the mixed 'good and naughty' table, the 'noisy' table and the table for the 'naughty ones' at which Marie also sat. There is also a table, the 'small' table, which seemed to have no clear identity where children presented a variety of academic, coordination and language difficulties.

As described above, although pupils were divided into five tables, the class was effectively divided into two groups which Marie described in terms of their different writing and mathematics attainment. The 'good' and the 'good and naughty' tables, in number twelve children, made up the higher-achieving group which was also reflected in their progression through mathematics and phonic work cards and reading levels. The 'naughty' the 'noisy' and the 'small' tables, numbering fifteen children, were on the lower levels. There was an overlap between the two groups of a few children on some of these achievement indicators. Not quite all children remained in fixed positions, however, for some of the 'naughty boys' on Marie's table were allowed to return to alternative places at another table, according to behaviour. Thus three children on the 'naughty table', described as 'intelligent' by Marie and whose behaviour was good so long as they were kept fully occupied, also had more or less permanently available places among the twelve higher-achieving pupils. They made up the 'naughty' element of what children described as the 'good and naughty' table.

There was in Marie's groupings, however, a more precise indicator of the difference between the two groups than writing or maths attainment and that distinction was concerned with those in the class who could work independently of Marie and those who, for whatever reason, were dependent upon her. This was clearly an important distinction for Marie, as illustrated in the following account of her social assessments of pupils.

The social assessment of pupils

Through informal discussions with Marie, I quickly became aware of some regular ways in which she discussed individual children in her class, in that she almost invariably made reference to a child's family. A semi-structured interview with Marie in which I asked how she viewed the progress of twelve children of varying attainment, selected by me, revealed a similar pattern. An initial analysis of factors which Marie considered predisposed children to underachievement or slow progress revealed categories roughly concerned with physical factors, interactional factors and what might be called organizational factors. Instances and stories cited by Marie were numerous and accounts lengthy, especially concerning those who were experiencing difficulties. However, in summary, some examples of physical factors included poor coordination, speech problems and physical immaturity. Interactional problems included dependency on peers – 'being carried', lack of interaction or too much interaction with peers. Organizational factors included inability to organize tasks or thoughts.

However, what was common to all of these judgements was that, as in informal discussions, in each case the part played by families, but usually by mother, in causing or exacerbating problems or tendencies was discussed. Again, accounts were lengthy but, briefly, Marie's concern in this respect covered various forms of 'babying' such as conversing in baby-talk, doing too much for the child and having indulgent attitudes towards the child's immature behaviour and demands. Alternatively she talked about 'neglect' in relation to the failure of mothers to properly feed and clothe the child for its comfort or health and failure to provide the conditions for the child to make sound friendships or develop proper social habits.

It seemed, moreover, that what all these descriptions of parenting had in common was that they reflected Marie's strong concern with children's dependency on her in the classroom. Interestingly, they also most clearly reflected the distinction between the two main groupings in her classroom. This connection seems to be confirmed by the following comments volunteered by Marie in the interview that immediately followed her account of the two groups and the writing problems experienced by the less able of the two.

> I always think it's very interesting, you know, when you look at a class and nine times out of ten, says she generalising, and I shouldn't, but anyway, that those children who are succeeding invariably are the ones who have independence, who are encouraged to be independent. You know, who come from a background where the mother intentionally encourages independence (examples of children given) – but it's not often in my experience that one comes across a child that is experiencing problems at school, if you look at the family, it's not often that there is a mother and a father, but obviously the father far less, that are doing the right thing and encouraging them to be successful, independent and so on and there are still difficulties. (Marie Tucker, teacher interview, Year 1, 1990)

Of course, all teachers would agree on the value of 'independence' in their pupils. However, I would not conclude from the study of Marie's classroom and from all the conversations that we had that independence in the form of, for example, autonomy of pupil thought or learning strategies was what concerned her in relation to this class. Rather, the ability to carry out designated tasks efficiently and without the need of too much teacher intervention was, as I show below, the sort of independence that was necessary to her sense of coping with this class. This latter type of independence is one that is of very real practical consideration for teachers and many studies show selection for 'ability' groups actually being carried out on the basis of a range of classroom behaviours, including conformity to rules, knowledge of siblings and physical appearance (Leiter, 1974; Ball, 1981; Troman, 1988). Indeed, Leiter (1974) found that teachers who social-typed children according to 'independence' did so for practical reasons because independent children freed them from the need to directly supervise. Teachers' accounts of children's independence were embedded in that particular social requirement.

However, Marie clearly did not hold the kind of deterministic view that children's problems can be sufficiently explained in terms of family background and are therefore beyond teacher control. I say this because to some extent she also located the source of their problems within the school. In both interviews she expressed regret that demands made upon teachers generally nowadays, from head teachers and from the introduction of the National Curriculum and national assessments, meant that some children's needs were being neglected. Marie felt that the pressures on teachers' time nowadays meant that:

> the child seems to be getting more and more pushed into the background. ... Something's got to go and, sadly, it does seem to be contact with the children. (Marie Tucker, teacher interview, Year 1, 1990)

Talking of the particular problems associated with this year's intake of pupils, she said:

> I find that having quite a lot of naughty children, I find it very frustrating too. And I know one does with any class, but because there are quite a few children with varying, quite marked co-ordination problems too, I find it very frustrating because I just don't feel that I am, sort of, fulfilling their needs sufficiently. One does one's best and that's all one can do. (Marie Tucker, teacher interview, Year 1, 1990)

In *The Social World of the Primary School* Pollard suggests that favourable or unfavourable typifications will be made according to the extent to which qualities in children enable teachers to cope and reward their sense of self. Indeed, Marie very much *needed* children to be able to cope efficiently with routine tasks given her inaccessibility and her need to cope with the queue, hear readers daily and at the same time keep her 'eagle eye' on some boys. She did not, of course, blame the children for her feelings of frustration. Nevertheless, in the context of day-to-day classroom interaction, those children who did not show the sorts of independence she required were not rewarding to her image of herself as a teacher nor to her sense of 'coping'. As we saw above, it was those children who did not cope with Marie's routines that gave her that sense of failure and frustration.

Thus, as I suggested above, these kinds of social assessments that teachers routinely make of pupils are not the neutral forms of diagnostic 'knowledge' that teachers often present them as. Nor, like other assessment processes, are they always beneficial in their outcomes. As we have seen the ways in which Marie differentiated pupils as dependent/independent was reflected in her groupings of pupils. Below I show how allocation to particular groups could have implications for academic outcomes for pupils.

6.4   THE MESHING OF COPING STRATEGIES AND DIFFERENTIATION

The analysis in this section shows that the National Curriculum levels achieved by pupils in Marie's class carried within them elements of the teacher-created context in which they were produced. It shows ways in which pupil coping strategies, in meshing with those of the teacher, can reinforce and amplify the differentiating effects of teacher strategies. The meshing of teacher and pupil coping strategies (Pollard, 1983) represents the set of social relations that underpin *working consensus*, or taken-for-granted aspects of classroom life, and that will also include 'routine deviancy'.

Mathematics grades

Children's maths attainment was measured by their rate of progression through a school-produced series of structured work cards. The series covered all aspects of infant years' maths. Tasks were mainly designed to be worked at individually though sometimes they required a partner. With the introduction of the National Curriculum, the colours, letters, etc. that had previously denoted certain areas of maths study and progressions had been reorganized a little and translated into National Curriculum attainment targets and levels of attainment. Maths tasks in Marie's class involved reading the card, copying the task from the card into an exercise book, carrying out the task and filling in the answers.

The Social World of the Primary School describes coping strategies of teachers as falling into three descriptive categories; 'routinization', 'manipulation' and 'domination'. From what has been described in terms of the structuring and organization of tasks in Marie's classroom it is clear that, from this perspective, her coping strategies could best be classed as 'routinization' (for other strategies see Chapter 10). The key features of 'routinization' are suggested to be:

> regularity in the organisation of work tasks and activities, the setting of occupational work rather than work that is more challenging, the appeal to tradition and precedent when controlling children, and a degree of distancing in relationships. (Pollard, 1985: 187)

The routines of the work card tasks, together with the division of children according to teacher dependence/independence and the organization of table places constituted the conditions for differentiation of academic outcomes.

Those in the higher-attaining group of twelve were, by Marie's definition, 'independent' and could cope efficiently with allocated tasks. They needed a minimum of help from the teacher and were in a quiet area of the classroom. They thus had the conditions under which they could work quickly and make rapid progress through the routine expectations of the classroom (see also Filer, 1993a). One could say that classroom conditions were *geared to accommodate* the attainments and work habits of this group, as indeed they were for the group of six 'naughty' boys of all 'abilities' who sat on the same table as Marie under her 'watchful eye'. As described above, three of these pupils, whose behaviour was deemed good *so long as they were kept fully occupied* had more or less permanent places among the twelve higher-achieving pupils. Now, whilst Marie still had to watch these three carefully, the fact that they were able to easily accomplish the work assigned to them was crucial to keeping them 'on task'. Indeed, as we shall see below, all of the twelve pupils could manage the routine and, for them, relatively unchallenging tasks characteristic of 'routinization'. Also helping to keep these three children 'on task' most of the time was the fact that they were with 'good' children and in the quiet half of the classroom. Marie's 'naughty' table, the queue, the 'noisy' table, the 'small' table, carpet activities and the door were all in the other half of the classroom.

Classroom conditions were not, on the other hand, geared to the attainments and work habits of those in the teacher-dependent group other than the 'naughty' boys. Those on the 'noisy' table and the 'small' table who struggled with handwriting, lacked confidence, needed reassurance, positive feedback and encouragement on task did not, as Marie acknowledged, have access to the level of teacher attention they needed. Their progress was slower than it might be under different conditions.

The above argument is not intended to deny the fact that in any class some children will make slower progress and have greater difficulties than others. The point being, rather, the extent to which, given other constraints, teachers are able to adopt strategies which accommodate those differences and the extent to which the accommodation of some pupils' needs is managed to the detriment of others.

Pupils' coping strategies

I now focus on some of the coping strategies employed by the two groups of children whereby they meshed with Marie's to reinforce the effects of differentiation. In *The Social World of the*

Primary School Pollard observes that the teacher coping strategy of 'routinization' produces corresponding pupil coping strategies which can generally be described as 'drifting'. 'Pleasing teacher' is relatively easy in view of the fact that tasks are clearly defined and goals attainable. Under these conditions, finishing the task is the main aim with something of an indifference to means and ends (Woods, 1979). In the class under study, however, this analysis had more application to the 'independent' group than to the 'teacher-dependent' group. Indeed for many of the teacher-dependent group, goals were not so easily attainable.

In order to examine the way in which children's coping strategies typically meshed with Marie's, it is useful to look more closely at the strategies of two children; a 'teacher-dependent' and an 'independent' pupil. I have selected children seen by Marie Tucker as particularly problematic, that is, one of her particularly 'naughty' boys and a boy from the 'noisy' table with 'marked coordination problems'. This selection helps to show that 'meshing' does not necessarily represent ideal pupil behaviour from the teacher's point of view. Rather it represents the 'working consensus' or taken-for-granted aspects of classroom life, including routine deviancy (Pollard, 1985).

As we have seen, for the six or so 'naughty' boys evading the 'watchful eye' was almost a moment-to-moment strategy. However, these children also had to have strategies for coping with the workload. In a study of John, we can see how he combined the apparently opposing tendencies of 'teacher opposition' and 'teacher pleasing'. We can also see how both of these strategies meshed with Marie's coping strategies to reinforce the effects of differentiation.

John was, for Marie Tucker, 'the bane of my life'. He was 'intelligent' but was also 'streetwise' and 'wayward' and because of his disturbed family background he was described by Marie as 'independent, because he has to be independent'. He was grouped accordingly in the light of Marie's management of 'naughty' boys who were also 'intelligent' and 'independent'. In interviews in which children showed me their work over the year, neatness, enjoyment of drawing, easiness of tasks and speed of accomplishing them all featured as areas of satisfaction for John, as did rewards in the form of house points, stickers and stars. In interview he also stated preferences for working with children who were 'good', 'on the highest work' and who got most house points. The following is an extract from the transcripts of John's interviews which illustrates his satisfaction with quickness and easiness. John was looking through his maths book:

> John   That's good, because the writing's good, because it's neat. (He then refers to another piece of work.) And I liked doing that.
> AF   Mmmm.
> John   Imps. [= easy, as in 'Impsy pimpsy']
> AF   Why did you like doing that?
> John   Because it was easy. It only took about (pause) ... Count how many seconds it takes.
> AF   (I begin counting as he pretends to write. I get to 'three'.)
> John   See? But I had to work it out so it took a couple of seconds. I liked doing that 'cos I got two house points and a sticker. . . . (He then refers to another piece of work.) I definitely liked doing these.
> AF   Weighing. Balancing.
> John   Yeah, I definitely like doing them. They're easy 'cos I got one house point.
>   (John, pupil interview, Year 1, 1990)

Something of the apparent mismatch between John's working strategies and his social strategies could be seen in his school record where Marie described him as 'cooperative' but in the next phrase 'very disruptive still'. It would seem though that John's coping strategies, both in relation to school work and his oppositional strategies, meshed perfectly with Marie's coping strategies. He complied with her academic aims and responded to her reward system of house points wholeheartedly, thus generally making rapid progress through tasks. (Indeed as I described above, whilst among the 'independents' he could very much more rapidly accumulate house points than on the 'naughty' table.) At the same time he rewarded and reinforced Marie's systems for managing 'naughty' boys; thus also reinforcing her image in her own eyes and in the eyes of others of being 'good with naughty children'. He also rewarded and reinforced her group arrangements for 'independent' children and the social assessments which gave rise to them. It is perhaps not surprising that she was 'very fond of John'.

Coping strategies will also include deviant acts which are not directly oppositional to the teacher and are a 'taken for granted' aspect of classroom life. Such 'routine deviance' will fall within the parameters of the working consensus and will be dealt with in a routine way. In Marie's class, such 'routine deviance' included talking too much, working slowly and 'dreaming' all of which are described as aspects of 'drifting' and, as such, are typical responses to teacher coping strategies of 'routinization' (Pollard, 1985). In addition 'fussing' about hair bands, ribbons, etc. was common and complained about by Marie. Disputes over rubbers, crayons, etc. were also common, these often resulting in physical struggles for possession, sometimes ending in tears.

As would be expected these deviations, especially the latter ones, were much more common in the 'teacher-dependent' group. Anything too loud or disruptive, too many talking too much or too many working too slowly were all causes of routine reprimand, either addressed to the whole class or to groups or individuals as appropriate. However, as long as a reasonable level of noise or disturbance was not exceeded and a reasonable number of children were in the queue with finished work, some children were able to indulge in routine acts of deviance for considerable lengths of time, thus doing a minimum amount of work or avoiding it altogether. Bearing in mind that most children in the 'independent' group tended not to deviate to any great extent and that the low-achieving, naughty boys were under close scrutiny on Marie's table, most, if not all, of the prolonged routine deviancy occurred on the 'noisy' table (hence its name) and on the 'small' table of four. In the latter case children's strategies tend to be of a quieter order than those of most children on the 'noisy' table.

Clearly there was a greater range of routinely deviant coping strategies to be found in the 'teacher-dependent' group than in the 'independent' group and some of these have already been described in Chapter 4 in Elizabeth's case study. Below I take a closer look at Simon's coping strategies as representative of the meshing of teacher and pupil strategies in the teacher-dependent group.

Simon had been assessed as a child with 'special needs' and diagnosed as having 'coordination problems'. He was one of several in the class who received daily help with handwriting in a small group with another teacher. Simon's home background was described by Marie in terms of neglect of his health, so, under the circumstances, she found Simon 'amazingly capable', since 'the odds are stacked against him'. He thought logically and was good at mental arithmetic she told me and she described him as 'keen' in his school record with respect to mathematics. However, she felt that he was very frustrated by his inability to write.

In order to complete the daily routine of mathematics tasks in Marie's class, all children first had to read the work card and copy the question into their exercise books. The following two episodes were noted by me during classroom observations. (Simon sat on the 'noisy' table):

> I notice Simon making little scribble in his exercise book, his pencil being held in his mouth for this. I ask Simon if he can read his maths card and he tells me 'no'. Nathan comes round the table and looks at the card but cannot read it either. He gives up and returns to his seat. I ask Simon how he is going to find out what it says, but Nathan replies: 'Write it down and ask Mrs Tucker. That's what I do.'

> Simon still does nothing. I help him to read the card and encourage him to write the six words necessary. The finished writing is disorganized and hardly legible. He takes it to Marie who writes it out again for him. Time taken to complete this task: 20 minutes plus whatever time before I came to him. Simon then proceeds to the sink. He talks to himself as he works: 'Where's the green pot?' He finds it. 'Fill the green pot.' He counts as he fills it from another container. 'One ... two ... three' [correct response] 'I done it. I'll do it again.' He repeats the operation and fills in the answer. He has worked quickly and efficiently at the mathematical aspect of the task. (Field notes, Year 1)

A week later Simon was having similar problems with writing. I checked that he could read the card. He could this time. I noted:

> This time I resist the temptation to intervene in order to see how long he will take before getting to the maths part of the activity. He copies a few words, large and sloping, filling the available space. He rubs them out and does nothing more. Sits making light scribbles on the table with his pencil. After 25 minutes plus whatever time before I observed, nothing completed and time to pack up for lunch. (Field notes, Year 1)

Exercise books were not collected at the end of the day; they went into the children's drawers at the end of sessions for continuation the next day. This is not to say that Marie was unaware of the waste of time but that Simon was not accountable for it; at least not in the short term.

Simon's problems here were threefold. He sometimes had difficulty reading cards, though clearly he did not have difficulty in remembering instructions once they were read to him. He found writing a slow and difficult process and the space available in his exercise book was too small for his writing. Strategies available to him to quickly accomplish the task were not taken up by him. He did not (at least on these occasions) ask the teacher or other pupils for help with reading the card (asking other pupils for help with reading and interpreting work cards was a strategy frequently employed in the class). Neither did he write what he could as quickly as he could and take it to Marie for her to write again if necessary. Whatever the reasons for Simon's failure to take up these options, his strategy of sitting for long periods doing nothing except making little scribbles, bending his work card and occasionally chatting and laughing were not helpful to him. Simon was very capable in mathematics, enjoyed the subject and worked quickly and efficiently at it but the proportion of time he spent in a mathematics lesson actually doing mathematics was negligible in comparison to that spent struggling with reading, writing or doing nothing.

It would seem then that Simon was first handicapped by Marie's coping strategies in the routinization of tasks with which Simon had difficulty coping and in the fact that her concentration was primarily on 'naughty' children, the queue and the readers. There were thus created the conditions for primary differentiation whereby Simon and others like him did not have ready access to the on-task teacher attention and encouragement they needed and were able to avoid seeking it out.

Simon's coping strategies meshed with those of Marie resulting in much slower progress in mathematics than he was capable of. As mentioned above, there were a number of children in the 'teacher-dependent' group who, like Simon, had difficulties with handwriting. In addition, there were many others in this group who took a long time over tasks for reasons concerned with their particular difficulties or social relations (see e.g. Elizabeth's case study). Thus there was, in the meshing of pupil and teacher strategies in this group, the creation of a system which acted as a *regulator* on children finishing tasks and joining the queue. However, without the *routine difficulties* and *routine opportunities* for sustained deviance, with which children's coping strategies meshed, Marie's queuing system would certainly have broken down. Marie's coping strategies were therefore, to some degree, sustained and reinforced by the coping strategies of the 'noisy'' and 'small' tables of 'teacher-dependents' just as they were, in a different way, by those of the 'independent' group.

6.5   CONCLUSION

In this chapter, I have presented data and an analysis that illustrates the theoretical approach that Pollard and I have taken to the question of 'Who is assessing?' and thus to the issue of 'pedagogy' in Figure 4.1. In it I use the concept of 'coping strategies' to illustrate ways in which policy change and conflicting role expectations for teachers are interpreted and mediated in particular settings and by individual teachers. It illustrates ways in which fundamental differences between teachers and the situations in which they find themselves, being reflected in their pedagogies, will in turn impact upon pupil responses and hence upon assessments.

In addressing the question of 'Who is being assessed?' in Chapters 3 and 4, we problematized what is involved in a teacher 'knowing' a child. We argued that 'the whole child' for assessment purposes cannot simply be 'read off' from classroom situations but has to be understood as the child *in context*. Hence our contention that teachers' social assessments of pupils are not neutral forms of diagnostic knowledge. Rather, as illustrated in this chapter, they are inseparable from the teacher-created settings which give rise to them.

The chapter also shows apparently objective differences between achievement outcomes of pupils as products of a differentiating effect arising out of teacher coping strategies which are geared to the needs of some pupils in ways that are detrimental to others. Using the concept of the meshing of teacher and pupil coping strategies, I show ways in which achievement outcomes are *joint achievements* of teachers and pupils. Thus the value of a holistic analysis, such as this, of the origins and effects of teacher coping strategies lies in its power to reveal the distinctiveness of classroom contexts and the different and differentiating affects of those contexts on individual pupils and groups of pupils. However, its value lies especially in its power to reveal the usually hidden role of the teacher in the production of classroom assessment outcomes.

In the following pair of Chapters, 7 and 8, Pollard and I go on to consider aspects of classroom assessment concerned with 'What is being assessed?' There we consider issues arising from pupils' socio-economic and cultural backgrounds and meet the cohort of children in their Year 3 class. In Chapter 10, however, we return for a consideration of aspects of Marie's pedagogy in comparing her pedagogy with that of the Year 2 teacher. That chapter is concerned with classroom language and the framing of educational knowledge in the two classrooms.

Chapter 7

What is being Assessed? – An Introduction

7.1 INTRODUCTION

In this third pair of chapters relating to Figure 4.1, we explore the question of 'What is being assessed?' The chapters raise questions regarding simplistic models of assessment in which pupils' responses are presented as self-evident products of existing ability, revealed through the stimulus of tasks, teacher questions or test items (Mehan, 1973). Rather, we explore the complex origins of pupils' responses to task expectations and the multiple social and cultural under-standings and relationships that shape and condition their production.

Through the chapter we discuss ways in which the activities, materials and questions of testing are not neutral tools for scientifically measuring pre-existing knowledge and skills but expres-sions of power relations that embody hidden values, social and cultural expectations and bias. We explore a range of contexts that research shows are important to children's developing personal and biographical understandings and learning. These wider sociocultural contexts are powerful in shaping children's spoken and written responses, the manner of their presentation and levels of social or emotional involvements in tasks. Such responses are, for example, embedded in and conditioned by gender, ethnicity and social class. Meanings are located in multiple contexts beyond the immediacy of assessment situations. Home, peers and community are ever-present evaluative contexts within which children locate their responses to classroom tasks and shape and communicate their developing sense of self.

In particular, in this chapter and through Chapter 8, we consider ways in which pupils' meanings and expectations that are located within peer-group relationships are in dynamic relationship with those derived from official classroom, biographical and wider sociocultural expectations.

Thus, ultimately, this pair of chapters reminds us that in observing the responses of individual children to assessment tasks or test items we might, to good effect, ask ourselves the question: 'What *else* is being assessed?'

7.2   SOCIOCULTURAL CONTEXTS OF PUPIL RESPONSES

In the field of assessment and testing, the term 'social context' is subject to broad interpretation. It may relate to the formally structured elements of test situations, the social context being embedded in, for example, test materials and questions. Alternatively it may relate to the wider interactional context in which assessments are made. In the latter case, 'context' will include interpretations, interactions, meanings, influences which are variously related in their intentions to the processes of the assessment task. An example of 'social context' in the former sense, that relating to test items themselves, might be the inclusion of items in a test which carry within them culturally specific meaning and understandings or gender bias. Test scores will also contain within them a measure of the social context, in the second sense, where interaction between the assessor and the assessed is called for in a test situation. Mehan (1973) described such tests and the scoring of them as:

> interpretive, interactional processes which should be approached and studied as such. (Mehan, 1973)

Research over many years has shown that in assessing pupils' academic skills teachers inevitably include a measure of other attributes and dispositions. Pupils' behaviour during a test, teacher knowledge of a child or its responses to a previous test, teacher interpretations of test material and pupil responses, the influence of other pupils are just some of the many contextual factors affecting scores or outcomes.

Context also relates to wider influences beyond the classroom and to the complex and diverse origins of pupils' written or spoken responses to classroom tasks. In this Halliday, for instance, (1978: 109) cites linguists throughout the century on the 'well-established concept' that context was not to be interpreted in terms of the concrete audio and visual 'props' surrounding a situation. It was rather to be understood abstractly in terms of its relevance to the text. The context of a situation, therefore, may be totally remote from what is going on in the concrete act of speaking or writing.

As we illustrated in Chapter 6 in the case study of the Year 1 teacher, Marie Tucker, 'context', in the form of the complex interaction of cultural, biographical and institutional factors, shapes the responses teachers elicit from their pupils and the way teachers interpret pupils' behaviour and responses. Research studies of pupil perspectives such as those within the *Identity and Learning Programme* show that children's biographies, sociocultural learning and experiences and peer relations also provide frameworks of reference and expectations beyond those officially related to classroom tasks. Considerations of classrooms themselves as sociocultural contexts and some of the well-understood classroom processes relating to, for example, the control of knowledge, the socialization and the social differentiation of pupils are discussed in relation to 'classroom processes' in Chapters 9 and 10.

Through this pair of chapters, therefore, we consider the importance of a range of sociocultural contexts, from the most immediate and visible to the most distant and intangible, in the shaping and conditioning of children's classroom responses. However, our focus in this is primarily on *pupil* meanings and interpretations in responding to assessment tasks. Meanings and interpretations for teachers are dealt with in the chapters relating to 'pedagogy' and to 'classroom processes'.

Our focus here also primarily relates to formal, National Curriculum assessment processes. Some of the more informal, 'social' and behavioural aspects of classroom assessment and their dynamic relationship with academic assessment processes have been explored through earlier chapters in relation to 'identity' and 'pedagogy'.

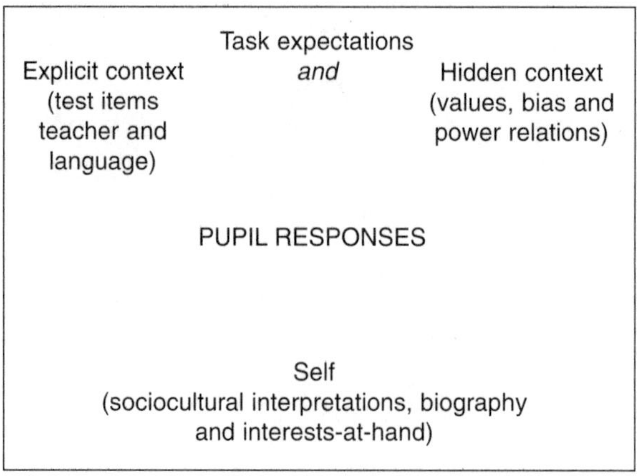

Task expectations
Explicit context   *and*   Hidden context
(test items   (values, bias and
teacher and   power relations)
language)

PUPIL RESPONSES

Self
(sociocultural interpretations, biography
and interests-at-hand)

Figure 7.1   *Task expectations and 'self': factors shaping pupil responses*

In further developing the model in Figure 7.1, therefore, we now focus on groups of factors we perceive pupils to draw on in their approaches to classroom assessment tasks. The groups of factors are those related to 'task expectations' and those concerned with 'self'. Readers comparing these factors with those of 'pedagogy' on the model will appreciate that both 'pupil responses' here and 'pedagogy' in previous chapters are represented by a synthesis of internal and external concerns whereby the external demands of a situation ('role expectations', 'institutional settings', 'task expectations') are mediated by personal and situationally strategic concerns (self).

Technologies of testing, values and power relations

Task expectations in this section of the model refers to any test, curriculum or teacher requirement upon the pupil for fulfilment of the task in hand. We are thus here concerned with particular academic requirements in the form of knowledge or skills of the kind required as 'evidence' in relation to National Curriculum attainments. Such 'evidence' could relate to ongoing classroom assessment situations (teacher assessment) or to externally set standardized tests.

Of course, tests and formal assessment requirements cannot be regarded as neutral tools. The development of test items and materials and the activity of testing, Madaus and Horn (2000) suggest, fit any instrumental definition of a technology. Thus technology and technological devices are tools, instrumental aids to human activity, drawing on specialist knowledge and activities, skills, methods and procedures. Assessment is a bureaucratic tool relying on this kind of craft knowledge. As such, Madaus and Horn argue, testing is both a *social technology* and a *technical craft*. The technology is embedded in such socio-technical systems as education, government and business. As indicated in Figure 7.1, the immediate and visible context of testing – the hardware – consists of test sheets and booklets, answer sheets, scoring machines and computers. Practitioners of testing share a common language, rationale, sets of practices, procedures and methods (Madaus and Horn, 2000). As also shown in Figure 7.1, the practices of technological elites embody hidden values of social and cultural bias and expectations.

However, as these and other authors point out, notwithstanding hidden values and bias, the mystique and legitimization of 'scientific' testing promotes acceptance of outcomes as accurate reflections of ability and, often, of prospects for future success (see also Madaus, 1994; Broad-foot, 1996; Filer, 2000). As discussed in Chapter 1, the analysis in Filer (2000), *Assessment: Social Practice and Social Product* draws attention to technologies of testing as an aspect of assessment practice that is often overlooked by many professional educators as well as by lay people. As Madaus and Horn (drawing on Winner, 1986: 5) comment:

> people generally do not concern themselves with either how a technology like testing, or for that matter light bulbs, telephones or cars, etc. are made or how they work. They believe such concerns are the province of those who invent, develop, build or repair them. Instead most people are primarily interested in the use of technologies. (Madaus and Horn, 2000)

Throughout this discussion of 'What is being assessed?', therefore, we need to bear in mind considerations of test technologies as an ever-present sociocultural process which can powerfully and differentially shape the responses of groups of pupils.

Such social and cultural values, perceptions, interpretations and power relations carry important implications for assessment processes and outcomes. A consideration of them presents insights into the fact that, as well as having educational purposes, assessment fulfils a range of political and social functions within modern societies. These wider functions are concerned with social differentiation and reproduction, social control and the legitimation of particular forms of knowledge and culture of socially powerful groups (Broadfoot, 1996; Filer, 2000) We need, therefore, to be aware when considering pupil responses that assessment is conducted 'on, by and for, inherently social actors' (Wiliam, 1997: 396).

We can now consider those aspects of the 'self' and the contexts pupils draw on which constitute those 'internal concerns' in their responses, bearing in mind also the above considerations of some of the hidden values and power relations embedded in the 'external demands' of assessment processes.

The 'self' and pupils' sociocultural identities

The processes whereby pupils assessed responses are embedded in, and conditioned by, gender, ethnicity and social class are well researched. Pupils' experiences and understandings of self come into play and account for differences in performance where assessment content is biased in favour of particular social or cultural groups. That is to say, even where pupils have the required knowledge or skills, assessment content in the form of the language used, test items, materials and illustrations may be more meaningful to some groups and less so to others (Swann report, 1985; Murphy, 1988; Gipps and Murphy, 1994; Black, 1998). For example, test items referring to particular situations, objects or processes can inhibit and affect performance. Thus, at different ages, test and other assessment content involving animals, botany, human, personal or social issues favours girls. Boys perform better if the subject of test items is mechanical toys, physical objects or impersonal essay topics (DES, 1988; Gipps and Murphy, 1994: 139-40; Black, 1998: 50).

Similarly cultural, social and class-based assumptions, understandings, conventions and language can be built into assessment questions in ways that bias in favour of or against certain groups. Cooper and Dunne (2000) discuss ways in which children from different socio-economic backgrounds interpret and respond to national test items. Problems in mathematics can arise where pupils use and import everyday knowledge of situations presented in test questions. Their findings indicate a social-class effect whereby, faced with 'realistic' mathematics test questions, many working-class and intermediate social-class children up to the age of fourteen fail to demonstrate knowledge that they have and can demonstrate in other contexts. The authors use the example of questions involving a series of pairings for mixed-doubles tennis matches. There may be a cultural disposition to engage realistically with such problems (Bourdieu, 1986) so that pupil responses include social-situational 'noise' where mathematical abstraction is called for. Such an example is also representative of situations whereby test items can be located in social or cultural situations of which some pupils may have no experience. Similarly, from the point of view of ethnic differences, Black (1998) suggests that a question concerning, for example, an old person living alone would represent an everyday situation in Western, white culture. It might, on the other hand, represent an odd case of exclusion from the family in other cultures giving rise to inappropriate responses from a tester's perspective (p. 50). As Cooper and Dunne conclude, test designers need to give careful thought to just what it is that they are testing (2000).

In Chapter 3 we discussed ways in which young children's gendered, ethnic and social-classed understandings of self are shaped by particular forms of social learning, experience and positioning. This was achieved within family, peer and school relationships and the mediation of wider forms of cultural knowledge and political and social discourse. These kinds of explanations are what Gipps and Murphy describe as the 'environmental hypotheses' for explaining the different performances of social groups (1994: 6). In relation to gender behaviour, for instance, expectations on the part of carers shape the provision of activities, toys and forms of feedback so that boys and girls come to attend to different features of the environment. Different out-of-school and within-school experiences regarding perceived male and female domains come to shape girls' and boys' attitudes and expectations of success within those domains. The authors suggest that whilst such hypotheses are used to explain gender differences they are also useful for considering some differences between ethnic and cultural groups (Wilder and Powell, 1989; Gipps and Murphy, 1994: 6).

Of course, as these authors point out, there are also a range of 'biological hypotheses' for differences among groups that are either genetic, hormonal or due to brain structure (Stafford, 1963; Petersen, 1976; Nyborg, 1988; Herrnstein and Murray, 1994). Though this approach has been discredited in relation to differences between ethnic groups (Gould, 1981; see also Fraser, 1997), biological causes of differential responses to context or content are still used by some people to account for differences between the sexes. For example, some maintain that boys are 'naturally' good at maths and sciences and that girls are 'naturally' better at languages and arts. However, data from international surveys and from changing patterns of results for 16-year-olds means there is now no arguable case for the biological hypothesis (Gipps and Murphy, 1994: 264).

The 'self' and pupils' biographies

In earlier chapters we discussed ways in which pupils incorporate and maintain their distinct identities within and through their classroom learning and responses. We pointed to a major finding of the *Identity and Learning Programme* concerning the importance of opportunities for the expression and affirmation of pupils' distinct identities and approaches to learning in classrooms (Chapter 3.3). As we illustrated with case studies, this was found to be particularly important where a child was withdrawn or marginal to classroom life or where a child's social identity was distinct from, or in tension with, that of the predominant peer culture.

Our own studies and those of others who attempt to access pupil perspectives on their learning show how their meanings are located in multiple contexts extending beyond the immediacy of any particular classroom task. In (Pollard *et al.*, 1996) for example, Maguire presents a study of three 8-year-old Muslim girls living in Quebec, showing their language, learning and social worlds as inextricably intertwined. The importance of opportunities for expressing and shaping identities through classroom tasks, the tensions and conflicts experienced and the nature of responses closely paralleled those of English pupils in Greenside and Albert Park Schools. In this, Maguire reveals the complexity, the personal and individual nature of the girls' responses to tasks. Their written and spoken responses reveal tensions between their personal and their social agendas and identities across home, community and school contexts and their responses are shaped by situations and events experienced in Quebec and Iran. Different teachers and the girls' individual relationships with teachers were variable in the opportunities they presented for exploring the different, often conflicting, cultural and social locations of their evolving identities. Across different classroom contexts and relationships they presented different personas, stances and representations of their lived situation. They used literature opportunities for making sense of their worlds as minority language users as well as for establishing relationships and expressing sociocultural understandings to others (Maguire, 1977). Readers might find it interesting to map these descriptions of classroom opportunities and relationships and pupils' means of expressing and exploring identity and difference on to the case-study vignettes of middle-class children in Greenside School in Chapter 3.3 (full case studies are presented in Pollard and Filer, 1999).

Perhaps because of the cultural and biographical differences between the Muslim girls and their Western teachers and peers (and the researcher herself), this study illuminates clearly ways in which young children's classroom responses are shaped by an awareness of a range of evaluative and relationship contexts. Through such studies we see that home, community, peers and friends are ever-present contexts within which young pupils locate their meanings and responses, shape and, where they have the opportunity, communicate to others their developing sense of self.

The 'self' and pupils' interests-at-hand

The Social World of the Primary School (Pollard, 1985) sets out pupils' 'interests-at-hand' (Figure 5.2 in this book) as a way of representing children's (and teachers') most significant and immediate concerns in the ebb and flow of classroom life (see Chapters 5 and 6). Pollard describes classrooms in terms of the relatively distinct social systems that coexist. The official system of school with its hierarchy, rules and particular criteria for evaluation exists alongside the less formal social system of the children, with its own hierarchy, rules and criteria of judgement (Pollard, 1985: 81).

As illustrated in Chapter 3.3 and through Elizabeth's case study, peer membership and acceptance is crucial for children for the solidarity and support it offers in countering vulnerability in the classroom and also for the enjoyment it offers. Moment to moment, meanings and expectations located within peer contexts are in dynamic relationship with those derived from official classroom, biographical and wider, cultural, sociocultural contexts. As we have shown through case studies, ours and those of others, the peer group is a powerful influence, along with other contexts, in shaping children's spoken and written responses, the manner of their presentation and the level of social or emotional involvement in tasks.

As well as being concerned with peer membership, pupil interests-at-hand are also concerned with such matters as self-image, dignity and autonomy in the classroom. Thus it is that our studies and those of others show children from moment to moment, shifting and modifying their responses. In so doing they seek to shape, project and, crucially, protect their sense of 'self' and status through changing contexts of teacher expectations, classroom relationships and peer appraisal. One detailed account of such a process comes from an observation reported by Pryor and Torrance of three small boys being assessed in their early language and mathematics skill. The task centred round the story of 'The Three Bears' (Pryor and Torrance, 2000). In this activity, holding 'Mummy bear', 'Daddy bear' or 'Baby bear' and the identification of self with bear became crucial aspects of the boys' responses. The playing out of gender roles and power relations and the jockeying for possession and position *vis-à-vis* teacher and peers reflected the 'overlapping discursive practices of home and school' (2000; see also Walkerdine, 1988). The authors show how classroom assessment, like other educational encounters, is socially situated and constructed. They point out that children's social positioning and understandings are also being assessed where the social interaction of a situation seems to construct failure and differentially affect outcomes. Whereas children's classroom responses are often treated as unproblematic sources of information regarding what a child knows or can do, in this, as in Cooper and Dunne (above) and in Chapter 10.4 in this book, children fail to demonstrate knowledge and skills that researchers observed displayed by those children in other contexts. In such assessment situations, the question is not what children know but what social learning and interpretations might be getting in the way of performance (Pryor and Torrance, 2000). They conclude that:

> Assessment is not an activity that can be *done* to children but is accomplished by means of social interaction in which the practices of the participants have a critical effect on outcome. The outcomes of assessment are actively produced rather than revealed and displayed by the assessment process. (Pryor and Torrance, 2000)

The following chapter presents an extended analysis of classroom talk in the context of Year 3 National Curriculum assessment of 'speaking and listening'. It shows how pupil responses are embedded in the wider contexts of the socio-economic circumstances of their families and community, in peer affiliations and statuses and classroom identities. It illustrates issues of identity, self-image and interests-at-hand of pupils where reputations and relationships are in the balance. The tension is between fulfilling teacher expectations, and National Curriculum definitions of classroom speaking, and fulfilling real social functions *vis-à-vis* an audience of peers.

7.3   CONCLUSION

The increasing pressure on teachers to formalize classroom assessment processes and recording procedures and for 'evidence' serves to obscure the reality of classroom life. The 'scientific' paradigm of testing disguises values and power relations, bias, inequalities and the sociocultural expectations of testers and the tested. Classroom assessments, from the most informal to the most formal, are interpretative processes. Knowledge, skills and performance are inseparable from social and cultural attributes and learning, gender and ethnicity. The relevant 'context' of influence is not to be taken simply as the immediate social or physical environment of an assessment activity but to include the wider contribution of family and peer affiliations, sociocultural biography and individual identity.

The exploration of the contexts of 'pupils responses' in this chapter combines with that of 'pedagogy' to develop a picture of classroom assessment outcomes as jointly constructed by pupils and teachers, and as part of wider fields of action and evaluative contexts beyond the immediacy of tasks.

The following chapter is the second of the pair concerned with the question of 'What is being assessed?' It relates to Ann Filer's PhD study and is set in the cohort's Year 3 at Albert Park School. The assessment being made relates to the National Curriculum attainment target of 'speaking and listening'. In it, children talk of their social purposes *vis-à-vis* an audience of peers which are embedded in the telling of their 'news'. We see how such purposes go beyond and often undermine the requirements of the task as envisaged by a National Curriculum attainment target.

Through previous chapters and in the following one, we have examined and theorized the impact of personal, social and cultural factors in shaping teacher and pupil interactions and interpretations and assessment outcomes. In the following chapter we also more explicitly begin to theorize classroom contexts themselves as cultural settings and classroom language as part of the social setting. These themes of language and classroom culture are further developed through 'classroom processes' in Chapters 9 and 10.

Chapter 8

What is being Assessed? – Peer Culture and the Assessment of Classroom Language

Ann Filer

8.1 INTRODUCTION

This is the second of chapter in the pair that poses the question 'What is being assessed?' It raises questions in relation to simplistic models of assessment in which pupil responses are presented as self-evident products of existing ability, knowledge and skills revealed through the stimulus of teacher and test questions (Mehan, 1973). Rather, in it I explore ways in which pupils' responses to task expectations are bound up in a multiplicity of social and cultural understandings and relationships that shape and condition their production. Thus in relation to any assessment of a pupil, we might well ask: 'What *else* is being assessed?'

This chapter further illuminates the importance of that question in presenting an analysis of 'speaking and listening' assessments in the context of the Year 3 'news' sessions at Albert Park School. In it I describe a 'communicative competence' (Hymes, 1971) model of language, on which, I argue, National Curriculum 'speaking and listening' assessment requirements are based. I also describe a model of language based on 'meanings' and 'functions in a social system' (Halliday, 1978) as a more appropriate basis for understanding classroom talk. Using Halliday's model, the analysis shows ways in which social and cultural factors in children's lives, related to their socio-economic status, gender and classroom identities, are also relevant to the contexts in which they are assessed. It illuminates ways in which the children's 'news' session had different meanings for different groups of children, which gave rise to academically and socially differentiated outcomes.

As with all case-study chapters, a wider theoretical and research background is provided in the previous chapter, where also a model of 'pupil responses' in relation to Figure 4.1 can be found. Whilst a reading of that chapter will further sensitize readers to the issues raised here, this chapter can be read independently.

An earlier version of the data and analysis presented here first appeared as ' "At least they were laughing": assessment and the functions of children's language in their "news" session' (Filer, 1997).

8.2 BACKGROUND AND SETTING

Halliday (1978) suggests that through language people in interaction:

> do more than understand each other, in the sense of exchanging information. ... By their everyday acts of meaning, people act out the social structure, affirming their own statuses and roles, and establishing and transmitting the shared systems of values and of knowledge. (Halliday, 1978: 2)

In this chapter I show pupils, in their 'news' sessions, doing as Halliday here suggests. If pupils are being assessed on their ability to 'exchange information' in this and similar assessment contexts, then they are also, at the same time, being assessed on the way in which they act out the social structure with respect to statuses, roles, shared values and knowledge.

The 'news' session in its various forms, whereby pupils show objects and tell the class about their out-of-school interests, events and activities, is a ubiquitous feature of English early years primary classrooms. In Albert Park School, as elsewhere, the 'news' session was used widely in developing the confidence of pupils in speaking before an audience of peers and their teacher, in listening and in asking and answering the questions of teacher and peers. As described in Chapter 10, the 'news' session, in its various forms, was one of the key situations in which 'speaking and listening' skills were formally assessed.

The National Curriculum attainment target of 'speaking and listening' would appear to be based on a model of language broadly aligned to a 'communicative competence' (Hymes, 1971) model of language. A communicative competence model of language is one in which, Halliday argues, language is perceived as 'knowledge in the head' of the subject (Halliday, 1978).

This analysis of classroom language of Year 3 pupils was undertaken to explore the possibility of an alternative model of language for understanding classroom language. That model is one suggested by Halliday (1978) based on *meaning* and *function* in a social system; that is a model that sees utterances as 'actions which are performed with language' (Stubbs, 1986: 145).

Using Halliday's *meaning and functions* model in the following analysis, therefore, I examined pupils' meanings in the context of the Monday morning 'news' session together with the meanings they attributed to other pupils' news. I show through this analysis that pupil's *purposes vis-à-vis* an audience of peers in a classroom go beyond the requirements of the task as envisaged by the National Curriculum attainment target of 'speaking and listening'.

The use of the theoretical position of symbolic interactionism in the study also suggested the key importance of pupils' differentiated perceptions of classroom situations (Chapters 1 and 3). Thus I also explored the different meanings and interpretations that an individual brought to, and derived from, the telling of news. This I did using Halliday's (1978) notion of language as a series of choices or *options* and through the conditions governing pupils' access to those options.

In the following section I compare the two models of language: a 'communicative competence' (Hymes, 1971) model and a 'meanings and functions' (Halliday, 1978) model. I argue that National Curriculum requirements for the assessment of 'speaking and listening' are based on an understanding of classroom language in terms of 'communicative competence'. I then present Halliday's comparison of the 'competence' model, with his alternative model of 'meanings and functions', as a basis for a more appropriate model for understanding classroom talk.

Two models of language

'Communicative competence' and the assessment of speaking and listening

The history of the term 'communicative competence' is complex, involving diverse but often interrelated schools of linguistic and sociolinguistic thought. A brief outline of the history of the term could start with Hymes (1971) who adopted it from Chomsky (1965) in order to describe the tacit knowledge that underlies linguistic behaviour. Hymes stressed a broader application of the term than Chomsky, however, who described such competence in terms of linguistic knowledge only. Hymes described it in terms of the knowledge of social conventions of language use in terms of what to say, when to say it, to whom, in what manner, etc. Such a model of language competence, broadly based on the Hymes (1971) model, I would argue, represents a model for the teaching and assessment of 'speaking and listening' in the National Curriculum.

The National Curriculum relating to Key Stages 1 to 4 describes the requirements for the teaching of 'speaking and listening' in the following terms:

> To develop effective speaking and listening pupils should be taught to:
> - use the vocabulary and grammar of Standard English;
> - formulate, clarify and express their ideas;
> - adapt their speech to a widening range of circumstances and demands;
> - listen, understand and respond appropriately to others.
>
> (Department for Education, 1994)

National Curriculum Levels 2 and 3 are considered appropriate for primary pupils of the age and attainment of the cohort in their Year 3. Therefore, moving on to the specific attainment targets against which these pupils were being assessed, we find that for Level 2, reflecting the above requirements, reference is made to the need to:

- show awareness of the needs of the listener;
- respond with increasing appropriateness to what others say.

For assessment at Level 3 pupils should:

- begin to adapt what they say to the needs of the listener, varying the use of vocabulary and the level of detail.

We can clearly see the roots of these aims in the Hymes model outlined above. We can see it in notions of 'adaptation', of 'circumstances and demands', in 'appropriateness' and in 'the needs of the listener'. Notwithstanding requirements to listen, it is I would argue, above all, a one-way, *performance* model of language whereby what is at stake is the development of an ideal, disengaged and efficacious speaker able to match speech to audience and to the purposes of the task in hand.

Now, whilst theories of communicative competence may incorporate factors such as social situations and social roles of subjects, they are essentially, Halliday (1978) suggests, about knowledge *carried in the head* of subjects. They take, that is, is a biological/psychological perspective on language which views it in terms of internal mechanisms and capacities. Though theories of communicative competence recognize that language takes place in a social context, questions concerning how to behave linguistically in certain contexts are viewed from inside the head, looking out at the social (Halliday, 1978).

Of course, a moment's thought tells us that any assessment of spoken language that seeks to attach a grade or attainment level to an individual child *has to assume* a 'within the head' competence model of language knowledge and skill. However, whether such a model is an appropriate one for understanding and assessing classroom talk is the subject of my analysis in this chapter.

An alternative model of language

If Hymes' 1971 theories of 'communicative competence' broadly describe language in terms of 'knowledge in the head', Halliday (1978) presents an alternative conception of language; one that is understood in terms of *meanings* and in terms of *functions in a social system*. He argues that in a 'competence' model, speech and the situations in which speech takes place are conceptually divisible. In a 'functions' model, language is inseparable from its social setting and language and society are inextricably bound together in meaning.

In the analysis which follows we see children talking about their use of language in the classroom in exactly the way Halliday suggests; in terms of functions in a social system. In situations in which their language is being assessed, they are seen to be *simultaneously* responding to teacher and task expectations (telling news) and also fulfilling a range of social functions in relation to the peer-group social system. The content of their news telling was imbued with meanings that drew on and had implications for their relationships and classroom statuses. This was quite apart from any meanings or functions related to filling teacher requirements for their talk, though with implications for how it was assessed.

An important element of Halliday's model for my analysis here, concerns the 'options' which were available to children with regard to the content of their news. For Halliday, what one 'can do' functionally in a situation is realized linguistically through the series of options available in that situation (1978: 27). People in interaction are, therefore, making choices in the environment of other choices and, because not all meanings are available to them, different social groups will have differential access and orientation to these options.

In the context of my PhD investigations, it seemed to me that Halliday's critique and alternative model of language had much to offer in relation to certain key areas of enquiry. In particular it had the potential for a better understanding of any relationship between, on the one hand, classroom talk and communication in assessment processes and, on the other, pupils' differentiated experiences and responses to classroom assessment processes. However, by the time the children were in their Year 3 class I had observed and analysed many 'news' and 'discussion' and similar whole-class teaching sessions with successive teachers (see Chapter 10), as well as observed, videoed and recorded virtually every other kind of classroom talk. However, I still had no idea where I might locate Halliday's 'meanings', 'options' and 'functions'. 'Pupil perspectives' were also key to my ongoing analysis and so it seemed to me that I might find out more if I simply asked them about their news sessions. I therefore interviewed all the children in the class individually, and some more than once. Below, I present an analysis of those interviews, following a description of the way in which 'news' sessions were conducted in Jenny Luke's Year 3 class.

The Monday morning 'news' session

On Monday mornings, with all pupils sitting on the carpet, those who wished to tell news, and this was the majority of them, took it in turns to tell it. Their teacher, Jenny Luke, expected that they should do so with minimum prompting or questioning from her. Unlike the teachers in Years 1 and 2, Jenny did not select a knowledge content to be focused on, for example, by means of teacher questions put to the listening class or to the teller of news (see Chapter 10). As I shall show though, this does not mean that pupils were not aware of teacher preferences for certain sorts of news. However, on the basis of much research evidence (Labov *et al.*, 1968; Strandberg and Griffith, 1968; Mueller, 1971; Lees, 1981; Wood and Wood, 1983; Tizard and Hughes, 1984; Dunn, 1996) and on the basis of earlier research with this cohort (Chapter 10), a situation in which the teacher is less controlling and in which there is increased personal involvement in the topic on the part of pupils provides a context in which pupils will talk more and with greater complexity. Within the limitations that pertain to any whole-class activity, therefore, the Year 3 news sessions as conducted by Jenny Luke would be likely to provide reasonably good conditions for maximizing pupil contributions and for assessing pupils' 'speaking and listening' skills as defined by the National Curriculum (see Chapter 9 for a fuller discussion relating to classroom language and culture).

At the time of the analysis I had been tracking the cohort on a weekly basis for nearly three years and they were now 7–8 years old. Where in the following I make reference to pupils' friendships and classroom status *vis-à-vis* peers, this is derived from sociometric questioning, interviews and observations. It is also supported by my knowledge of the children developed prior to the events they recount and my continuing knowledge of them through their primary years, as described throughout this book.

8.3   MEANINGS AND FUNCTIONS OF 'NEWS' IN THE PEER CULTURE

What follows is an analysis of two rounds of interviews, though primarily it relates to the second of these. Both rounds were conducted with individual pupils, the first with six pupils, the second across the whole cohort. The interviews were semi-structured and designed with the aim of investigating Halliday's notion of 'options' within the 'meaning potential' of the news session. That is to say, I wanted to know:

- What the possibilities were for what children could mean and be doing in their news telling?
- What were the factors that affected pupils' and groups' differential orientation and access to meanings?

The first round of interviews were exploratory in nature regarding children's experiences of news telling and were carried out in depth. The value of these initial interviews was that they began to alert me to the presence of something that looked like Halliday's 'options' and 'meanings'. These insights occurred in relation to decisions that children seemed to be making about what news to tell and the need for some circumspection in their choices in relation to an audience of peers. They seemed to be concerned with what children were meaning and doing *vis-à-vis* an audience of peers as well as in relation to the official agenda.

For example, Peter in interview began discussing his Grandma's stroke with me but, he told me, he would not talk about this in news time. He told me that 'the problem is the teacher'. Peter's mother had told Ms Luke about the stroke, he said, and:

> She (Ms Luke) keeps asking questions and everybody keeps asking questions and gathers round. . . .
> I don't mind one or two people that I can trust asking about it, like on the way home or whispering in
> the playground. (Peter)

Peter was, of all the children, perhaps one of the most sensitive to different speaking and listening contexts. It was, for example, two years after his entry to school before he was happy to volunteer a question or comment in a whole-class situation (see Chapter 10). Martin, on the other hand, was one of the highest achievers in the class, and certainly so with respect to spoken language skills. He, for example, was the child that successive teachers most often sent around the school with messages and he always commanded high status with his peers. Yet he too felt at least some circumspection concerning the content of his news. He told me about decisions he made about whether to tell certain things because:

> Sometimes I worry that other children will think that the things I have done are babyish. (Martin)

It was responses such as these, in the first round of interviews, which told me that some pupils at least were having to consider the content of their news telling in the light of peer responses. They suggested where, in the news session, I might locate Halliday's options. However, these interviews only told me about personal choices and individuals' feelings. For Halliday, 'meaning' is conceptualized in a less individualistic way than in symbolic interactionism. Thus in order to explore the relevance of Halliday's model, I needed to discover *shared meanings* among the children and, from there, ways in which children's utterances *functioned in a social system*. Already, however, references in National Curriculum requirements (above) for the need for children to 'adapt to the needs of the listener' and to 'respond with appropriateness to what others say' began to appear to be a somewhat simplistic understanding of what might be going on in classroom talk.

The next set of interviews, those conducted with each child in the class, were, as described above, designed to clarify what children could be meaning and doing in their news telling and the factors affecting pupils' and groups' orientation and access to meanings.

Analysing the interviews

Children's evaluation of the content of the news of their peers fell into two main categories. These two main categories are what I have called *special events* and *common events*. The notion of *special* and *common* are constructs which I arrived at through analysis of pupils' accounts of what constituted 'good' and 'not so good' telling of news. *Special events* referred to those outings, treats, purchases, etc. which to a greater or lesser extent fell outside the routine experiences of the children's lives. *Common events*, on the other hand, were the routines of, for example, family life and out-of-school play that all the children were familiar with, together with the ordinary outings, purchases, etc. which most experienced as a matter of course. Both *special* and *common* can be further analysed to cover all other examples of news cited by the children. Thus further categories will be derived from this main distinction.

In the following analysis I have only used data which refers explicitly to the content of news. Comments such as 'interesting', 'exciting' or 'boring' which could refer to the process or to content I have excluded. Making a distinction between their teacher's views and their own, I asked the children to nominate pupils who they thought were good and pupils who they thought were not so good at telling news and to give the reasons for their choices. They were also asked about the content of their own news and how 'good' or 'not so good' theirs could be. Children were allowed to nominate as many children as they wished as either good or not so good news tellers. The model presented in Figure 8.1 sets out the children's news telling in terms of Halliday's 'options' and 'functions' in the social system of the peer group.

Twenty-six children were interviewed. Ten children explicitly made the sort of distinction between *special* and *common events* that I have outlined. The following will help to elucidate the two main categories (or *options*) in news telling.

David nominated six pupils as being good at news telling because:

> They go to interesting places. (David)

Peter nominated three pupils because:

> They always seem to say exciting things. ... 'Cos they, like instead of saying like 'I called at Stuart's house' – I'm only making this up – they say like 'I had a barbecue' and they tell you what they had. (Peter)

Peter went on to cite one boy who did not tell good news:

> Well the problem is he says things that everyone's done like 'I went to the zoo'. (Peter)

We see in Peter's explanation that positive evaluation of the news of peers is about novelty value. Similarly, Nicola explains:

> Well, say someone said they went to a safari park, that would be interesting. But if they said they went out on their skateboard, that's boring. (Nicola)

In a similar way, Nicola explained:

> Elizabeth's is a bit boring sometimes. The other day she was on about getting new trainers. (Nicola)

Ricky came in for criticism from several peers for being boring. Bobby, for instance, said scathingly that:

> He talks about pencils and crayons for news. (Bobby)

This notion that some items are invalid as news can also be seen in Tina's criticism of Louise:

> She doesn't really tell news. She just says things like 'I went on my bike'. Things like that. (Tina)

Altogether, fifteen children, just over half the class, were cited as telling news that was good because it was interesting in these sorts of ways and there was a strong consistency of opinion in responses regarding the children that told of these *special events*.

Although, clearly, there was status in telling of special events, the children who did so did not necessarily escape criticism. Six children make negative comments about the news of individual children in this category. Martin's news, for example, was generally highly rated for interest and excitement, having more positive mentions in this way than anyone else in the class. Martin was one of several boys involved in organized, out-of-school sport. He sometimes told about his weekend football matches and clearly this was not of such universal popularity as, say, a visit to Alton Towers might be. Robert rated Martin's news as:

> Boring, because he always tells about football results. (Robert)

Nicola similarly rated Martin's football stories as 'boring'.

Children whose socio-economic circumstances allowed them access to the higher status of telling of special events were in line for a different sort of criticism as well as that related to personal interests of listeners. They could be accused of 'showing off'. David, a close friend of Martin and also highly rated as a teller of special events, was accused of showing off by Graham and also by Nathan:

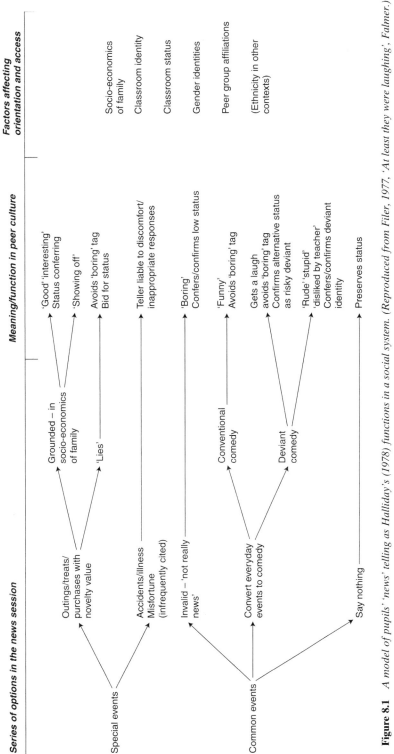

Figure 8.1 A model of pupils' 'news' telling as Halliday's (1978) functions in a social system. (Reproduced from Filer, 1977, 'At least they were laughing', Falmer.)

AF	Who do you think does not tell news so well?
Nathan	David. He shows off.
AF	Shows off? In what way?
Nathan	He takes his Grandma's dog for a walk. He shows off. He says 'I went to a party'. He walks down the road real cool. He's a show off.

Concern about consequences such as being regarded as a 'show off'' could, in this way, cut across and reduce pupils' options for news telling even though their socio-economic status gave them access to them. Peter's news, for example, was rated highly by the above 'cool' David, himself a teller of special events, because:

> Peter always goes to interesting places. (David)

On the other hand, Peter's news was rated negatively by Robert as 'showing off'. He complained:

> He (Peter) always goes swimming and tennis and telling what he's got. (Robert)

However, high-status David, who rated Peter's news highly, was not a *friend* of Peter's. Peter was a somewhat marginalized, low-status child among his peers. He was in the same loosely structured friendship group of low status, fairly low-achieving boys as Robert, his critic here. Though usually rejected by Robert, Peter always vied for his friendship with another boy in the group. For reasons to do with sensitivity to criticism and the maintenance of friendship, therefore, Peter was learning to be circumspect in selecting his news. He told me:

> I say things that people are not going to go on about. Like I said about my bed (Peter had been telling me about his new cabin bed) but they did, like, 'Can I come over your house? Can I come over your house?' Nathan or Bobby or John get jealous and say things to my friends like 'You don't want to go over his house' and say what better things they have got. (Peter)

Thus Peter was prepared to forgo some measure of status that the socio-economic circumstances of his home life gave him access to in favour of the much needed support and friendship of some of his low-status peers.

One option apparently open to those who aspired to the status of telling of special events was to lie. Three boys between them accused seven others of lying. Stuart told me:

> They tell things that they haven't been on and that. They just wish they had. Every bit of news Thomas tells is lying because he lives next door to me and he's always in and he can't go to the places he says he goes to. (Stuart)

Nathan was quite confident that he could detect a lie. He told me:

> If they say it in a certain sort of way you know they're lying. (Nathan)

Another option to avoid the label of being boring, cited by several children, was to say nothing. Alison was a child who was cited by her peers as going to interesting places and she said of herself that she went to exciting places and told exciting news. I asked her if she had ever done it not so well. She told me she hadn't because:

> If my stuff is boring I don't say anything otherwise they will think 'Oh this is *bor-ring*'. (Alison)

However, it was possible to tell of *common events* without acquiring the tag of being boring and that was done by converting such events into comedy. There were two distinctly different sorts of comedy cited. First there was what might be described as *conventional comedy*, against which could be contrasted *deviant comedy*. Two girls fell into the former category. School records and observations showed that Katie had, over the past two years, lacked much involvement in speaking activities involving the whole class. However, over the weeks of news telling as organized in Jenny Luke's class she developed a reputation for telling comic stories about her family. Six children cited Katie as being good at news telling because she was funny. Elizabeth told me:

> I like Katie's news best because she's got this little sister and she tells about her Dad. He steps in dog's mess. You should have heard. He went in the bushes to do a wee and he came out and stepped in dog's mess. (Elizabeth)

As alluded to here, Katie also told a series of stories about the naughty things her toddler sister got up to. My observations of news sessions left me with the impression that, over time, the facts of some of these 'naughty sister' news stories were increasingly being embellished by Katie to make good stories and amuse her peers. However, no pupil accused her of 'lying'. I also observed Elizabeth, also cited as telling comedy, giving a funny and animated account of hiding amongst furniture stacked up for house decorating so that her parents could not find her. Though these girls were making reference to very ordinary day-to-day events, by developing the comedy in them they avoided the label of 'boring'. Six children cited incidents of this sort, comedy of everyday events, as being funny and the best sort of news.

In addition to these two girls, six boys derived comedy from day-to-day events, but in the telling of what I have termed *deviant comedy*. Their news was nominated by five children with approval and by seven with disapproval. Children who liked this sort of news best were not necessarily in any way deviant in their own classroom behaviour. News that fell into this category included exaggerated, dramatized accounts of fights, accidents and misbehaviour. Helen gave an example:

> I don't like John's and Adrian's. Like John always says he goes to the park and fights or crashes into lamp-posts and his teeth fell out. (Helen)

Caroline also disliked this sort of news:

> Always messing about and saying rude, sort of stupid things in their news and everybody laughs. Some people don't laugh. (Caroline)

There was a strong consensus of opinion that Ms Luke did not like news about fighting. Lara told me about what was approved and disapproved of:

> Thinking about something to do with all your family, really. Sometimes she doesn't like it. If you say 'Yesterday I got in a fight', she doesn't like it. But if you say 'Yesterday I fell off a horse', that's okay. And if you say 'Yesterday I went on a picnic', she will say 'I wish I could come', and things like that. (Lara)

Teacher disapproval often meant that the news was cut short. Nathan, a teller of *deviant comedy* told me:

> If it's funny, like about fighting, she'll say 'Next!'. If everyone starts laughing she says 'Next!'. (Nathan)

At the time of the interviews Nathan and Thomas had recently been involved in telling an item of news which had been the subject of much disapproval on the part of both Jenny Luke and many of the children. It was frequently cited in interviews with children and later with Jenny. Thomas gave me his account:

> I do it different. I tell what I do to my sister. I hit her sometimes and sometimes I hide in a cupboard and see her undress and see her bare. The others tell me to bring in a picture but I didn't take one. (Thomas)

Thomas told me that his sister is sixteen and about to leave school. I asked him what Ms Luke said about his news. He replied:

> She says 'Thank you. Get off that chair. See you next year.' (Thomas)

The events of that afternoon at Thomas's house also involved Nathan and Thomas subsequently 'being rude to Thomas's Nan'. Becky disapproved and told me the story and told me that Ms Luke had said 'I don't want to hear any more of that.' Nathan told me his version which I did not altogether follow or capture in notes but which centred more on the events involving the grandmother:

> Sometimes I do it boring. Sometimes I do it funny. Sometimes middles ... Then I said (to the class) 'There was this old lady (Thomas's Nan) and she sat on a chair and she went Bang!' And they all laughed. Some people were laughing. Some weren't. That's okay. At least they were laughing. (Nathan)

Thus, despite teacher disapproval and that of many peers, from the point of view of Nathan, as well apparently as for Thomas, the story was a success.

Options – meaning and doing in the news session

In summary (see Figure 8.1), a typology of news items for this cohort consists of a primary distinction between *special events* and *common events*. Some telling of special events might be *lies* and common events can be made into *comedy*. Both of these options, lying and comedy, avoid the tag of 'boring' which otherwise holds for common events. Comedy can further be categorized as *regular comedy* and *deviant comedy*.

In this typology can be seen a set of meanings that can be related to Halliday's concept of 'options', in that children were making choices in the environment of other choices (Halliday, 1978).

According to Halliday's model of language, there will be social functions being realized through the choices made. We see in pupils' accounts functions beyond the immediate and obvious imperatives to fulfil the requirements of the lesson and the teacher. With respect to the audience of peers we see functions beyond the immediate needs of the audience for interest, amusement, etc. We see rather, as Halliday suggests, functions in the social system. Statuses, identities and affiliations are being shaped and reinforced both positively and negatively. Reputations and relationships are in the balance.

Groups, options and orientations

According to Halliday's conception of language as function, different social groups will have different orientations to and draw different meanings from the function of language in a given context. Options are not open to all but rather there will be in the situation conditions which affect the access of different groups to the options. From the perspective of the children, which I have outlined above and from a further analysis of the data, there begins to emerge a picture of conditions affecting access to the options. Clearly access to the sort of *special events* cited by the children was largely dependent upon socio-economic circumstances of the family. In the number of children who cited it and contrasted it with the boring and commonplace, clearly too it had high status. The fact that some children who told of *special events* were accused of showing off or lying confirms its potential for conferring status, whatever the truth of the accusations. Clearly as well, at least half the class seemed to have access to the option of telling of *special events* on a fairly regular basis.

My close knowledge of the families and socio-economic status of ten of the children as well as a more generalized knowledge of the others indicates a range of financial resources across the class. For example, trips to the United States and Disneyland had been enjoyed by several children and riding lessons, computers, electronic toys and holidays abroad were standard fare for a sizeable proportion of the children. Others in their dress and grooming had more of the appearance of poverty compared with their wealthier classmates and in the words of one teacher, 'are lucky to get a crust'. Four children in the cohort, at this point in the study, had a father or both parents who had been long-term unemployed.

As Halliday suggests to be the case, different pupils will have different orientations towards and draw different meanings from language in a given context. With respect to the telling of *special events*, what was good, exciting, status-conferring news for some, was resented by others as 'showing off'. As the data shows, socio-economic status did not always guarantee automatic access to the option of telling of higher-status news. The classroom status of oneself and one's immediate reference group may impose the need to be circumspect and avoid alienating those whose friendship and support you need.

As well as socio-economic conditions and classroom status, gender also appears to have had an affect upon access to options. Results of my analysis are speculative, and for that reason not reported in full here (see Filer, 1997). However, a key issue in relation to children's access and orientation to the options was that girls clearly did not have access to the same alternatives that were available to many of the boys. They did not, for instance, accuse or stand accused of lying about special events. Not only did they apparently not lie about special events, but also they did not have the option of telling deviant comedy. Deviant news belonged primarily to those boys in this cohort who, since their entry to school, to a greater or lesser extent had been regarded as 'problems' and who had represented a challenge to successive teachers (see Chapter 6). Whether or not any of the girls had the sort of risky/deviant out-of-school experiences upon which they could have capitalized, none in this cohort displayed the sort of behaviour in the classroom that traditionally attracts teacher disapproval and the 'deviant' label.

The assumption that 'problem' boys *chose* deviant comedy may not be a strictly correct one. Given the low status that telling about common events attracted, especially among the boys, and, in the absence of high-status special events to tell of, in avoiding the former and being 'boring', pupils may have been forced to choose between the good opinion of a teacher and their status in the eyes of their peers.

Clearly the above analysis may not cover all varieties of news that pupils might tell. The nature of the questions put to the pupils, for example, in requesting information about 'good' and 'not so good' news telling, may mean that some options were omitted from their response. An example of a category omitted may well be the sort of news such as that which Peter discussed with me in the preliminary interviews. Such news would cover such events as family misfortunes and accidents generally and some children did tell this sort of news from time to time. This sort of news could be classed as *special events* though, of course, without socio-economic, status-conferring factors coming into play. Two children mentioned this sort of news with respect to accidental injury to themselves and expressed a reluctance to tell it because of other pupils' inappropriate laughter at their misfortune. Stuart described his experience of such unintended comedy in news telling:

AF	What do you do if you haven't done anything interesting?
Stuart	I just say I haven't got any news today.
AF	Have you ever done it not well?
Stuart	Yeah. I broke my leg and I didn't like telling all the class how I'd done it because it was dangerous. I fell off a climbing frame and a big fat man jumped off a trampoline and landed on top of me and they had to cut open my leg because they couldn't get an X-ray.
AF	Why didn't you want to tell them?
Stuart	Because they was all laughing.

Clearly the groups that were definable in terms of their various access to meanings did not include all the groups which might be found in schools generally. Here, for example, I have described some of the differences between groups of children in terms of socio-economic status, gender, classroom status and affiliations. However, as I indicate on the model (Figure 8.1), within a multi-ethnic cohort of pupils, groups and the meanings they have access to would go beyond those identified with this cohort. Nevertheless, I would see the *functions* which pupils are carrying out *vis-à-vis* their peers as the same within this sort of classroom situation, whatever the social or cultural make-up of the group. I would see those common functions as those cited at the beginning of this chapter and being concerned with 'acting out the social structure', 'affirming statuses and roles', 'establishing and transmitting the shared systems of values and knowledge' (Halliday, 1978: 2). This would also accord with Halliday's notion of language performing a limited number of functions within the social system, and as the critical means by which individuals become members of, and are shaped by, the group.

In summary then, the meanings and groups which have been identified reflect the Halliday model with respect to the following.

- Meanings in the news session in this class can be represented as a system of choices, access to which was circumscribed by socio-economic circumstances, classroom identities and affiliations and gender identities.

- Language was being used for functions within the peer group concerned with establishing and maintaining status, identities and peer relationships and this in addition to any purposes with respect to teacher requirements.

The question arises as to what extent functions *vis-à-vis* school requirements and functions *vis-à-vis* peers were compatible. If they were not compatible, then clearly we are in a situation whereby a teacher is not necessarily accessing the sort of language she is trying to assess (see also Chapter 10). What we see, of course, is that for some pupils, those of high socio-economic status and high classroom status, the options to which they had access were compatible with teacher requirements. Clearly though for some pupils there were tensions between teacher expectations and favourable peer-group evaluations of their news. For some, that is, the options of saying nothing or telling deviant comedy were preferable to telling news that was acceptable to the teacher. Many children were having to choose between maintaining self-respect and identity within the peer culture and pleasing the teacher.

As well as giving rise to issues of academic differentiation, the news session was also socially differentiating. Not only did different groups draw different meanings from the *content* of news sessions as described above, but also the news session itself had different meanings for different groups of pupils. For some it was a situation in which they could both fulfil teacher requirements and at the same time positively reinforce high standing and identity in the peer culture. For others, even when fulfilling teacher requirements, it may well have been a negative experience, confirming their lesser status in the peer culture.

8.4   DISCUSSION

The importance of the listener's perspective and the circumstances and demands of the situation feature prominently in the National Curriculum (DfE, 1994) attainment target of 'speaking and listening' because clearly they are central to any notion of effective communication. However, the perspectives of children on their news sessions as described and analysed in this chapter shows that a pupil's purpose *vis-à-vis* an audience of peers embodies considerations that go beyond any particular task as envisaged by the attainment target. It is, moreover, difficult to imagine a situation in which audience and context awareness with respect to official tasks could be isolated from audience and context awareness with respect to meanings and social functions associated with membership of a peer culture. Halliday (1978: 109), for instance, cites linguists going back to Wegener (1885), Malinowski (1923, 1935) and Firth (1957) on what he describes as the 'well-established concept' that context was not to be interpreted in terms of the concrete audio and visual 'props' surrounding a situation. It was rather to be understood abstractly in terms of its relevance to the text. The context of a situation, therefore, may be totally remote from what is going on in the concrete act of speaking or writing (Firth, 1957: 182).

Though Halliday believes that different models can coexist serving different goals, he argues that a biological/psychological perspective is not a necessary one for the exploration of language which is part of the social system. Both he (1982) and Stubbs (1986) would argue for a meaning/function model of language as one relevant to education. Halliday states, for instance, what Chomsky has always made clear, that the linguistics of formalism and notions of 'competence' originally associated with his name have little relevance for education. Language has to be accepted 'for the typically human mixture of order and chaos that it really is' (Halliday, 1982: 11).

Awareness of the impact of the complexity of classroom life on pupils' responses need not prevent teachers from confidently making assessments of their pupils' strengths and weaknesses, their achievements and needs. What such awareness does mean though is that teachers will recognize the provisional and context-related nature of the assessments they make. However, where policy seeks to measure, grade, and rank pupils as users of language, the assumption has to be that classrooms represent a neutral social and cultural backdrop against which efficacy of speech can be judged. In that case, of course, the complexity of classroom life will not be addressed.

8.5   CONCLUSION

In exploring the question 'What is being assessed?', this chapter takes as its focus some ways in which pupils' classroom responses are located in multiple contexts and fulfil multiple social purposes extending beyond the immediacy of a classroom task. However, I argue that National Curriculum requirements for 'speaking and listening' are based on a model of 'communicative competence' (Hymes, 1971) that fails to address the social complexity of classroom language and assumes a 'performance' model of language and the development of an ideal and efficacious speaker. Through this chapter I present an analysis of children's accounts of their news telling using an alternative model of language (Halliday, 1978); one that enables us to see classroom talk in terms of 'meanings' and 'functions in a social system'. This allows us to see pupil purposes beyond the immediate and obvious imperatives to fulfil teacher and task requirements, and that are embedded in the wider contexts of the socio-economics of families and community, peer affiliations and classroom identities. Through this analysis we see tensions between functions related to teacher requirements and a range of social functions *vis-à-vis* an audience of peers.

The chapter illuminates ways in which the news session represented different meanings for different groups of children. It illustrates issues of identity, self-image and interests-at-hand of pupils where reputations and relationships are in the balance and give rise to academically and socially differentiated outcomes for pupils.

Chapter 9

How does Assessment Function in Classrooms? – An Introduction

9.1   INTRODUCTION

This is the fourth pair of chapters relating to Figure 4.1 and through them we explore the question of 'How does assessment function in classrooms?' In Chapter 4.6 we saw that assessment simultaneously fulfilled several functions in Elizabeth's life. As well as the explicit roles in supporting learning and monitoring attainment and progress, assessment practices also acted to communicate expectations for behaviour to Elizabeth, to parents and to peers. It thereby acted to socialize Elizabeth into appropriate, gendered, pupil roles and relationships: to monitor simultaneously Elizabeth's social learning and her academic learning.

In this chapter we explore the theoretical connections between assessment and other classroom processes in terms of the power relations which bind them together. The power relations we explore relate to 'ideology', 'language' and 'culture'.

Through our theoretical enquiry into 'classroom processes' we consider ways in which particular forms of assessment give rise to particular forms of relationships and interactions for teaching and learning and different goals for learning. We analyse ways in which these different social forms and goals can act to polarize pupils' attainment and to promote or inhibit pupils' verbal responses. In this, therefore, we also address processes of differentiation and social and cultural reproduction.

Throughout this chapter we draw on sociological and sociolinguistic understandings of assessment and other classroom processes established over some 30 years of enquiry. We assert their continued relevance for current assessment practice within which 'evidence' of attainment represents the outcome of a range of differentiating and polarizing classroom processes. Thereby, perhaps one of the key functions of 'evidence', and other 'objectified' forms of assessment recording and reporting, lies in the ways in which it acts to obscure what we know about assessment *processes*.

9.2   ASSESSMENT, CLASSROOM CONTROL AND LEARNING

In this and the following chapter we further develop our model of 'assessment in a social context' (Figure 4.1) by addressing the question of 'How does assessment function in classrooms?' In

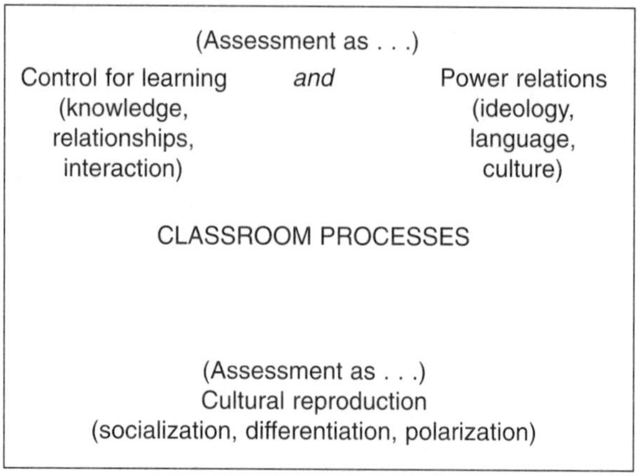

Figure 9.1   *Classroom processes as control for learning, power relations and cultural reproduction*

considering ways in which assessment functioned in Elizabeth's life in Chapter 4.6, we explored some outcomes concerned with her identity as a pupil, her classroom status and relationships and her approaches to learning and to various tasks. All of these social, motivational and attitudinal outcomes were shaped in a dynamic relationship with official outcomes concerned with her academic progress and attainment. Through Elizabeth's career we tracked a similar inter-connection between the explicit functions of assessment in supporting learning and monitoring outcomes and implicit functions as a mechanism of socialization. We saw, for example, ways in which forms of verbal, written and symbolic feedback (e.g. 'stars') relating to academic attain-ment and progress served also to evaluate her adaptation to school expectations, control her behaviour and transmit school and individual teachers' values and norms for pupil behaviour.

Thus questions related to the functions of assessment in classrooms involve us in exploring the relationships between assessment and a range of other classroom processes and outcomes. In Figure 9.1 we summarize our approach to analysing such relationships in terms of 'classroom processes' which are bound together in three sets of factors concerned with 'control for learning', 'power relations' and 'cultural reproduction'. In each case 'Assessment as . . .' precedes each set of factors on the model. This serves to remind us of our analytic premise: forms of assessment permeate and shape processes of teaching and learning and a range of social as well as academic-related outcomes.

Control for learning on the model expresses the set of functions that are simultaneously managed in the process of teaching. These functions are shown on the model to be concerned with the control of knowledge and with the forms of teacher–pupil relationships and interaction through which particular ways and states of knowing are realized in classrooms. In this chapter we use Bernstein's (1975) conceptions of 'education codes' to theorize the interconnectedness of these functions. 'Education codes' enable us to see ways in which the functions are bound together in patterns of authority and control. They also help us to conceptualize ways in which particular approaches to the control of knowledge and relationships for learning are related to particular approaches to assessment. In exploring such connections we make use of Bernstein's (1975) three 'message systems' of 'curriculum', 'pedagogy' and 'evaluation'.

We have conceptualized the functions associated with 'control for learning' in the model as being bound together in patterns of authority and control. *Power relations* on the model (Figure

9.1) draws attention to the means and indeed, the *logic* by which assessment and other functions are bound together. First in this we consider the ideological connectedness of the functions. We use 'ideology' here as Bernstein used it, which is 'not (as) content but (as) a way in which relationships are made and realised' (1996: 31). Then, in considering 'language' and 'culture' on the model we draw on well-established sociolinguistic understandings regarding ways in which teachers' language simultaneously fulfils a range of pedagogic purposes. In this we consider the taken-for-granted assumptions in Western culture regarding how lessons are accomplished and learning takes place.

In exploring *power relations* we also use Bernstein's (1975) concept of the 'framing of educational knowledge' and consider frame *strength*. The framing of educational knowledge refers to the degree of control teachers and taught possess over the selection, organization and pacing of educational knowledge. Thus an analysis of frame *strength* enables us to differentiate between pedagogic approaches to the control of knowledge in teaching and assessment with some important consequences for pupils' responses that teachers are assessing.

Cultural reproduction on the model relates to classroom processes which help to reinforce and perpetuate social and academic disparities. It draws attention to the processes whereby particular forms of knowledge capital and social relations are reproduced. Thus some of the differentiating process involved in cultural reproduction are concerned with the polarizing effects of different forms of pedagogic and assessment practices on the learning and motivation of pupils. They are also concerned with pupils' differential acquisition of the forms of the interaction and cultural meanings through which knowledge and teacher expectations are communicated, with implications for pupils' verbal responses and engagements in assessment situations.

Throughout this chapter we examine a range of theoretical understandings related to classroom processes and their effects on learning which have been established over some 30 years of enquiry. Drawing on our own and others' research, we established their relevance to current changes towards 'performance goals' in primary schools and for challenging some current assumptions embedded in the drive for formal, 'evidence'-based assessment practices. The theoretical analysis presented here draws attention to some of the hidden classroom processes which shape assessment outcomes but which are obscured by 'ticked boxes' and objective-looking recording and reporting practices.

We organize our analysis in this chapter around the set of factors in Figure 9.1 concerned with 'ideology' and 'language and culture'. We do so because, as discussed above, an analysis of these 'power relations' enables us to perceive ways in which the functions involved in 'control for learning' are bound together. Such an analysis also enables us to perceive ways in which processes of cultural reproduction are set in train.

Whilst the language and analysis throughout the chapter are concerned with issues of power and control, we have shown elsewhere that these are not absolutes but are also shaped by expectations external to the classroom. In this, of course, they are also open to challenge from pupils. Therefore, negotiation and renegotiation of teachers' authority to establish routines, procedures and forms of relationships are part of the everyday reality of classroom life. Such issues we have discussed in earlier chapters and explored in detail through the case studies in Chapters 4 and 6.

Assessment: ideology and control for learning

We begin our consideration of 'classroom processes' by establishing the links between assessment practices and a range of other classroom practices in classrooms as 'ideological' connections. In exploring such connections, the PACE project (*Primary Assessment, Curriculum and Experience*; Pollard *et al.*, 1994; Broadfoot and Pollard, 2000) adapted Bernstein's (1975) conceptions of education 'codes' and the associated 'message systems' of 'curriculum', 'pedagogy' and 'evaluation' through which the codes are realized.

Bernstein's 'collection codes' and 'integration codes' characterize ideological connections between particular views of knowledge (transmitted through the message system of 'curriculum') and particular views with respect to how knowledge should be delivered (transmitted through the message system of 'pedagogy'). 'Collection codes' and 'integration codes' will also embody different forms of assessment which support and bring into being the desired knowledge outcomes and pedagogic relationships.

Put very simply for our purposes here, *collection codes* are characterized by views of knowledge and types of curricula that are 'rigid, differentiated and hierarchical in character' (1975: 82–3). Views of knowledge have a direct relationship to views of the instructional processes and learning relationships through which particular forms of knowledge can be realized. Thus pedagogy within a 'collection code' is likely to be didactic and to emphasize 'states of knowing' in pupils. Groupings for learning are likely to be rigid and there will be an emphasis on teacher authority in the student–teacher relationship.

We can contrast these views of knowledge and curriculum and styles of pedagogy under a 'collection code' with those related to an *integration code*. Under the latter, the knowledge content of the curriculum will be more open, less differentiated and emphasize 'ways of knowing' rather than the 'states of knowing' of 'collection codes'. The traditional primary school 'topic' work and other cross-curricular approaches are examples of 'integrated codes'. Pedagogic processes within 'integrated codes' are likely to include flexible groupings and greater student self-regulation, status and autonomy in the learning relationship.

Relevant to our understanding of the ideological interconnectedness of assessment and other pedagogic processes is the observation that there are two kinds of pedagogic discourses embedded within each of the above codes. Within each code, a 'regulative discourse' is concerned with the creation of a particular kind of social order and an 'instructional discourse' is concerned with achieving particular knowledge outcomes (Bernstein, 1996). Thus both regulative and instructional discourses are bound together in collections of pedagogic practices which are ideologically mutually supportive. Indeed, Bernstein argues that they are bound together as *one discourse*; that

> the instructional discourse is embedded in the regulative discourse, and that the regulative discourse is the dominant discourse. ... Often people in schools and in classrooms make a distinction between what they call the transmission of skills and the transmission of values. These are always kept apart as if there were a conspiracy to disguise the fact that there is only one discourse ... not two. ... Most researchers are continually studying the two, or thinking as if there were two: as if education is about values on the one hand, and about competence on the other. (Bernstein 1996: 46)

In this assertion of Bernstein's that there is only one discourse, we can most powerfully see the relevance of our observations regarding assessment processes in the case study in Chapter 4. There we described ways in which functions of assessment concerned with socializing Elizabeth into appropriate girl–pupil relationships and behaviour were inextricably bound up with those related to her academic attainment and progress.

Focusing more precisely now on our question concerning 'What are the functions of assessment in classrooms?' we can draw on Bernstein's (1975) argument that 'evaluation' is the 'purest form of pedagogic control'. Thus changes in the regulative and instructional discourse(s) in classrooms are most powerfully brought into being through changes in assessment practices

(Broadfoot and Pollard, 2000). Thus, Broadfoot and Pollard explain, in the context of current changes in primary schools, the change in assessment language and practices towards 'levels', 'standards' and target setting can be expected to bring about changes in the instructional discourse and ways in which knowledge and skills are inculcated. The changes in assessment practices can also be expected to bring about changes through the regulative discourse, in relation to the social order, in social relations and social identities. Indeed, the PACE data reflects just such an inexorable change in both the instructional and the regulative discourses in English primary schools. A move towards the explicit, categoric assessment outcomes gives rise to a 'performance'-orientated pedagogy. Increasingly, if with difficulty (see Chapter 5), teachers are having to accept the 'instrumental goals' of 'levels' and the achievements of 'targets' as important aspects of their professional identities (Broadfoot and Pollard, 2000).

For our purposes in this chapter, however, we are primarily concerned with the affects of changes in assessment and classroom practices on learning outcomes for pupils. The Bernstein (1975) model indicates that it is through the operation of explicit assessment procedures that learners are made aware of the outcomes that are desired and valued. Their performance will be a means of locating them in terms of hierarchical judgements. Again, the PACE study reflects just such changes. Children are becoming more 'performance orientated' with an increased focus on the 'instrumental goals' of test outcomes and levels of achievement and away from 'learning-orientated' goals (Pollard and Triggs, forthcoming).

Many other authors present theoretical models and research findings to support the kinds of direct relationship between assessment, pedagogy and pupils' approach to learning that we describe here. In the following section we set out some of these perspectives with a closer examination of the assumptions and processes embedded in contrastive approaches to assessment. At the same time we explore some understandings of the differentiated social and learning outcomes that different approaches to assessment can give rise to.

Assessment: learning and motivation

Bernstein's analysis and those of others above remind us that teaching and assessment practices are intimately bound up with patterns of authority and control (Bernstein, 1975) and reflect the prevailing social, moral and economic order of nations (Pollard *et al.*, 1994: 24; see also Filer, 2000). However, teachers' varying approaches to classroom assessment and testing embody assumptions about learning processes that are usually more implicitly held. Of course, individual teachers' pedagogic styles are complex in their origins (see Chapters 5 and 6) and very different in the detail of their realization (see Chapter 10). Nevertheless, in broad respects, pedagogies inhabit a limited number of forms based on taken-for-granted, contemporary Western cultural assumptions regarding the nature of teaching and the functions of assessment.

For instance, we can begin by comparing some of the practices inherent in 'linear' and 'constructivist' approaches to the development of knowledge and in implications for children's learning outcomes. Torrance and Pryor (1998) identified the different forms of assessment associated with 'linear' versus 'constructivist' approaches to learning as 'convergent assessment' and 'divergent assessment'. In 'convergent assessment', assessment functions to find out *whether* a child knows, understands or can do a predetermined thing (1998: 153). Thus convergent assessment is associated with closed questions and tasks, tick lists, 'can do' statements and quantitative feedback. It implies behaviourist models of the sequential acquisition of knowledge (1998: 153). Convergent or linear assessment, it is suggested, promotes 'shallow learning' associated with success in tests based on short-term memorization (Entwistle, 1992; White, 1992).

In 'divergent assessment' the focus is on the learner's understanding rather than on the agenda of the assessor. Thus assessment functions to understand *what* the child knows, understands or can do (Torrance and Pryor, 1998: 154). It is thus characterized by an awareness of the learner's perspectives as well as teacher and curriculum agendas. Divergent assessment can be located within a constructivist view of the acquisition of knowledge which stresses the importance of the ZPD (Zone of Proximal Development) (Vygotsky, 1978). Teacher awareness of the ZPD for individual children can be achieved through joint accomplishments in which lower-order skills take on meaning in the context of the shared intellectual work of the group (Resnick, 1989). Within a constructivist approach, the acquisition of knowledge is perceived, not sequentially, but with existing knowledge providing a 'scaffolding' for future knowledge which is interpreted and restructured to make new meanings. Divergent, constructivist assessments are thus formative in relation to potential development and are deemed to be more likely to promote 'deep learning' (Entwistle, 1992; White, 1992).

In addition to formal and explicit forms of assessment, a range of classroom evaluative practices are deemed to have significant effects on students with implications for learning, motivation and confidence. Extrinsic reward systems, for instance, have been found to have detrimental effects on intrinsic motivation (Lepper and Hoddell, 1989). They appear also to promote learning strategies related to 'performance goals' and the gaining of favourable judgements from others rather than strategies related to 'learning goals' concerned with the gaining of competence and understanding (Dweck, 1989; Nicholls, 1989; Urdan and Maehr, 1995). Evidence also suggests that 'performance goals' are fostered by competition and through normative comparisons with peers (Dweck, 1989). These different strategies for learning have both short- and long-term implications for success (Crooks, 1988). As Broadfoot and Pollard point out a narrow 'performance orientation', whilst satisfying short-term requirements for high-stakes assessment for example, may also have the unintended consequence of undermining long-term dispositions to learn through life. This is especially so for those who are less successful in the current system (Broadfoot and Pollard, 2000).

A consideration of less-successful pupils bring us to the point that pupils' motivation to achieve is differentially affected by consistent patterns of evaluation. The approaches to assessment associated with 'performance goals' within which pupils are hierarchically located by their performance are likely to be highly motivating for some but damaging and demotivating to the learning of others.

For example, such effects were very apparent among the class cohort of pupils studied at Albert Park School. As described in Chapter 6.2, the pedagogy of the children's Year 1 teacher was clearly located within a 'performance discourse', as were many other teachers' practices in the school. From the point of view of the 5- and 6-year-olds, the seating arrangements, the grading of tasks and the numbering of exercise books filled, together with the house-point system, provided highly public measurements of their place in the official hierarchy of the classroom. The children who found routine tasks easy to accomplish (see Chapter 6) and made fast progression through work cards and filled exercise books quickly were highly motivated to work quickly, compete fiercely and win the high-profile status associated with their achievements. For example, Alison and Martin, two children who were consistently well in front of the rest of the class on maths schemes, work cards, etc. vied with one another throughout their primary school years to pull ahead of the other in filling books. For Martin, in Year 1, the highly graded organization of tasks meant that even the writing of Monday morning 'news' was something he could 'be ahead' in by 'getting on to' the next exercise book. Here Martin is responding to a question from Ann Filer regarding whom, from among his peers, he might get help:

Martin   When I was littler William used to help me but now I'm ahead of everybody else on sounds (phonics) and on number and a bit on news. I went on to blue book 2 (his second 'news' exercise book) and somebody else came on to it (their second exercise book) just the other day so I am a little bit ahead on blue books.

(Pupil interview, Year 1, 1989)

Here is Alison's mother talking in Year 6 about the competition to keep ahead sustained by Alison and Martin through their school years:

Mrs Gough   With the maths, they've got the book and they can just carry on at their own pace. As I said in the (research) diary, especially with the competition with Martin, I think that's good. A little competition does them good, I'm sure it does. Yes, you know, Alison says that he'll come up to her and say 'Oh, I did *that* page last week'. And the next week she'll say to him 'Oh, I've gone past *that* page'. I don't think it does them any harm at all.

AF   Neck and neck isn't it.

Mrs Gough   That's right. All the way. And it's a shame it can't happen with all subjects at school. I know it can't because, especially when they are doing topic work, things are being done as a whole group. But at least in some subjects she can get on.

(Parent interview, Year 6, 1995)

As we see here, Alison's mother considered that competition for grades and to stay ahead did no harm. However, such highly public measurements of each child's progression was certainly harmful to the motivation and self-esteem of the children at the lower end of the hierarchy, and especially to their sense of themselves as learners. In the following extract from an interview with Christopher, Ann Filer has asked him about the move into the Year 2 class the following term:

Christopher   It's not going to be very good.

AF   Why is that?

Christopher   I hate changing classes because I start crying in the class and I'll be straight back on number 1 (exercise books) again.

AF   Isn't that good? Because everyone else will be on number 1, won't they.

Christopher   No, 'cos everyone else will be in front of me and I'll be right behind because they is doing it all fast. . . . I don't chat. I try not to chat but others try to get me to chat.

AF   Does it matter that some get ahead like that?

Christopher   Yes, 'cos Alison and Martin is on number 8.

AF   How do you feel about that?

Christopher   Nasty and Angry. Peter is on number 4 and I feel angry with him.

(Pupil interview, Year 1, 1990)

As we can see above, hierarchical grading systems and normative comparisons of 'perform-ance goals' were shaping pupils self-esteem, motivation and sense of self as learners in increasingly polarized ways. Moreover, this was apparent in Year 1, before the pupils had any experience of National Curriculum 'levels' or had undergone any formal national testing. For Christopher and others, progression against measured output became more a matter of *regression* as the difference between himself and fast-working peers got ever wider through the year. Christopher and others like him were clearly displaying symptoms of 'learned helplessness' that are created and reinforced by repeated experiences of failure against 'performance goals' (Licht and Dweck, 1983; Elliott and Dweck, 1988). It is perhaps no wonder that pupils such as

Christopher usually remove themselves from the education system as soon as they are able. Indeed, many give up trying and remove themselves spiritually well before that.

Assessment: language and culture

In Chapter 7, the question 'What is being assessed?' explored the socio-economic contexts of, and some of the meanings children brought to, their 'news' sessions at Albert Park School. The chapter argued that National Curriculum 'speaking and listening' attainment targets assume a model of classroom language that fails to take into account the multifunctional nature of language. That is to say it fails to take into account the fact that pupils have purposes *vis-à-vis* an audience of peers which go beyond fulfilling the requirements of a particular task or teacher expectations.

Similarly we have well-established understandings regarding ways in which teachers' language, when assessing pupils, simultaneously fulfils a range of pedagogic purposes. From the late 1960s and through the 1970s, there was much research interest in demonstrating ways in which classrooms were inadequate contexts for assessing children's verbal competence. Barnes (1969) had shown that the closed questioning, which was a feature of most formal teacher–pupil exchange, put constraints upon pupil's responses (see following section). Sinclair and Coultard (1975) later demonstrated that much teacher–pupil talk fell into a pattern of teacher initiation, pupil response, teacher evaluation (IRE). Indeed, there is in Western culture an almost taken-for-granted expectation that learning will take place in schools by means of direct questioning followed by a pupil's verbal response.

Much subsequent classroom research has revealed that teacher question-and-answer routines are not simply concerned with instruction and ascertaining what pupils know. For instance, Torrance and Pryor (1998) draw on the work of Mehan (1979) and Edwards and Mercer (1987) in analysing ways in which pupil responses are appropriated, and adjusted if necessary, to suit teacher purposes in accomplishing the lesson. In this, teaching and assessment functions are realized simultaneously with functions concerned with the management, pacing and sequencing of lessons and the control of, perhaps, a large class of children. Teacher purposes in accomplishing a particular lesson or assessment may mean that the relevance of pupils' responses may be denied where they do not accord with teacher definitions of what knowledge is appropriate to the lesson (Keddie, 1971; Young, 1976; Filer, 1993b). In this we can appreciate that further functions of question-and-answer sequences are concerned with the control of knowledge, what counts as relevant knowledge and with focusing attention on the teacher as the holder and arbiter of that knowledge (Filer, 1993b; see also Chapter 10).

Thus we can appreciate that, as with 'ideology', the power relations embedded in the language and culture of classroom assessment are realized in relation to the control of 'knowledge' and 'relationships' and in relation to social control (Figure 9.1). We can consider also that in relation to young children, question-and-answer sequences in assessment also serve the function of socializing young children into the interactional codes (Edwards and Furlong, 1978; Edwards and Westgate, 1987; Torrance and Pryor, 1998) through which classroom relationships and learning are conducted.

Thus to establish again our original point that teacher talk, like that of pupil talk, performs multiple functions in assessment contexts, we can appreciate Halliday's assertion, cited in Chapter 7, that:

People do more than understand each other, in the sense of exchanging information. ... By their everyday acts of meaning, people act out the social structure affirming their own statuses and roles, and establishing and transmitting the shared system of values and knowledge. (Halliday, 1978: 2)

We can also appreciate the relevance of Berstein's (1996) assertion, discussed above, that there is only one pedagogic discourse and that the 'transmission of skills' and the 'transmission and values' are indistinguishable processes.

Assessment, language and sociocultural differentiation

A useful way to conceptualize the simultaneous functions of teachers' questions is to employ Bernstein's (1975) conceptions related to 'framing of educational knowledge'. As discussed above, Bernstein refers to educational knowledge as being realized through the three 'message systems' of 'curriculum', pedagogy' and 'evaluation'. 'Frame' in this context is used to determine the structure of the message system of pedagogy. It refers to the degree of control teacher and taught possess over selection, organization and pacing of educational knowledge and to the strength of the boundary between what may or may not be transmitted in the pedagogic relationship as educational knowledge. Bernstein points out that an important aspect of framing with respect to boundary maintenance concerns the degree to which teachers insulate educational knowledge from their own and their pupils' everyday knowledge. Framing will thus be weak to the extent that pupils are allowed to incorporate and sustain contributions from their own personal and everyday experience. This may be contrasted with the stronger framing inherent in the kind of 'question and answer' sequencing that we discussed above, where one 'right' answer is pursued.

The concept of frame *strength*, therefore, enables us to differentiate between pedagogic approaches with regard to some important implications for eliciting the pupil responses that teachers are assessing. We can now make connections between strong framing, teacher approaches which are highly controlling with regard to what counts as knowledge, and Barnes' (above) findings that closed questions put constraints on pupils' responses. Thus we might assume that strong framing means that teachers are *less likely* to access the responses they are trying to assess. Conversely we might assume that weaker framing, in which pupils are able to sustain contributions from their personal and everyday experiences, means that teachers are *more likely* to access the responses they are trying to assess. Such an assumption is supported by the work of Cazden (1972) who also drew on the work of Mueller (1971), Labov *et al.* (1968) and Strandberg and Griffith (1968) to show that, as well as using more complex language, children communicated more successfully when they had some personal interest in the topic under discussion. They look, listen and engage their attention more effectively at such times. Other studies have shown that there are cultural considerations to be brought to bear in any assessment of or through children's language. The Western culture that takes it for granted that teaching will take place through questioning is not universally shared. The defensiveness and silence of some American Indian groups (Dumont, 1972; Philips, 1972), working-class Black Americans (Labov, 1969) and Hawaiian children (Boggs, 1972) in such contexts has been compared with their extensive use of language out of school. Such research has shown that the mode of educational transmission and the power relations embodied in it can be at odds with cultural expectations with regard to valued modes of expression (Labov, 1972; Philips, 1972) and to appropriate forms of address (Boggs, 1972; Dumont, 1972). Through such research the 'cultural deficit' theories of the 1960s which were supposed to account for the differentiated classroom performances and learning outcomes of Black and American Indian children were overthrown.

The strong framing of 'question and one right answer' modes of teaching and assessment is also problematic for many young children even among those brought up in a Western culture. Young children will differ in the extent to which they have gained the kinds of procedural competence necessary for understanding and managing the interactional codes of classrooms (Edwards and Furlong, 1978; Edwards and Westgate, 1987; Torrance and Pryor, 1998). Familiarity with the codes is also likely to depend on social class and pre-school experience (Wells, 1986). Of course, in addition, where the framing is strong in classroom questioning many children will say nothing rather than risk being 'wrong' (Filer, 1993b; see also Chapter 10).

The above, therefore, represents something of a paradox for assessment situations where teachers are trying to elicit pupils' knowledge and understanding through talk and questioning. For, it seems, the stronger the framing of educational knowledge and the more that teachers focus their questions around and pursue explicit categoric responses, the less likely they are to access what they are trying to assess. On the other hand, the weaker the frame, the more open the questions and the more pupil responses, however 'irrelevant', are accepted and sustained, the greater the chance that teachers will be able to access what a pupil knows (Filer, 1993b and 1993c). The following chapter demonstrates just this principle in operation. During her PhD tracking of the children at Albert Park School, Ann Filer found that a change of class and a switch to weaker framing of educational knowledge in class 'discussion' sessions meant that formerly silent children began to make lengthy contributions and all children spoke at greater length and on a greater variety of topics. Of course, the 'strong framing' teacher and the 'weaker framing' teacher received very different impressions of children's 'speaking and listening' skills and assessed them accordingly.

Indeed, such findings accord well with other research findings showing that within different relationships, the same child will show very different powers of social understanding and communicative and reflective behaviour. The crucial difference being the quality of supportive interest (Tizard and Hughes, 1984; Dunn, 1996). They also accord with theories of 'linear' and 'constructivist' approaches to assessment described above. As Torrance and Pryor put it, the teacher who is more interested in the *child* will elicit more valid responses than the teacher who is more interested in the *attainment* (1988: 157). From their studies of the language of classroom assessment, and the many other sources they cite, they conclude

> the assumptions of those currently determining policy on assessment, that teachers can easily interpret pupil behaviour and ask clear questions that elicit clear and discrete answers, are not well founded. (Torrance and Pryor, 1998: 45)

This review of research into classroom processes demonstrates what has been argued elsewhere (Filer, 1993a, 1993b, 1995); that the message which historically has emanated from sociological and sociolinguistic studies of assessment and classroom processes has been disregarded or forgotten. It is clear that the preoccupation with the *content* of assessment, with 'evidence' and the 'ticked boxes' or their equivalent relating to many and varied Statements of Attainment, is obscuring what we know about *process* (Filer, 1993b: 195–6).

9.3   CONCLUSIONS

In the case study in Chapter 4, we observed that as well as having an explicit function with regard to learning and attainment, assessment practices simultaneously acted to monitor and control Elizabeth's social learning and socialize her into appropriate pupil roles and relationships. In exploring the question of 'How does assessment function in classrooms?', therefore, we have focused the theoretical enquiry in this chapter around 'classroom processes' and analysed understandings of the relationship between assessment and a range of other pedagogic functions.

We have drawn on a number of theoretical perspectives and research findings in analysing ways in which assessment and other classroom processes are bound together in patterns of authority and control. Our analysis has focused around ways in which these functions are bound together in the power relations of ideology, language and culture.

We contrasted ways in which particular forms of assessment give rise to particular patterns of teacher–pupil relationships and interactions in the teaching process and different goals for learning. We analysed ways in which such patterns associated with 'performance goals' can act to polarize pupils' attainment and promote learned helplessness in some. In particular, we considered some important ways in which contrastive forms of teachers' language in assessing pupils can act to promote or inhibit pupils' responses. In this we addressed processes of cultural reproduction arising from pupils' differential access to culturally specific forms and patterns of interactions in teaching and assessment.

Throughout this chapter we draw on sociological and sociolinguistic understandings of assessment and other classroom processes established over some 30 years of enquiry and assert their continued relevance for current assessment practice. As we concluded in Chapter 7, the pressure on teachers to formalize classroom assessment processes and recording procedures for 'evidence', serves to obscure the reality of classroom life. The preoccupation with the *content* serves to obscure what we know about the *processes* of assessment.

The following chapter is the second in the pair which explore functions of assessment and ways in which they are bound up with a range of other classroom processes. It shows ways in which forms of language for teaching and assessment are bound up with patterns of control and social relationships in the classrooms, with important consequences for pupil's verbal responses. In this, it extends the analysis in this chapter concerning classrooms as problematic contexts for assessing children's verbal responses.

Chapter 10

How Does Assessment Function in Classrooms? – A Comparison of Two Classroom Contexts

Ann Filer

10.1 INTRODUCTION

This is the second of the pair of chapters which explore some functions of assessment in classrooms, together with some implications for pupils' responses. In this, the chapter illustrates some key aspects of the theoretical analysis developed through Chapter 9. It thus takes us beyond assessment's explicit roles in classrooms with a consideration of its embedment in a range of other classroom processes.

The chapter is concerned with classrooms as language environments within which functions of assessment are bound together with other pedagogic functions related to the control of knowledge, classroom interaction and relationships (see Figure 9.1). Teacher talk, therefore, is deemed to be concerned not simply with processes of instruction and with ascertaining what pupils know or understand. Rather, in this chapter, classroom language is seen to be simultaneously involved in the pedagogic control of knowledge and with particular patterns of social interaction through which that control is maintained. Bernstein's theory of 'the framing of educational knowledge' is used to conceptualize these simultaneous functions of teacher language. In addition, Bernstein's concept of 'frame strength' enables a comparative analysis of different patterns of control and forms of interaction. The importance of these different forms of control and interaction is shown in their different effects on pupils' verbal responses and, hence, on the classroom assessments made by the teachers that used them.

The analysis in this chapter relates to the assessment of the National Curriculum attainment target of 'speaking and listening'. The classroom language environments in which 'speaking and listening' assessments are made are analysed for the cohort of children as they pass through Year 1 and Year 2 at Albert Park School. The classroom contexts are first analysed briefly in terms of teachers' 'coping strategies' but predominantly in terms of their 'framing of educational knowledge'. Between them, these approaches help to indicate the range and the nature of classroom situations in which children's language was assessed in each classroom. Comparisons are made between the two contexts as teacher-created language environments, contrasting the quantity and distinctive quality of verbal responses each evoked from the pupil cohort. The analyses of classrooms is followed by a case study of one child in order to examine in some detail the potential impact of different patterns of language and control on assessment outcomes.

Whilst the analysis in the chapter relates to the assessment of 'speaking and listening' it also, of course, has implications for other classroom assessments where pupil knowledge or understanding is inferred by teachers from verbal responses to their questioning.

A theoretical background to this chapter is presented in Chapter 9 and arguments are only briefly rehearsed here, as necessary, in introducing and drawing conclusions from the analysis. Thus whilst a preliminary reading of that chapter will help sensitize readers to the issues, as with other case-study chapters, this one can be read independently of its wider theoretical context.

10.2   BACKGROUND AND SETTING

In this chapter I compare the impact of two teacher-created language environments on the verbal responses of the class of pupils studied at Albert Park School. The data and some aspects of the analysis which I present here first appeared in different forms (Filer, 1993b and 1993c) and relate to the first two years of my PhD study at Albert Park School. The class of children was tracked through their Year 1 and Year 2 classes and beyond, during weekly visits to the school. The children were very familiar with both teachers before moving into their classes. The data supporting the following accounts of classroom life are taken from field notes, interview material and classroom observations. They also draw on video transcripts and documentary evidence in the form of pupil records and reports. The data relate to the first two years of Key Stage 1 national assessment following the 1988 Education Reform Act. However, with the continued and increasing pressure for teachers to formalize their assessment procedures for producing 'evidence' (see Chapter 5), the analysis and conclusions drawn here become ever more relevant with the passage of time.

This analysis should not be read as an indictment of a teacher's practice by suggesting that one teacher was somehow 'better' than the other because the chapter inevitably reflects only one aspect of classroom life, this would be both an unfair and an untrue interpretation. Similarly, as described in Chapter 9, the patterns of classroom interaction described here are common features of classrooms across the country. In both forms they are typical of culturally embedded but often taken-for-granted assumptions, regarding the nature of knowledge and appropriate relationships and interactional forms for teaching and learning.

Since the introduction of the National Curriculum, classroom assessment, for primary school teachers, has meant matching and grading children against detailed statements of attainment. Since that time also, teacher assessments certainly have gained the *appearance* of being more objective than those made pre-National Curriculum. Records, often in the form of ticked boxes, based on observations with 'evidence' to back them up and carefully worded records and reports to parents have long since replaced the 'frequently generalised, laconic statements' (Alexander *et al.*, 1992) that parents and subsequent teachers traditionally received (see Chapter 12 for examples). However, over the years, the focus on *content*: on 'ticked boxes' and objective-looking statements of children's attainments, has acted to obscure what we have known for many years about the classroom *processes* that underlie them.

As described in Chapter 7, the problem with assessing classroom language begins as soon as one moves away from an abstract, ideal notion of what language competence might mean and it begins to be tied to specific situations and social events. In that chapter I explored the socio-economic contexts of children's 'news' telling at Albert Park School. I argued there that National Curriculum 'speaking and listening' attainment targets assume a model of classroom language that fails to take into account the multi-functional nature of language; that pupils have purposes *vis-à-vis* an audience of peers quite apart from those related to an assessment task or teacher requirements. Similarly, in Chapter 9 Pollard and I described teacher language in assessing pupils as being bound up with and inseparable from a range of other pedagogic functions concerned with the management, pacing and sequencing of lessons and the control of the knowledge content.

The two classroom contexts are each analysed briefly in terms of coping strategies but more explicitly in terms of Bernstein's theory of the framing of educational knowledge. Between them, these approaches help to portray the range of classroom situations and the social and emotional climate in which children's language was assessed in each classroom. In particular the concept of frame strength allows us to differentiate between pedagogic approaches with regard to some important implications for pupils verbal responses. In our analysis in Chapter 9, Andrew Pollard and I associated *strong framing* with functions of assessment for ascertaining 'states of knowledge' (Bernstein, 1975); that is knowing *whether* a pupil knows or understands something (Torrance and Pryor, 1998). Framing will be strong, therefore, where teachers focus their questions around and pursue explicit categoric responses in relation to a predetermined item of knowledge or skill. We associated *weak framing* with functions of assessment for understanding 'ways of knowing' (Bernstein, 1975); that is for accessing '*what* a pupil knows or understands' (Torrance and Pryor, 1998). Framing will be weaker, therefore, where teacher questioning is open and pupils' contributions are accepted and sustained. The implication of frame strength for classroom language is that where framing is stronger, pupil responses may be inhibited; where weaker, the teacher is more likely to be able to access what pupils know. This connection between teacher questioning and pupil responses is supported by many sociolinguistic studies of children's language (see Chapter 9 and Filer 1993b and 1993c for reviews of such studies).

Coping strategies

In comparing the two classroom contexts, below, I give a brief description of the coping strategies of each teacher. This will help to support an analysis of the distinctive language environments of the two classrooms and the social and emotional climates in which teacher–pupil communications took place.

As we described in Chapter 5, coping strategies constitute the broad base of classroom policy which teachers construct and which subsumes and informs their moment-to-moment decisions and actions. Pollard (1985) analysed coping strategies adopted by teachers as falling into three descriptive categories; 'routinization', 'manipulation' and 'domination'. 'Routinization' refers to routine in organization of work tasks and activities, the setting of occupational work rather than work that is more challenging, the appeal to tradition and precedent when controlling children and a degree of distancing in relationships. A detailed example of 'routinization' was given in Chapter 6. In the case of 'manipulation' a considerable amount of effort goes into issues such as how to motivate children, how to present work in attractive and stimulating ways and how to create a positive classroom climate. 'Domination' is a strategy which explicitly attempts to use the expected power differential between teacher and pupils and which is employed rather more obliquely and implicitly in other approaches. It can occur in the form of commands and threats, insistence on conformity to behavioural rules and sometimes in 'showing up' children. Of course, these are not mutually exclusive categories and teacher's strategies may, either routinely or occasionally, show elements of more than one approach.

The framing of educational knowledge

As Pollard and I discussed in Chapter 9, classroom language simultaneously fulfils a range of pedagogic functions. Teacher talk is not simply concerned with processes of instruction and with ascertaining what pupils know. It is also concerned with the control and management of the knowledge content, controlling the pacing and sequencing of interaction and managing the teacher–pupil relationships through which the lesson is achieved. As Pollard and I suggested, a useful way to conceptualize these simultaneous function of teachers' language is to employ Bernstein's (1975) conceptions relating to the 'framing of educational knowledge'.

The 'framing of educational knowledge' allows us to see a range of classroom processes in terms of the control of knowledge. Bernstein (1971) refers to educational knowledge as being realized through the three message systems of 'curriculum', 'pedagogy' and 'evaluation'. 'Frame' in this context is used to determine the structure of the message system of 'pedagogy'. It refers to the degree of control teacher and taught possess over selection, organization and pacing of educational knowledge and to the strength of the boundary between what may or may not be transmitted in the pedagogic relationship as educational knowledge. Bernstein points out that an important aspect of framing with respect to boundary maintenance concerns the degree to which teachers insulate educational knowledge from their own and their pupils' everyday knowledge. Framing will thus be weak to the extent that pupils are allowed to incorporate and sustain contributions from their own personal and everyday experience. This may be contrasted with the stronger framing such as is inherent in a 'question and answer' sequencing of lessons, the more so where only one answer, the teacher's, is pursued. However, I do not want to differentiate, as Bernstein does, between 'educational knowledge' and 'everyday knowledge' in the following analysis as that is not an altogether appropriate distinction for examining frame strength in an infant classroom. Rather, I differentiate between what I term 'curriculum knowledge', that is what has been decided will be taught, whether National Curriculum, school policy or teacher inspired, and 'pupil perspectives, knowledge and interests', however these might stand in relation to curriculum knowledge.

In Table 10.1, I present a chart which summarizes and compares the data and my analysis of each of the classroom contexts.

10.3   A COMPARISON OF TWO CLASSROOM CONTEXTS

The cohort's Year 1 teacher: coping strategies

My classroom observations of daily and weekly routines, of the physical environment and of the means of control of the pupils together with interviews and informal conversations made a coherent picture of the Year 1 teacher's coping strategies. These can be described in terms of 'routinisation' (Pollard, 1985) and embody formality and a sense of order and control. Classroom tasks were generally formally structured, featuring individual progressions through work cards and highly visible grading of levels of achievement. Children sat at designated places and were grouped by achievement. Few unstructured, exploratory/play activities took place.

When not teaching the whole class, the teacher, Marie Tucker based herself at one end of the table where a group of more difficult to control boys sat, and from where she monitored class

Table 10.1   *The assessment of 'speaking and listening': a comparison of two classroom contexts.* (Reproduced from Filer, 1993b, 'The Assessment of Classroom Language', *International Studies in Sociology of Education)*

	Year 1	Year 2
Coping strategies (teacher)	Routinization	Mixed routinization/ manipulation/domination
Framing of educational knowledge (teacher)	Strong	Weaker
Context of assessment	Some social and emotional distancing	Volatile
	Assessed within routine social/ knowledge contexts	Assessed within more varied social/knowledge contexts
Language response – whole class	Short answers	Long answers
	Eight children do not contribute to discussions voluntarily	One child does not contribute to discussions voluntarily
	Little evidence of home/child cultures	Content of classroom talk more varied
Case study: assessments of Peter's speaking and listening	Silent 'Lacks knowledge' 'Lacks understanding' 'Cannot organize' 'Return to reception' recommended	Participates 'Good in groups' Teacher 'enjoys his conversation' 'Nothing wrong' cognitively

behaviour, whilst hearing readers and dealing with a queue of pupils with work to be marked (see also Chapter 6).

The cohort's Year 1 teacher: the framing of educational knowledge

In this section I first describe frame strength in the Year 1 class with respect to the broad classroom context. This together with the above description of coping strategies will give a good indication of the range of situations in which teacher–pupil communication took place and in which pupils' language skills could be assessed. I follow this with an analysis of teacher–pupil interaction in those whole-class situations in which most assessments relating to speaking and listening in Year 1 were grounded.

Marie Tucker's classroom was not a place where a lot of informal teacher–pupil conversations took place. Some of the reasons for this can be seen in the above descriptions of classroom routines whereby access to the teacher for much of the day was limited by the queuing system and the maintenance of classroom norms of behaviour was depersonalized. In addition to this, it was school policy to encourage parents into the classroom at the beginning and end of the day and Marie could usually be seen talking with parents, rather than pupils, during those times. Evidence of home life from children's perspectives and child culture were similarly excluded from the classroom in the absence of personal possessions such as small toys and novelties, pencil cases, etc., which are a feature of many primary classrooms. However, Marie encouraged children to bring in items of interest for the purpose of 'showing' to the class, for example during 'news' sessions.

Interaction between teacher and pupils in this setting was thus strongly framed with respect to the maintenance of boundaries between curriculum knowledge and children's experience and perceptions of the world outside of school across a range of social as well as educational classroom contexts.

Next, I can consider frame strength with respect to curriculum knowledge in the context of whole-class sessions which took place on the carpet. In this area children sat on the floor for whole-class teaching and discussion activities, including 'news', story time and registration.

Teacher records and interviews, together with my knowledge of classroom routines as described above, all confirmed that 'news' and discussion sessions on the carpet were the situations most used for assessing children's speaking and listening skills. It was also a situation that the teacher talked of as being beneficial for children in the development of their spoken language skills.

Below is an extract transcribed from a video recording of one such session on the carpet. I have chosen it because it illustrates several routine practices which functioned to maintain the boundary between curriculum knowledge and children's knowledge, perceptions and interests. It also shows how assessment under such circumstances functioned to ascertain 'states of knowledge' (Bernstein, 1975) in the pupils; that is, *whether* children knew or understood a teacher-determined item (Torrance and Pryor, 1998). The extract takes the form of a question-and-answer routine whereby Marie is trying to elicit from the children one particular answer to her question. Although such IRE (initiation, response, evaluation: see Chapter 9) sequencing was routine in this classroom, it would be unfair to suggest that the protracted and convoluted nature of the routine in this extract was typical.

Afternoon registration had taken place and Nicola had brought a doll into school to show to the class. The doll, called Cricket, told stories when a tape was inserted into its side. Nicola stood beside her teacher, Marie, and explained to her in a quiet voice that she bought the doll with £50 birthday money. Marie took the doll from Nicola, held it up to show the class and relayed this information to the children. She then demonstrated the number 50 by asking five children to stand up and hold up fingers for everyone to count together. Still holding the doll, she talked to the class about some of its features. During this talk, Nicola tried to handle her doll but was gently restrained from doing so by her teacher, who then proceeded to question the class:

Teacher	How do you think Cricket can talk? Hands up. (… inaudible …) I'm going to choose Sam 'cos he's sitting up nicely.
Sam	Um. Batteries.
Teacher	D'you think the batteries would make her talk?
Pupil 1	(Laughs.)
Teacher	That makes me cross if you laugh.
Pupil 2	He's trying.
Teacher	I know. I always tell you, as long as you have a try. What would the batteries do, Sam?
Sam	Make it go.
Teacher	Yeah, batteries would (pause). So what's in batteries?
Pupils	Electric
Teacher	Good boy. The batteries have got?
John	It's not electric for everything. It's acid.
Teacher	Yes, I know, but it's a sort of electricity. The batteries have got the power to make them work. They don't actually make her work, Sam. What d'you think actually makes her talk?
Pupil 3	Um. I know.
Teacher	Rebecca.
Rebecca	(… inaudible …) [She mentions a tape]
Teacher	A tape. (pause) What else? (pause) I've got one in my bag actually. But if I've got a tape, will that make her talk?
Pupils	[Chorus] No.

Teacher	What else d'you need? You need batteries. You need a tape. But what else?
Pupil 4	Electric.
Teacher	Well, you've got electric in the batteries.
John	Buttons.
Teacher	We've got buttons. We've got batteries. We've got a little tape (pause). If you pretend that this was a little tape (she holds up a small book) would it work on its own?
Pupils	[Chorus] No.
Teacher	What else do we need?
Ricky	(... inaudible ...)
Teacher	No Ricky. Think. You're all right.
Pupil 5	I know. [= I know that we are right]
Teacher	But there's something else that we need.
Elizabeth	Knobs.
Teacher	Knobs are the same as buttons, Elizabeth.
Elizabeth	A fuse.
Teacher	You have a fuse in there but there's something else. (She points to a child)
Pupil 6	You need a case.
Teacher	What sort of case?
Pupils	(Answers indistinguishable)
Teacher	And what do you call it? If you want to play a tape at home and if you have got a stereo (pause) Who has got one?
Pupils	(Hands go up.)
Teacher	What do you put into it, Caroline? What do you do with the tape?
Pupil 7	There's a tape recorder in there. [This is the response Marie has been waiting for but it goes unnoticed.]
Pupil 8	A plug.
Caroline	There's a brown thing.
Teacher	What d'you call it?
Pupil 8	A plug.
Teacher	No.
Pupils	(Derisive laughter)
Teacher	What d'you call the brown thing?
Pupils	(Quiet talk amongst themselves)
Teacher	Listen, Who's got a little (pause) a little **tape**?
Pupils	[Chorus] Me.
Teacher	Right. Put your hands down. What do you do with Cricket if you want to play a tape? You choose a tape and what?
John	You put it in the case. (Corrects himself) Take it out Cricket. (He laughs at his confusion.)
Teacher	You take it out the case and where do you put it?
John	(Laughing, and emphatically) You – put – it – into – Cricket.
Pupils	(Join in laughter)
Teacher	Put it in the ...?
Pupil 9	Tape recorder.
Teacher	The *tape recorder*. So what do you think she's got in her side?
Pupils	[All chorus] A *tape recorder*.
Pupil 7	That's what I said, a tape recorder. [See above where this sought-after response went unnoticed.]
Teacher	No you didn't.

(Video recording, summer term, 1990)

The focus of the session changed at this point as Marie went on to outline activities for the afternoon.

The first feature of this exchange, which was typical of situations in which children had something to 'show', is that Marie invariably took the object from the child and held it. Whether the object was a personal possession or school work, the object remained in the hands of Marie who also made any necessary demonstrations of the object. The restraining of children to prevent them handling objects was also a common occurrence, recorded on a second video of sessions on the carpet and also in field notes.

Relevant to the notion of frame strength is the way in which, in those situations in which one would most expect to see children's knowledge and interests surfacing as in 'showing', 'news' and other child-initiated interactions, Marie maintained a position of the holder of knowledge. She focused attention upon herself as such, not only physically, as described above, by the appropriation of objects but also in the way in which priority was given to teacher-selected knowledge. Of a number of features of an object or subject under discussion, the tendency was towards a process of early identification and homing in on an area of possible ignorance whereby children's knowledge and perceptions were marginalized, excluded or made 'wrong'. Boundaries between curriculum knowledge and children's knowledge and perceptions were also maintained in question-and-answer sequences through the practice of 'skating over' responses which challenged the teacher's knowledge or attempted to debate an issue. An example of this 'skating over' is John's 'It's not electric for everything. It's acid'. This practice was also recorded in other lessons and has been discussed elsewhere (Filer, 1993c, ch. 7).

Other authors have discussed ways in which, in the privacy and immediacy of classroom life, teachers may deny the relevance and validity of pupil challenges to the teacher's definition of what knowledge is appropriate to the lesson. As Delamont points out, teachers, on reading transcripts of their lessons, may well wish they had responded differently to pupil challenges (Delamont, 1983; also Keddie, 1971 and Young, 1976). However, it is not usually the challenge to their knowledge, in itself, that is problematic for teachers. Indeed, in other circumstances, Marie was quite prepared to reveal her ignorance on particular issues and pursue further understanding with pupils. Rather it is the case that, in circumstances such as the above, such challenges can represent a threat to a teacher's need to control both a large class of children, some of whom present a challenge to teacher control and, at the same time, the pace and direction of the lesson. Thus also, as was discussed in Chapter 9, in the process of assessing knowledge and understanding, teachers' questions simultaneously function to socialize young children into the interactional codes through which teaching and learning take place.

The above classroom processes, therefore, reflect existing research summarized in Chapter 9 and ways in which in question-and-answer sequencing pupil responses are routinely appropriated and adapted to suit teacher purposes in accomplishing the lesson. Having initially implied that batteries, tape and buttons were not correct answers to her question of what makes the doll talk, the teacher then needs to reduce pupils' increasing confusion and concede that they were all right answers. However, they were still not *the* right answer and not accorded the status of the long-awaited, emphasized and repeated 'tape recorder'.

The strong framing of the 'one right answer' routine here meant that children prepared to answer risked both having their perfectly appropriate answers declared 'wrong' and also the laughter of other pupils which, though frequently deplored by Marie, nevertheless often occurred.

To summarize thus far: the above transcripts demonstrate some ways in which strong framing with respect to curriculum knowledge versus children's knowledge, perceptions and interests was maintained by the Year 1 teacher. The episodes selected represent those whole-class speaking and listening situations in which one would expect to find the weakest framing, in that such situations arose out of children's personal out-of-school experiences. The analysis of the data focuses upon four processes by which the teacher took and maintained control of the knowledge content in these situations:

(1) She physically held the item.
(2) She selected the knowledge content.
(3) She pursued one right answer by marginalizing others, thus making them 'wrong'.
(4) She 'skated over' and closed off pupil challenges which might have diverted progress towards the 'right' answer.

In the following section I compare the strong framing of educational knowledge of the Year 1 teacher above with the weaker framing of the children's Year 2 teacher. The comparison shows different approaches to the control of knowledge, bound up with different patterns of inter- action, classroom relationships and control strategies.

The cohort's Year 2 teacher: coping strategies

Despite some similarities, the coping strategies of the cohort's Year 2 teacher, Peggy Major, cannot be as easily categorized as those of the Year 1 teacher. Elements of 'routinization', 'manipulation' and 'domination' (Pollard, 1985) coexisted.

'Routinization' could be seen in the formal organization and grading of tasks which, because it to a large extent reflected school policy, was similar to that of the Year 1 teacher. The Year 2 teacher, however, devised many and varied rewards systems and the control of children was more verbal, featuring discussion and explanation to a much greater extent than in the Year 1 class. This together with the more public and personal criticism of individuals meant that a much higher profile was given to misdemeanours in this class (see Chapter 4.4). Thus, in the control of children, elements of 'manipulation' and 'domination' coexisted.

In Peggy Major's Year 2 class, therefore, there was a much more volatile classroom atmos- phere, with emotions closer to the surface than in Marie Tucker's Year 1 class. The teacher and hence the children were much more physically demonstrative than in the previous year and Peggy Major was much more mobile than the Year 1 teacher. She placed herself at different tables and worked with small groups, especially for writing tasks. There was a general feeling of more freedom of movement in the class and a greater variety of tasks was under way at any one time. For many of these tasks there was therefore less close supervision than was the case in Marie's class. As can be assumed from this account of her coping strategies, the Year 2 teacher interacted with pupils in a much greater variety of situations than was the case in Year 1.

The cohort's Year 2 teacher: the framing of educational knowledge

Because of the sudden hospitalization of the Year 2 teacher during the summer months, I do not have a video of a situation comparable with that analysed for the Year 1 class. Nevertheless, direct comparisons can be made from my field notes of a similar situation; one that was typical of those in which a child is 'showing' an object.

In contrast with the framing of educational knowledge in Marie's class, which was strong, framing in Peggy's class was considerably weaker. The following therefore reflects the kind of assessment context, described in 10.2 above, which appears to function to support 'ways of knowing', as opposed to 'states of knowledge' (Bernstein, 1975). That is to say it would function to access *what* a pupil knows or understands rather than *whether* a child knows or understands a predetermined thing (Torrance and Pryor, 1998).

Again, a child had brought something of interest into the classroom to show to her teacher and peers. The following is an extract from my field notes taken at the time.

> A child has brought in a programme of the Nutcracker Ballet. The teacher (Peggy Major) asks the child about her mother's trip to London to see it; whether she enjoyed it. She asks the class if they remember the Nutcracker story that her class of last year performed for the school. 'What was special about the Nutcrackers in the story?', she asks. The children respond with descriptions of ordinary nutcrackers, a description of breaking nuts by stamping on them and an apparently unconnected story about a pet cat killing a bird. All responses are accepted and the teacher describes the workings of another sort of nutcracker; a screw device. She asks the children about benefits of nutcrackers over stamping on nuts (which one child had described). Several contributions from children, summarised by Peggy as 'the right sort of pressure does not squash the nut'. Her original question (What was special about the nutcrackers in the story?) was abandoned. Children's responses mostly fairly lengthy. (Ann Filer, field notes, Year 2, spring 1991)

Thus in classroom contexts focused around children's interests, such as telling news or showing objects, the Year 2 teacher differed from the Year 1 teacher in the following ways:

(1) She usually held objects up for children to see but did not exclude the owner from it, allowing them to demonstrate, manipulate it, etc.
(2) Year 2 teacher selected the knowledge content to be the focus of attention as did the Year 1 teacher but she tended to abandon her line of questioning in the light of the direction of pupil response.
(3) Whole-class discussion sessions in Year 2 were therefore more unpredictable and conversational rather than following a strongly framed teacher question, short pupil answer, teacher evaluation format. Pupil contributions were all accepted, none was 'wrong'. No one laughed at the contribution of others.
(4) I have no record of children making challenges to teacher knowledge in the Year 2 class. However, it seems reasonable to suggest that where they occurred the tendency for this teacher to use a more 'elaborated' language of control (Bernstein, 1975), as described above, would mean that challenges would have been incorporated and discussed, rather than curtailed.

Through this comparison of two language environments we can distinguish some key differences with regard to frame strength in maintaining the boundary between teacher-generated curriculum knowledge and children's knowledge, perceptions and interests. In Year 1, even in sessions where one would expect to see children's knowledge, perceptions and interests coming to the fore, strong boundaries existed to maintain the focus of attention upon the teacher as the holder and arbiter of relevant knowledge. In Year 2 in similar situations, weaker boundaries enabled these privileges to be shared between the teacher and the children.

In the following section I compare the impact of this strong and weaker framing of knowledge on children's verbal responses in the two classrooms, and hence on teachers' experience and perceptions of their 'speaking and listening' skills in each context. I do so first with respect to the response of the cohort in general classroom situations and then with respect to whole-class teaching situations such as those analysed above. I then go on to present a case study of one child who, of all the cohort, was perhaps the most sensitive to the difference between the two teacher-created language environments.

Pupils' verbal responses: comparisons between Year 1 and Year 2

General classroom context

As might be imagined from the above description of the two teachers' practices, there were clear changes in both the form and the content of the children's language as they moved from Year 1 to Year 2. There was in Year 1, compared with most infant schools, something of a social and emotional distancing and restraint in their approach to adults in the classroom. I was not able to recall, for instance, an occasion when a child initiated any physical contact with an adult in the classroom. Nor did the children, whilst in the classroom, show any marked tendency to engage adults in conversation other than that arising out of the immediate classroom context.

In the emotionally and physically less restrained atmosphere of the Year 2 classroom, not surprisingly, children's language underwent a corresponding change. Children made more demands on me, initiated conversations as well as requests for help and made more physical contact. Children's out-of-school experiences were more to the fore in their conversations. Early in the autumn term, during classroom observations, I recorded that a child asked my opinion on football teams and that others were having conversations about a child's neighbours, about dogs and about spaceships whilst they worked. This in itself is pretty unremarkable primary classroom activity, and I would not claim that such conversations never occurred in the Year 1 class. However, I had not recalled nor ever recorded such conversations in the previous year. These behaviours came as something of a novelty with the change of classes, worthy of recording in field notes. I also recorded in field notes that 'telling teacher' was a feature of this class rarely observed in the more controlled and calm atmosphere of Year 1.

Whole-class teaching on the carpet

In Year 1, where question-and-answer routines were the norm, short answers prevailed. Apart from those few children who held forth at length in telling their 'news' without teacher prompting, ten words were the maximum length of pupil responses to teacher questioning recorded in two videos and in field notes. An analysis of teacher records relating to individual children's 'speaking and listening' skills showed that eight children, nearly a third of the class, did not ever voluntarily contribute to class discussions.

The less determined, more fluid nature of whole class discussions in Year 2 tended to allow for children's perceptions and knowledge and interests to surface rather than the pursuing of one right answer. As well as being qualitatively different, answers tended to be lengthy in comparison with those in Year 1. In comparison with the end of year reports in Year 1 where eight children did not contribute to class discussion, in the autumn reports of Year 2 all the children except one volunteered contributions to group discussions.

In the above analysis of two classes as teacher-created language environments we begin to get a strong sense of teachers' power to generate a range of contexts which may elicit or suppress particular language responses on the part of pupils. However, the possibility of such changes coming about as a result of the maturing of the children rather than as a result of a change of teacher needs to be addressed. I would argue that, for several reasons, this does not seem to be the case. First, as a regular observer of both classes I experienced the change as abrupt and distinct; identifiable at the beginning of Year 2 but not some five to six weeks earlier in Year 1. Second, I would argue that the sorts of changes observed were not age-related changes. Of course, one would expect to see developmental changes in children's language as they move up the school. These changes would include, for example, increased articulacy, reasoning powers and precision in questioning. The language I have described which children used in Year 2, in terms of length of responses and range of content, were not of that order. The language, in the respects I have described, would have been no more remarkable in a reception class of 4-year-olds than it was in a Year 2 class. What these changes do, in terms of increased range of content and increased length, of course, is to allow the teacher *access* to a child's developing articulacy or reasoning powers. The case study below demonstrates just this process. I would also argue for there being no necessary connection between chronological or cognitive development and increased numbers participating in class discussion. Though children clearly may learn to manage the linguistic demands of classrooms with more confidence as they mature, we also know that large sections of classes not participating in this way can be found across the school years and even into higher education.

Of course, as discussed in Chapter 9, there is, in fact, no reason to find it surprising that these sorts of changes in children's language occur with a change of teacher. Lees (1981) and Wood and Wood (1983) described the way in which, when teachers changed their style to become less controlling in conversation with children and to ask fewer questions, pupils talked more frequently and revealed more of their views and ideas. As I have described above, as well as being less controlling in this way than the Year 1 teacher, the Year 2 teacher also allowed children's knowledge perceptions and interests to surface. Mueller (1971) found that the likelihood of getting a conversational response from young children was affected by the topic under discussion. Personal involvement in the topic on the part of the child was a strong influencing factor. In addition, Labov *et al.* (1968) and Strandberg and Griffith (1968) showed that with a greater degree of personal involvement in a topic there is a corresponding greater degree of structural complexity in the language used. This finding applied to children of all ages. Dunn (1996) and Tizard and Hughes (1984) have shown that within different relationships, the same child will show very different powers of social understanding and communicative and reflective behaviour. The crucial difference being the quality of supportive interest where adults are trying to understand what children are attempting to say and to help them make sense of their experience. Or, as Torrance and Pryor (1998: 157) put it, the teacher who is more interested in the *child* will elicit more valid responses than the teacher who is more interested in the *attainment*.

10.4   ASSESSING PETER'S 'SPEAKING AND LISTENING': A CASE STUDY

Year 1 teacher experience and assessments of Peter's 'speaking and listening'

Peter was one of the youngest children in the class, having a July birthday. The Year 1 teacher's perception of Peter was that much of the time he did not know what was going on in the classroom and did not seem to understand what was expected of him in any situation and was bewildered. She said that with regard both to topic work and general classroom activities, 'I don't think he's got any idea what we're talking about, really. It just seems to go over his head.' These classroom responses of Peter's led the Year 1 teacher to the opinion that he would be better provided for if he could be returned to the Reception class for a while. She had approached the head teacher several times proposing this, but without success.

Formal assessment of Peter's 'speaking and listening' made in school records during the autumn term stated that his vocabulary was 'limited'. Similar assessments made in the summer term reported 'increased vocabulary' and that he 'shares news'. It was also reported that though he appeared to listen he failed to absorb or understand what he heard.

My experience of Peter's speaking and listening abilities

In the spring term, midway between the two assessments of Peter's vocabulary as 'limited' and 'increased', and before I knew anything of the Year 1 teacher's perception of Peter, I was, on the basis of interviews with Peter outside the classroom, beginning to form a different perception of him in this respect. After asking Peter questions concerning who helped him, and who he helped in the classroom, I recorded the following in field notes:

> Peter (5 yrs 6 mths) seems to be a very articulate child in that in talking to me he qualified his answers with the words 'eventually' and 'occasionally'. (Field notes, spring term, 1990)

Later in the year, as I became more aware of the discrepancy between the Year 1 teacher's experience of Peter's language capabilities and my own, I frequently made a point of observing Peter during sessions on the carpet. During these observations Peter did not make any contribution to lessons, always remaining perfectly still and apparently attentive. Outside the classroom, in interview, he always talked freely and expanded on the topic of conversation. He always took a lively interest in the research process, questioning me on note taking and the workings of the tape recorder, for instance. Throughout the 'tape recorder' episode analysed above, Peter, as usual, sat attentively and said nothing. Marie might well have considered that it was 'all going over his head'. In contrast to this, a few weeks before that episode, Peter, during an interview with me, brought up the subject of the tape recorder I was using and told me about using one at home:

> We put the tape in and we say things and it tape records. It says it. It says, like, the things we said. (Peter)

Later in the same interview, whilst operating the recorder himself, he peered into it and asked me:

> How does my voice get winded on?'

Clearly Peter had the potential to offer experience and intelligent questioning to a class discussion on tape recorders. Clearly, also, Marie's question-and-answer routines, strongly framed in a way that marginalized or excluded children's knowledge and interests, were not situations in which Peter, or any other child, could have asked perhaps the most relevant and intelligent question of all: 'How does my voice get winded on?'

Year 2 teacher experience and assessment of Peter's 'speaking and listening'

After nearly a year of seeing Peter sitting silent and still on the carpet, the first thing I saw of him in the new class at the beginning of the autumn term was that he was standing in the middle of the carpet, holding a book that he had brought into school and recounting the story of 'The Lion, the Witch and the Wardrobe' that his parents were reading to him.

Also during the autumn term, the Year 2 teacher said that Peter was 'good in groups', that in writing tasks he was the one in his group to come up with all the ideas. Formal assessments in the autumn term state that he listens well in a group but sometimes has trouble retaining instructions.

My observations showed that Peter took full part in discussions where child knowledge, perceptions and interests were to the fore. Formal assessments recorded that he voluntarily contributed to other curriculum discussions and I observed him to answer correctly or appropriately when called upon, showing that he was following proceedings. The Year 2 teacher told me that 'Peter has got it all up the top' and in the summer term she reported that he had a good background general knowledge.

In the light of the teachers', and my, very different experiences and perceptions of Peter's language competencies and cognitive development, readers might like to return to, and review, the question that Pollard and I posed in Chapter 3.3:

- What is involved in a teacher 'knowing' a child?

10.5   DISCUSSION

This analysis and comparison of two teacher-created language environments illustrates some of the problems inherent in assessing children's verbal competencies in classrooms. By extension, of course, where *any* assessments are made through teacher–pupil talk, the problems remain the same. A full review of the theoretical background to the analysis here, and other supporting research, was presented in Chapter 9.

Perhaps the fundamental importance of this analysis is that it illustrates ways in which children's classroom language is conditioned by patterns and forms of control which are embedded in teachers' everyday routines and interactions with pupils. This has implications for ways in which we approach and interpret classroom assessments involving teacher–pupil talk; for it follows that such assessments are always jointly accomplished by teachers and pupils. As Bernstein (1990) points out, in their classroom talk, teachers are not culture-free, ideal speakers. No one is. Teachers do not represent a neutral linguistic background against which children can be assessed.

Given this understanding, we can perceive that increased formalization in assessment recording and reporting, the drive for supporting 'evidence' and the 'ticked boxes' deceive with their appearance of 'objectivity' and thus actually serve to obscure the role of teachers in the *production* of assessments. Beyond this, the pressure upon teachers for greater formality in assessment practices (see Chapter 5) is driving teachers to pursue more explicit and categoric expressions of pupils' knowledge, as seen in the change towards 'performance goals' (Broadfoot and Pollard, 2000; see also Chapter 9). The implications of this change are that 'frame strength' as I have described it here must increase and assessment will increasingly function to ascertain 'states of knowledge' (Bernstein, 1975) and *whether* pupils know a predetermined item of knowledge (Torrance and Pryor, 1998). It is *less* likely to be required to function to understand 'ways of knowing' (Bernstein, 1975) or *what* a child knows or understands. As I have illustrated here, in many cases the former may well serve to inhibit responses, to confuse and to limit teacher access to what they are trying to assess. Elsewhere (Filer, 1993a and 1995), I have examined assessments of pupils' written responses where frame strength is strong, with similar conclusions.

10.6   CONCLUSION

This chapter has analysed and compared two classrooms as teacher-created language environments together with their influence on the verbal responses of a cohort of children. Within the classrooms, functions of assessment are seen to be bound up with other pedagogic functions in the control of knowledge, relationships and interaction. Bernstein's (1975) conception of the 'framing of educational knowledge' is used to conceptualize these simultaneous functions of teacher language. 'Frame strength' allows a comparative analysis of different patterns and forms of control which have different effects on the level and quality of pupils' verbal responses.

The analysis in this chapter extends that in Chapter 7 and Chapter 9 in showing that National Curriculum expectations for classroom assessment assume a model of classroom language which fails to take into account its multi-functional nature. Teachers, like pupils, have social purposes in their utterances which, in turn, shape assessment outcomes in important but hidden ways.

Throughout this pair of chapters relating to functions of assessment, we have been concerned with issues of power and control in pedagogic relationships. As we have pointed out though, power and control are never absolutes in classrooms. Thus in the final pair of chapters that follow, we consider a wider 'audience' of assessment outcomes and the families, peers and wider communities who are active in interpreting and mediating them.

Chapter 11

How are Assessments Interpreted and Mediated? – An Introduction

11.1   INTRODUCTION

The issues which we address in this final pair of research chapters relate to an under-researched area of assessment activity. Our question, 'How are outcomes interpreted and mediated?', addresses ways in which academic and social outcomes of assessment are differentially shaped within a matrix of family, school and wider community perceptions, expectations and relationships. In relation to the model in Figure 4.1, therefore, 'interpretation and mediation' relates to the processes that *initial* assessment outcomes are subject to before recursively affecting individual pupil's social and academic identities and sense of selves as learners.

Through this pair of chapters, therefore, our analysis is concerned with the possibility of what we have termed 'transformative processes'. We introduce the concept of an 'audience' of families, peers and local communities who are active in the lives of individual pupils, interpreting and mediating, supporting or challenging the official and unofficial voices of school assessment. In this we draw attention to the sociocultural and professional power relations through which professionals and power elites legitimate, control and disseminate assessment outcomes and which delimit 'audience' powers to interpret, mediate, contest and contribute to assessment outcomes.

Through these chapters we also conclude that current policy and government discourses that position parents as consumers of assessment outcomes fail to capture their potential for contributing in more active and collaborative ways in the assessment of their children.

11.2   POWER, CONTROL AND THE OUTCOMES OF EDUCATIONAL ASSESSMENT

Assessment – social processes and social outcomes

Through the chapters in this book we have shown ways in which assessment practices give rise to outcomes beyond those concerned with marks, grades and statements of academic achievement. As we discussed in Chapter 9, in addition to those overt functions, processes of assessment also give rise to outcomes relating to the motivation, self-esteem and sense of self-as-learner of individual pupils. Assessment also gives rise to particular perceptions and expectations held of groups of pupils from particular sociocultural groups. In Chapters 3 and 4, in relation to 'Who is being assessed?' we discussed ways in which children's social and academic identities as pupils and their culturally defined and gendered identities as pupils are shaped within the context of successive minor and major cycles of formal and informal assessment practices. Again, in Chapter 9, we drew on our own research and that of others to show ways in which those processes and cycles of assessment differentially shape pupils' responses and engagements with tasks and act to polarize achievement outcomes. Of course, these effects in relation to learning and social outcomes are not confined to classrooms but go on to present differential educational and career opportunities and socio-economic statuses throughout life. Thus a powerful function of all forms of educational assessment lies in its role in the social and cultural reproduction of societies (Bourdieu and Passeron, 1977; see also Broadfoot, 1996; Filer, 2000).

In Chapters 9 and 10, where we posed the question 'How does assessment function in classrooms?', we discussed some of the assessment and classroom processes that give rise to differentiated learning and social outcomes. There, we used Bernstein's (1975) conceptions of 'evaluation' as the 'purest form' of pedagogic control to elucidate the multiple social as well as academic functions of assessment, as well as some of the power relations that underpin them.

Legitimation and contestation

However, as we also pointed out in Chapter 10, power and control are not absolutes in classrooms or in state policy within democratic societies. Thus outcomes perceived as unfair or oppressive will, to varying degrees, be subject to contestation by, or on behalf of, those whose lives they most adversely affect. On the other hand, acceptance of outcomes will depend on perceptions of the '*legitimacy*' of systems of assessment. The concept of 'legitimacy' is crucial in this as, throughout history, the outcomes of assessment have been economic and social rewards for some, reduced access to educational and occupational opportunities for many. The mass categorizing and social differentiation of populations have needed to be accepted as broadly just, in particular by the *loser* in the assessment stakes (Filer, 2000). As we also discussed in Chapter 7, such public acceptance has been underpinned by perceptions of technologies of mass assessment as a scientifically neutral and reliable means of measuring learning and of drawing conclusions about capacities for future learning (Filer, 2000).

Of course, the important issue of 'legitimation' does not just relate to systems of mass assessment. As we found through the *Identity and Learning Programme* case studies at Albert Park and Greenside Schools, parents evaluated ongoing assessments of their child's attainment in the context of a *particular teacher's class*. In this they drew on their own evaluations of their child's capabilities and potential, their perceptions regarding the provision of appropriately challenging work and teacher support for progression. These assessments made by parents of *their child and teacher together* formed a basis for decisions to support or challenge the day-to-day judgements teachers made of their children. Our analysis in this chapter presents a fuller account of the judgements parents brought to bear in this decision-making process.

Transformative processes

In further developing the model in Figure 4.1 therefore, this pair of chapters is concerned with the processes that *initial* assessment outcomes are subject to before they recursively affect

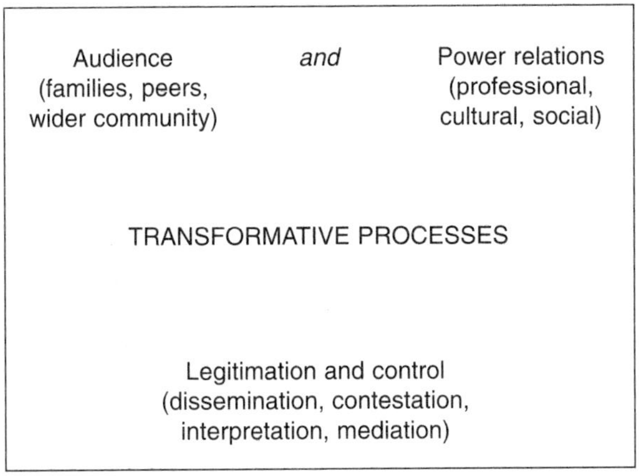

Audience   *and*   Power relations
(families, peers,   (professional,
wider community)   cultural, social)

TRANSFORMATIVE PROCESSES

Legitimation and control
(dissemination, contestation,
interpretation, mediation)

Figure 11.1   *Audience, power relations and legitimation and control: three factors shaping transformative processes*

individuals' self-perceptions and academic and social identities as pupils. Thus the question we pose here of 'How are assessments interpreted and mediated?' relates to 'transformative processes' in the cycle of assessment in a social context (Figure 4.1). It relates to *audiences* which may bring different sets of values and expectations to assessment processes. It relates to the social, cultural and professional *power relations* and to issues of *legitimacy and control* which delimit the powers of 'audiences' to question, mediate and contest assessment processes and outcomes. We present these factors in the model of *transformative processes* in Figure 11.1.

'Audience', interpretation and mediation

Through the *Identity and Learning Programme* we have broadened theoretical conceptions of social influences on assessment through a consideration of issues of *audience, interpretation* and *mediation*. Through the case studies presented in *The Social World of Children's Learning* and *The Social World of Pupil Career* and through this book, it can be seen that assessment is not a one-way process. Teachers, parents and pupils are all involved in making judgements about, mediating and interpreting the official and unofficial voices of school assessment.

For example, the case studies show that teachers interpreted and mediated formal measurements of achievement to pupils and parents with regard to their importance and what constituted a satisfactory outcome. Teachers could thus exercise a good measure of influence over ways in which parents perceived their child's attainment and progress, over what they should be concerned about and what they should act upon. Teachers also controlled and mediated the dissemination of a range of informal assessments. As we described in the case of Elizabeth (Chapter 4.4), how much of teachers' perceptions were available to pupils, peers and parents, varied from teacher to teacher, with important consequences for Elizabeth's home and peer relationships, her academic identity and classroom status.

The case studies also show the involvement of parents as well as teachers in assessing their children, in attributing success and failure, rewarding and encouraging competitiveness or comparisons with peers. Responses to school assessment practices and outcomes were therefore shaped in the contexts of family culture, relationships and experience, as well as in the context of local socio-economic and cultural interpretations and expectations.

In addition to assessing their children, parents also evaluated teacher and school assessment practices. As we described above, nearly every parent evaluated their child's progress *in the context of a particular teacher's class*. Such judicious judgements were made in decisions to support, ignore or contest teacher judgements or to offer alternative interpretations to the child or teacher.

The case studies also showed ways in which teacher assessments, both formal and informal, were mediated by those of peers who provided alternative sources of identity. The values and evaluations of the peer group were powerful influences that existed in dynamic relationship with the official voices of teachers and school assessment and those emanating from the cultural and material circumstances of home and community. In Chapter 4.4, for example, we illustrated the power of peer evaluation in the case of Elizabeth where assessment outcomes were embedded in the values and relationships of the peer culture, as well as in teacher requirements for tasks.

Thus our case studies show assessment as a multi-dimensional process, whereby individual pupils' perceptions and responses to assessment practices and outcomes were differentially shaped within a matrix of family, peer group, school and community perceptions, expectations and relationships.

Discourses and contestation in the public arena

Of course, in their responses to school assessments, families draw on wider discourses and debates than those presented by family and local culture. Their perceptions and expectations will also be informed by perceptions of the *legitimacy* of assessment processes and outcomes (see above) and debates and levels of contestation in the wider society. We can draw on the writing of UK and US writers in *Assessment – Social Practice and Social Product* (Filer, 2000) in exploring ways in which the nature of contestation and pressure for change in societies varies across time and across different national contexts. For instance, until the changes brought about by the 1988 Education Act, assessment procedures in England remained virtually unchallenged for decades (Broadfoot, 1996: 52–3). We might contrast this, and indeed the nature and extent of current public contestation in the UK, with the situation in the USA. There, from the 1970s onwards, different interest groups have actively questioned the role of assessment in their own and others' lives and contested the expansion of testing (OTA, 1992: 67). Challenges have arisen there in relation to the inequitable power relations embedded in practices that are ill-understood by those that use them and from decision-making processes that are remote from the populations they act upon. For example, in the USA, controversy has surrounded the lack of privacy in relation to test results and students' lack of power and control over them. Scores can be used, or misused, by anyone with access to student records, whether or not that person knows anything about a particular test. American interest groups and academics powerfully articulate and challenge the lack of public discussion and knowledge of a highly technical arena in which there is no unanimity among professionals concerning what is good practice (OTA, 1992: 69–71). Such a discourse hardly exists within education in the UK, let alone in wider public debate. A further key aspect of public contestation in the USA has come from cultural minorities resentful of having their histories and cultural meanings represented in curricula by white, governing elites of European descent (Berlak 1995, 2000). LaCelle-Peterson (2000) also raises concerns related to the problem of disparities between centralized assessment policies and the needs of linguistic minorities. The above analysis draws on Filer (2000), where US and UK authors present a fuller, macro analysis of legitimation, control, power relations and cultural reproduction in assessment than is possible or appropriate here.

Meanings, interpretations and parental strategic mediation

As we discussed in Chapters 7 and 8, pupils engaging in assessment practices draw on a field of action that includes their families, peers and wider communities within which they shape their identities. Their responses to task expectations are thus shaped by their awareness of a range of evaluative contexts so that home, community, peers and friends are ever-present contexts within which children locate their classroom meanings and responses (Filer, 1997; see also Pollard with Filer, 1996; Maguire, 1977; Nicholls *et al.*, 1996; Pollard and Filer, 1999).

However, the potential for families to shape assessment outcomes can also take more direct forms. In the following chapter, for example, we describe ways in which parents variously support, act upon, contest or ignore the official and unofficial voices of school assessment. The chapter shows parents' successes and failures in their attempts to negotiate higher or different achievement outcomes for their children, together with some implications for home–school relationships. It also describes the ambivalence and antagonisms that can coexist with appreciation for teachers' work and which can run beneath apparently supportive strategies and relationships. Assessments were thus being interpreted and mediated within family settings and in interaction with teachers in ways that could powerfully influence children's self-perceptions and achievement outcomes, both positively and negatively.

Parental roles in assessment processes

Notwithstanding the insights which the analysis in the following chapter offers, we would argue that parental participation and influence in assessment processes should not hinge on their ability to deploy successful strategies. Of course, English education policy has made much of the role of newly empowered parents in their children's education, their partnership with schools and their shared responsibilities for the education of their children. However, research suggests that there are no real gains in parental power and relationships with schools over the 1980s and 1990s. As we have described elsewhere (Filer and Pollard, 2000) in the case of most schools, the rhetoric of partnership amounts to little more than the expectation that parents attend school events and are passive recipients of information, rather than co-constructors of a shared understanding of their children (Barber, 1996; Johnson and Barber, 1996; Vincent and Tomlinson, 1997; see also Hughes *et al.*, 1994; Hughes, 1996). Vincent and Tomlinson argue that schools' 'soft rhetoric' of partnership has, through successive Conservative and Labour politicians, become translated into mechanisms for defining good parenting, directing family life and emphasizing complete parental responsibility for their children's behaviour and achievements. This emphasis on parents as 'responsible consumers' (DES, 1992; Vincent and Tomlinson, 1997: 369) can be seen as an aspect of the current discourse of target setting, 'standards', home–school 'agreements' and in the context of the 'moral panic' about disruptive pupil behaviour (Broadfoot and Pollard, 2000).

Hughes (1996) points out that although the role of parents in their children's education has received a vast amount of attention within public debate, we know comparatively little about how parents themselves view their supposed new roles. We also know little about how they view the assessment initiatives that are supposed to support them. Hughes (1996) and Hughes *et al.* (1994) found in a study of 150 children that parents had learned 'nothing new' from SATs but wanted a closer, more interactive relationship with schools. In a further study of around 240 children in a variety of schools, parents particularly wanted a more active role in assessment through providing additional information about activities and interests at home (Desforges *et al.*,

1994 and 1996). Teachers in that study though were generally not aware of such desires, were unwilling to change practices and in any case generally found them inappropriate. Some thought that parents had little to offer in the field of assessment. Overall the study findings reflected those of a study fifteen years earlier (Tizard *et al.*, 1981 and 1982) that teachers' sense of professionalism kept them from acknowledging what parents had to offer (Hughes 1996: 108). However, that parents have both the knowledge and the potential to contribute to school understandings of their children's achievements is very well established. West *et al.* (1998) made a study of the educational activities of 107 children in their homes other than those directly associated with school work. They found a range of activities including cooking, music, library visits, writing, art and craft. They found no significant difference in the range of activities undertaken between parents in terms of their social class or mother's educational level. A study by Hirst (1998) confirmed and extended the research of others (e.g. Delgado-Gaitan, 1996; Huss, 1997) in finding that ethnic minority families were involved in extensive home literacy practices and much learning was happening at home. These practices were neither understood, valued nor built on in schools. However, whereas most families in these studies were interested in their children's learning and eager to be involved in home–school collaboration, schools often took a deficit view of the attitudes to education of ethnic minority families.

Thus, as we argue in Chapter 12, assessment policy and public discourse in England has, for some years, been based on misconceptions of 'what parents want' and that parents are potentially more willing *partners in learning* than their positioning as 'consumers' allows. We also argue that whilst government policy remains driven by the ideology and discourse of 'performance' (Broadfoot and Pollard, 2000; and see Chapters 5 and 9), then teachers are likely to remain within its yoke. At the same time, however, the power to influence assessment outcomes will be accorded to those parents who can mobilize the most successful strategies for intervention in their children's education. We analyse such strategies in the following chapter.

11.3   CONCLUSION

We have presented here a short chapter which begins to conceptualize an under-researched area of assessment activity through a consideration of 'transformative processes'. In it we set out some of our conclusions relating to ways in which assessments are mediated and interpreted within a matrix of family, school and wider community perceptions, expectations and relationships. In so doing we also address issues of sociocultural and professional power relations and those of legitimation and control which together delimit dissemination, mediation, contestation and contribution to assessment outcomes.

In particular we draw on our own research and that of others in presenting an account of the gap between the rhetoric and the reality of parental power and involvement, and between their *actual* and *potential* role in relation to school assessment practices. In a policy context which fails to value parental knowledge and has a limited appreciation of their contribution to their children's learning, the power to intervene and influence assessment outcomes remains with those who can employ the most successful strategies. The strategic responses of parents in relation to assessments of their children is the subject of the following chapter, the second which poses the question 'How are assessments interpreted and mediated?'

Chapter 12

How are Assessments Interpreted and Mediated? – Parental Strategic Action

12.1   INTRODUCTION

This is the second of the pair of chapters in which we address the question 'How are assessments interpreted and mediated?' In it we show ways in which classroom assessments are differentially shaped within a matrix of family, school and local community perceptions, expectations and relationships. It presents an analysis of the strategic approaches of parents at Greenside and Albert Park Schools as mediators and interpreters of assessments of their children as they progress through primary school. In this, the analysis further develops the model in Figure 4.1 in exploring processes that teachers' initial assessments are subject to, before recursively affecting children's academic and social identities as a pupil. It thus further illuminates our conceptualization of 'transformative processes' developed through Chapter 11.

In this chapter we draw on conceptual models of the 'dimensions and dynamics of strategic action' that we developed for *The Social World of Pupil Career*. This enables us to cut across the more usual structural analysis of home–school relationship in terms of power inequalities of working and middle-class families. At the same time it allows us to problematize the simple dichotomies of 'supportive' or 'problem' families that prevail among politicians, practitioners and in popular discourse. We also consider parents' successful and unsuccessful strategies for influencing teacher perceptions of their children in the light of the lack of official recognition of the knowledge and understandings of their children that parents have to offer.

In Chapter 11 we presented a theoretical and research background to this chapter and relevant arguments are only addressed here as necessary for purposes of introduction or discussion. We recommend a preliminary reading of that short chapter in order to further contextualize the case-study analysis here.

The data and analysis presented in this chapter has been adapted from a chapter first published as *Assessment and Parent's Strategic Action* (Filer and Pollard, 2000).

12.2   BACKGROUND AND SETTING

Over the last decade research into classroom assessment in England and Wales has been concerned primarily with issues relating to new forms of national testing, in particular those associated with their impact on teachers' work and pupils' learning. One particular focus for attention has been the work of primary school teachers for whom the Education Act of 1988 brought about the most revolutionary changes. This necessary focus on understanding momentous changes in national assessment practices has meant that comparatively little research has been undertaken into ways in which parents use and respond to new forms of assessment. As Hughes (1996) notes, this is somewhat surprising, since parents have certainly received huge amounts of attention from policy perspectives.

Over the last decade there have been two main aspects of governmental rhetoric regarding parental power through assessment. First, assessment data has been constructed as the currency of an education market place whereby parents as 'clients' of the education system are supposedly free to 'choose' successful schools, allowing those less successful in league tables to sink. This exercise of choice has been explored by, among others, Gewirtz *et al.* (1995), Allatt (1996), Reay and Ball (1998). However, policy changes to make assessment the key to parental power has not just been about programmes of national testing and league tables of schools' results. In addition to new forms of national testing externally set and marked, teachers themselves have become accountable to parents in very categoric ways. These changes have had particular impact with respect to primary school practice (see Broadfoot and Pollard, 2000; Osborn *et al.*, 2000). Teachers have been trained in careful observation and review of 'evidence' in order to match pupils' work and achievements against curriculum specifications and levels. Many primary teachers began to take a pride in their new professional skills. Parents of primary school pupils began to receive reports on their children with more carefully worded and detailed descriptions of attainment than those formerly criticized as 'frequently generalised, laconic statements' (Department of Education discussion paper by Alexander *et al.*, 1992). In Figure 12.1 we offer typical examples of old-style followed by new-style reporting and readers will no doubt agree that, as well as being more detailed, the latter certainly has an *appearance* of greater 'objectivity'.

However, data gathered through the *Identity and Learning Programme* between 1987 and 1995 revealed that, whilst parents were quite pleased to receive more detailed reports on their children's activities and attainments, they made little use of the information such reports contained. In evaluating teacher perceptions of their children's 'abilities' and achievements, there was no change between old-style and new-style assessment and reporting with regard to what parents used, how they expressed satisfaction or dissatisfaction or information through which they intervened for change. Notwithstanding changes intended to provide more detailed and valid assessments, to make teachers more accountable and to empower parents, the parents in our study responded to and used information just as they had previously. That is, they were *particularly* influenced by more tangible indications of their children's progress and teachers' perceptions – such as reading book and maths scheme levels, spelling lists and other categoric information gathered informally from teachers, their children and their own observations.

In this chapter we explore the responses of parents to ongoing informal assessments of their children, as well as more formal statements of attainment. As we described in Chapter 2, ten key pupils from each cohort at Greenside and Albert Park Schools were tracked year on year through their primary school experiences. Through this time they were monitored regarding ways in which they progressively shaped their school identities and careers in the context of judgements made by teachers, families, friends and peers who variously supported, acted upon, contested or ignored the official and unofficial voices of school assessment. In addressing the question of 'How are assessments interpreted and mediated?' in Chapter 11, we provided a fuller theoretical and conceptual background to this analysis of social influences on assessment outcomes.

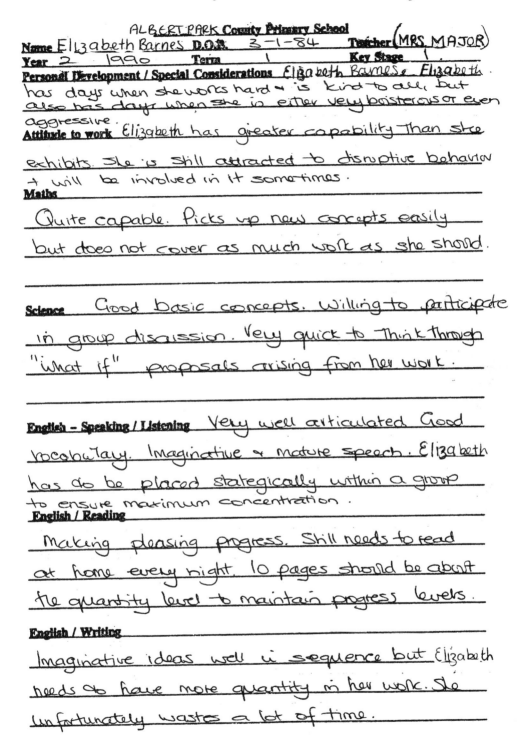

ALBERT PARK County Primary School

Name Elizabeth Barnes D.O.B. 3-1-84   Teacher (MRS. MAJOR)
Year 2   1990   Term 1   Key Stage 1.

Personal Development / Special Considerations Elizabeth Barnes. Elizabeth has days when she works hard – is kind to all, but also has days when she is either very boisterous or even aggressive.

Attitude to work Elizabeth has greater capability than she exhibits. She is still attracted to disruptive behavior + will be involved in it sometimes.

Maths

Quite capable. Picks up new concepts easily but does not cover as much work as she should.

Science Good basic concepts. Willing to participate in group discussion. Very quick to think through "what if" proposals arising from her work.

English – Speaking / Listening Very well articulated Good vocabulary. Imaginative + mature speech. Elizabeth has to be placed stategically within a group to ensure maximum concentration.

English / Reading

Making pleasing progress. Still needs to read at home every night. 10 pages should be about the quantity level to maintain progress levels.

English / Writing

Imaginative ideas well in sequence but Elizabeth needs to have more quantity in her work. She unfortunately wastes a lot of time.

Figure 12.1 *'Elizabeth's two Year 2 reports from 'Mrs Major'. A comparison of typical old style and new style primary school reporting.*

English / Spelling Can spell some common words. Uses a spelling line but increasingly uses invented spelling. Makes good attempts + uses her phonic knowledge effectively.

English Handwriting Makes very valiant efforts in formal practise + is developing a maturing hand but will revert to print in her free work

Humanities Good basic knowledge. Likes to participate in class + group activities.

Technology Has made plans + executed models. She was single minded in this activity + stayed uninterrupted on task for some long while.

Music

  Can keep a steady beat.

Art Creative. Can produce lovely detailed drawings Imaginative use of other materials.

P.E. Good. Well balanced on lrg apparatus. Imaginative floor work.

Remedial action taken :

Discussion with parents – date........................

Parents comments

_____ _____

_____

_____

Figure 12.1   (continued)

ANNUAL REPORT 1991

School Name: Albert Park Co P	
Pupil's Surname: BARNES	
First name: ELIZABETH	D.O.B 3.01.84 END OF KEY STAGE 1

	COMMENTS	P.C.	LEVEL
ENGLISH Speaking and Listening Reading Writing	Elizabeth can participate as a speaker + a listener in group activities. She can describe real or imaginary events. She can follow more complex instructions. She can read a range of material with some independence, fluency, accuracy + understanding. She can describe what has happened in a story + what may happen next. She can produce independently, pieces of writing parts of which show correct use of sentence making. She can sequence her work chronologically She is beginning to understand the basic structure of story writing. She can spell many common words	2 1 2	2
MATHEMATICS Number and Measure Shape and Data Handling	Elizabeth can select the materials + the mathematics to use for a task (Level 2). She can add + subtract objects to 10. She can talk about her own work + make predictions based on experience. She can explore + use patterns in addition + subtraction facts to 10 (Level 2). She can compare objects for weight length + capacity without measuring. He can sort 2D + 3D shapes, state position + recognise the outcome of random events.	1 1	1
SCIENCE Exploration Knowledge and Understanding	Elizabeth can formulate hypotheses (Level 3). She can record findings in charts + other appropriate forms. She can identify simple differences. She can select + use simple instruments to enhance observations. She can use standard + non-standard measures. She can list + collate observations. She knows there are a wide variety of living things + her own individuality. She is aware that humans produce waste products. She has basic concepts of weather conditions, push + pull, electricity + magnetism, sound + energy. We have studied Earth in Space.	2 1	2

The above are the results of statutory assessment procedures

TECHNOLOGY	D.T Elizabeth has planned + made models. I.T She has used the computer as a word processor.
GEOGRAPHY	These two subjects are undertaken as part of the whole class topic for the term. We have studied The History of Transport + The Lives + Times of the North American Indians.
HISTORY	Elizabeth has difficulty maintaining concentration, which is a pity because at times she has good contributions to make to class discussion. She is usually interested in the topic work. Basic Map work has been undertaken.
RE	Term 2 We studied "Gods Wonderful World". Term 3 We studied "Flowers for Beauty, Food, gardens, shops + special occasions.
ART	Elizabeth has a natural flair for art work. She is very precise in her execution + has good control of the materials.
MUSIC	She has participated in percussion activities. She can nearly hold a more complicated rhythm. She has participated in class productions.
PE	Elizabeth is very well balanced + has well developed large motor skills. She is supple + innovative in small group floor work.

GENERAL COMMENTS ; Elizabeth failed to attain Level 2 reading because she could not meet the necessary requirement in use of the dictionary. She, has gained a good assessment in English + Science. Her maths one could also have been Level 2 had she worked more quickly through the school maths scheme. She must endeavour to concentrate in class, & apply herself to the task in hand.

CLASS TEACHER(S) (MRS MAJOR)   HEADTEACHER ——————————

Figure 12.1   (continued)

12.3   PARENTAL ROLES IN ASSESSMENT PROCESSES

In Chapter 11 we presented research which showed that, despite the government rhetoric of partnership and shared responsibility for the education of their children, there have been no real gains in parental power relationships with schools over recent decades (Barber, 1996; Johnson and Barber, 1996; Vincent and Tomlinson, 1997; see also Hughes *et al.*, 1994; Hughes, 1996). Studies of the range of educational activities provided for children in their homes contribute to now well-established understandings that parents have knowledge and potential for contributing to understandings of their children's achievements (Delgado-Gaitan, 1996; Huss, 1997; Hirst, 1998; West *et al.*, 1998). Research also indicates that parents would like a more active role in assessment by supplementing teacher knowledge of their child (Desforges *et al.*, 1994 and 1996). Yet, as we also described in Chapter 11, English education policy continues to support expectations that parents should be passive recipients of information rather than co-constructors of shared understandings of their children. At the same time, teachers' sense of professionalism keeps them from acknowledging what parents have to offer (Hughes 1996: 108; also Tizard *et al.* 1981 and 1982; Desforges *et al.*, 1994 and 1996).

As described in Chapter 2, the families in the *Identity and Learning Programme* are drawn from two distinctly different parts of a city in the south of England, and facing very different socio-economic conditions. In the light of the above it is worth looking at the way their respective schools viewed the populations of parents of their pupils and their involvement in their children's education. An important consideration in this though, as other studies remind us, is that not all teachers within schools share the same perspective. Whilst the following perceptions were typical of unofficial staffroom and informal conversations with us as researchers over seven years in the schools, there were of course exceptions to them. By the same token, not all families were seen in the same light. However, at Albert Park, the predominantly skilled, working-class parents were generally viewed, en masse, as active in their children's schooling but in entirely the 'wrong' way. Many staff held a critical view of parents as very confident, vociferous and challenging to school in relation to their 'rights' with regard to such issues as the wearing of school uniform and selection for sports teams. On the other hand, they saw most parents as lacking concern and less likely to raise issues with regard to academic decisions or outcomes in relation to their children's attainment.

> If their son doesn't get selected for the football team fathers that you never see will be up here like a flash. (Teacher at Albert Park, 1991)

Further, some staff in the school expressed opinions that, though poverty and unemployment were not a great problem for most families in Albert Park, families for the most part exhibited a kind of shallow consumerism, a lack of 'culture' in their recreational pursuits. It is perhaps worth noting that this community represented the socio-economic group then described as C2s which were much courted by Thatcherism and then by New Labour. For one teacher, many families had:

> plenty of money but not much couth – if that's not being unkind. (Teacher at Albert Park, 1991)

It is worth noting that in our sample, as well as attending the usual children's local and church organizations of Brownies, Cubs and sporting activities, children were involved with their parents and sometimes with more distant communities in a number of educational activities.

These included amateur dramatics, light opera production, music and marching bands, photography, crafts and computer activities. We have no reason to believe that these were exceptional. Certainly, however, in our study we found parents at Albert Park School to be often *apparently* more accepting of teacher assessments and perceptions of their children than those at Greenside School but, as we shall see later in this chapter, the picture was not that simple.

However, if Albert Park School parents were criticized for not contesting or raising issues in relation to their children's attainment, the parents at Greenside School came in for some criticism for being *too* active. Though the ethos and the school intake changed somewhat over the time of the study (see Pollard and Filer, 1999) many parents in the community of Greenside were perceived by school staff (and indeed among themselves) as 'pushy', of having unrealistic expectations and of putting undue pressure on their children. A parent in our study was denounced for questioning the reading level attributed to her child as being:

> one who would take over her child's education if she could. (Teacher at Greenside School, 1989)

As this chapter shows, teachers were often perceived by Greenside parents to be on the defensive, even in one case 'unprofessional' when parents questioned their children's levels of achievement or what they were capable of. Indeed, parent intervention in their child's education in Greenside School often led to a deterioration, at least temporarily, in home–school relationships.

At a relatively simplistic level then, our schools, in their different ways, both reflected other findings (above and Chapter 11); that teachers do not consider that parents have much to contribute to the assessment of their children's achievements. Indeed, some of the parental data from Greenside that follows illustrates some teachers' sense of affront to their professionalism when parents questioned their views of children's capabilities.

Notwithstanding the specific circumstances of our two case-study schools, the issues in relation to social class and parental intervention in children's education reflect issues from other research. In spite of the expectation that parents call teachers to account, it is still middle-class parents who are most active in this. This is seen as a reflection of, on the one hand, the cultural capital of middle-class parents and, on the other, the unwillingness of working-class parents to question professional knowledge (see e.g. Crozier, 1997; Vincent and Tomlinson, 1997). However, as Vincent and Tomlinson point out, explanations such as these regarding differential power relations among teachers and parents have clearly failed to engage the teaching profession. Rather, a working-class deficit model of parental involvement and parenting has grown up over the years whereby some groups of parents are designated as lacking in interest or involvement and failing to provide the kind of home life and discipline that supports their children's education. As Broadfoot and Pollard (2000) describe, this has intensified in an atmosphere of target setting and competition among schools for pupils that will enhance their standing in league tables.

Notwithstanding the relevance of existing studies of social class and school expectations of parental involvement, the longitudinal design of this study enables a more dynamic analysis of parental involvement in their children's education than that offered by an analysis of social-class differences. It also at the same time problematizes simple dichotomies of 'problem/uninterested' and 'supportive/active' parents which prevails in both political and practitioner discourse.

In illustrating some of the dynamics of home–school relationships, we also hope to offer some insights aimed at supporting an improved 'partnership' between schools and parents and the potential for a less adversarial response to parental intervention and a more collaborative use of parental knowledge and skills in assessment processes in primary schools.

In the following section we offer a model of the 'dimensions' and 'dynamics' of parental strategic action. This has been extended from a similar conceptualization of pupil strategies that we have developed, and it is helpful here to review the key features of this pupil model.

12.4   DIMENSIONS OF PUPILS' STRATEGIC ACTION

In *The Social World of Pupil Career* we constructed a four-part typology of pupils' strategic and adaptive responses through their school careers to a range of curricular and social structures and expectations of the primary schools. These strategies can be summarized as follows:

- *anti-conformity*: some rejection of school career structures, expectations and norms; oppositional learning and social agendas, characterized as deviance.
- *non-conformity*: some indifference and lack of concern about school career structures, expectations and norms; little perception of risk because pupils have their own learning and social agendas, characterized as independence.
- *conformity*: reification of school career structures, expectations and norms; low-risk conformity to others' learning and social agendas, characterized as adaptation.
- *redefining*: personal identification with school career structures, expectations and norms; high-risk strategies for influencing learning and social agendas, characterized by negotiation and challenge.

12.5   DYNAMICS OF PUPILS' STRATEGIC ACTION

The 'dimensions of pupils' strategic action' do not describe *children*, nor do they represent psychological 'types'. They describe relatively coherent patterns of strategies which pupils adopted. Pupils tended to use particular dimensions consistently, in so far as the *meaning* of the context remained the same for them. However, patterned responses were liable to disruption where, for instance, changing classroom contexts and expectations meant that a pupil's accustomed orientations and strategies became no longer appropriate or viable.

Thus the seemingly static typology of 'dimensions of pupils' strategic action' can be extended and used to plot the *dynamics* of strategic action for individual children – as derived from longitudinal case-study data (Figure 12.2).

Pupils, for example, moved towards greater or lesser conformity in response to a particular pedagogic style or learning context. For similar reasons, a switch might occur from, for example, a redefining position of negotiation and challenge towards anti-conformity and deviance.

The model is also designed to depict the way in which the gaps between conformity and anti-conformity, non-conformity and redefining are potentially sites of tension. Such tension may occur between an individual pupil and a teacher or between individual pupils and their peers as a result of, for instance, a learning stance or expression of identity which contravenes the structural norms or relationship expectations of classroom or playground.

We found that the typology and model also provided a useful analytic framework for characterizing the strategic action of parents as interpreters and mediators of their children's assessment and school experience generally. These could be set against simplistic assumptions and caricatures of parents as 'lacking interest' or 'pushy'; 'supportive' or 'non-supportive'. Also it shows them in dynamic interaction with teachers, just as pupils were in dynamic interaction with a series of teachers.

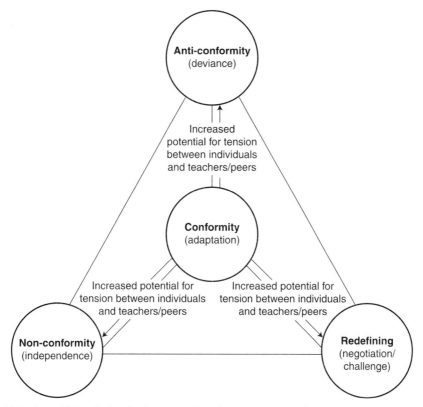

Figure 12.2 *A model for plotting the dynamics of pupils' strategic action. (From The Social World of Pupil Career: strategic biographies through primary schools*, Pollard and Filer, 1999)

12.6   DIMENSIONS OF PARENTS' STRATEGIC ACTION

The dimensions of strategic action and orientation which typify pupil adaptation and response to classroom and learning contexts can be extended to characterize the strategic responses of parents as mediators and interpreters of assessment and school experience generally. We can take the characteristics of those dimensions and map them on to a typology of parental strategy as follows.

Redefining: characterized by 'identification', high-risk strategies for influencing a shared agenda, negotiation and challenge

Some parents, whilst they identified with and supported school assessment procedures and curricular expectations generally, often disputed the school's or a particular teacher's interpretation of satisfactory *levels* of achievement, either for pupils generally or for their own child in particular. In Greenside School, this sometimes happened in the context of anticipating entrance exams for independent schools. Parents were involved in negotiating higher achievement outcomes and school expectations, for instance through requests for extra homework, a focus on some particular area of weakness for their child or for faster progression through maths or reading schemes for their child.

The following are examples of redefining strategies:

Mrs Keel One thing I have noticed (different) from last year – some of David's spellings – I've noticed they've been quite easy, whereas Ms Luke used to grade them a bit more. I think in that way he needs to be pushed a little bit more.
(Albert Park School, Mrs Keel, parent interview, November 1994, Year 6)

Mrs Keel I went in to see Mrs Hutton to ask her if he could have some more difficult spellings to do, because he was finding them too easy. And so I did go and mention it at open evening, that if he could have some more difficult.
(Albert Park School, parent interview with Mr and Mrs Keel, July 1995, Year 6)

I was disappointed with Mary's progress after she had been back at school for a few weeks. This is because I had been told (and also thought) that she was bright, interested and her attitude was just right and she should 'take off' with her reading at any time and it just hadn't happened. I went to see Miss Scott to talk about this. Anyway, her progress has been a lot better recently and she seems to be more interested again. (Greenside School, Mrs Inman parent diary, October 1988, Year 1)

(At the above meeting) a somewhat stormy encounter between Mrs Inman and Miss Scott took place, with Miss Scott believing that Mrs Inman was making Mary over-anxious. Nevertheless, following their discussion, Mary received a steady stream of books to take home and more attention at school.
(Reproduced from *The Social World of Children's Learning*, Pollard with Filer, 1996: 59)

Mary's parents' data show that redefining could be a relatively high-risk strategy for parents. Managed carefully and in the context of mutually respectful parental–teacher relationship, it was able to influence outcomes and achievement levels for their children. Where there were many such parents, as in Greenside School, it was also likely to have been highly influential in raising levels of school expectations for pupils generally. Managed poorly, however, it was interpreted as criticism, viewed by teachers as 'deviant' and could lead to antagonistic home–school relations. Which brings us to anti-conformity.

Anti-conformity: characterized by 'rejection', high-risk strategies associated with oppositional agendas and 'deviance'

Some parents' *alternative* views or expectations regarding their child's achievements represented a challenge to school assessments. Anti-conformity largely represented a failed interventionist strategy to redefine; parental attempts to negotiate for change were interpreted by the school as 'deviant'.

The case of Harriet provides an example:

After a year of schooling, Harriet's reading achievement in relation to the graded reading scheme did not accord with Mrs Morley's estimation of her potential. Mrs Morley's wry assessment of the situation was:

She is nearly up to the standard she was when she left playgroup last year.

There was a gulf between what Harriet's mother thought she should be reading and school reading level expectations. The level of graded reading books being selected by mother and daughter for home reading lead to accusations that she was 'pushing' Harriet, contributing to strained relations with teachers generally.

Mrs Morley took into school a newspaper article suggesting that 'children respond to more of a structured approach'. She sought Harriet's teacher's opinion on the issue:

Mrs Morley That went down terribly. Mrs Powell interpreted it as I was finding fault with Mrs Long (teacher of Harriet's sister). I never mentioned Mrs Long but there is so much tittle-

> tattle in that school. I was called in by Mrs Long – did I have any complaints about her teaching? It was awful. So unprofessional.
> (Greenside School, interview with Harriet's parents, July 1988, Reception. Reproduced from *The Social World of Pupil Career*, Pollard and Filer, 1999: 235)

Such patterns of interaction occurred more often in our more affluent middle-class Greenside sample than in Albert Park. This was also reflected in the schools' perceptions of the communities they served. As described above, some of the teachers in Greenside School saw parents as variously 'pushy', 'taking over' their child's education, holding educational ideologies and expectations for outcomes that pressurized their children, as well as themselves as teachers.

Non-conformity: characterized as a measure of 'indifference' and 'independence', and parents holding their own agenda

Some parents expressed a measure of indifference to school agendas for success and attainment outcomes, and this was sometimes an expression of dissatisfaction with the evaluations of school as irrelevant to the cultural norms or educational ideologies of the family.

   Robert's mother provides a good example of nonconformity:

> Though pleased with Robert's early school reports and evidence of his fast developing reading skills, Mrs Osborne expressed doubts about early formal education either institutionalised or in the home:

> I would say he has got on very well, because I think it is very young to be bothered with that. I think it is very young. I mean, I am not a teacher, I know nothing really about education in that sense, but you know, you hear about people teaching them at playschool how to read and mothers teaching children to read before they go to school, and what is the rush really? (Greenside School, Mrs Osborne, parent interview, March 1988, Reception)

> There was a consistency between Robert's parents' attitude to his early learning as expressed here and their attraction to some elements of the Steiner school of educational philosophy. (Reproduced from *The Social World of Pupil Career*, Pollard and Filer, 1999: 171)

Sometimes nonconformity represented an adaptation to a lack of responsiveness on the part of the school to pupil or family concerns for learning – again, a failure to 'redefine'. For instance:

> Alison's parents felt that school assessment of her attainment was not in accordance with her ability and that she was frustrated by the pace of school expectations for her. They were asked how they interpreted that situation for their daughter and how it was managed.

Mrs Gough	Well, what we used to do was, we used to say that she'd have to do what the teacher told her but then what she wanted to do we did at home.
AF	Ah, right.
Mrs Gough	The next stage we did at home, so that way she was doing both and she was still getting what she wanted.
AF	One step ahead of school and doing what she wanted. And does it continue in that way?
Mrs Gough	Yeah, and now she's ready to go to senior school – now. (Senior school begins in Year 7 – over a year away for Alison).
Mr Gough	She was ready last year really. I feel she was. She finds some things still menial at school and she helps others, as you're probably aware. But while she's helping others she's not getting ahead herself is she? And we feel that you shouldn't hold anyone back who's got the ability. I know it's difficult in a class of thirty children for a teacher to cater for every individual child, she's got to go with the majority and clever children are a minority in most classes.

(Albert Park School, Mr and Mrs Gough, parent interview, July 1994, Year 5)

*Conformity: characterized by 'reification' and adaptation to procedures and curricular
expectations and low-risk strategies in conformity to the agenda of school*

Many parents (particularly in Albert Park School) appeared to generally support school
assessments and trust teachers to objectively assess and report their child's achievements.
   For instance:

AF	So, reflecting on those results, and the sorts of teachers' assessments that you've had over the years generally, have you always felt that they are a reflection of Chris's achievements. Or of Chris's abilities?
Mr Kennedy	I think, I suppose I'd have to say that the teachers who dealt with him at the time know him best for what he achieves in class. And we can't comment on that, but we've – you know, it's our place to listen to their opinion. At (his brother's) secondary school, I questioned one particular teacher about the way things were done when we visited the school, but not at Albert Park.

(Albert Park School, Mr and Mrs Kennedy, parent interview, July 1995, Year 6)

   As we have described, therefore, and as we discuss at greater length later in the chapter, there
was nothing fixed or inevitable about parental patterns of response. Neither indeed did surface
appearances of conformity or 'good' and 'supportive' home–school relationships always reflect
parents' underlying and more complex feelings about teachers' evaluations and expectations of
their children and of them as parents. We discuss some of this complexity and its implications for
ways in which school assessments could be interpreted and mediated within families in the next
section.

12.7   PARENTAL MEDIATION AND INTERPRETATION OF ASSESSMENTS

'Conformity' at Albert Park School was often strategic in relation to teachers but was contra-
dicted by parents' mediation and interpretation of assessments to their children. Parents' sincere
concerns for their children's progress were often mixed with a desire to hold off pressure, on
teachers as well as their children, and for good relations at school and home. This meant that poor
achievement evaluations made by teachers, or underachievement generally, might be interpreted
as 'not important so long as you're trying' or mediated, for instance, 'just like my report when I
was a kid'.

   Apparent conformity also usually hid ambivalent, antagonistic feelings and oppositional
agendas (anti-conformity) which ran beneath what were, on the surface, supportive home–school
relationships. The case of Adrian Rowe provides an example of this.

   Throughout his primary career, Adrian's failure to apply himself to tasks meant his attainment
was well below what teachers and parents knew he was capable of. His parents had frequent
contact and relaxed, supportive relationships with teachers. However, Mr Rowe explained:

> (I get told) he's been fighting in the playground, or he hasn't done his work, he should have sent some
> homework in. And sometimes you think I shouldn't be put in that position. And I never feel hostile to
> teachers or anything, because I'm a professional myself, I deal with children and I know how difficult
> it is. So I'm not going to go round there saying 'Why haven't you flipping *made* him do his work?' But
> you do wonder sometimes. You think, 'Well, why should I? I'm a parent and I'm supposed to love him
> and protect him and care for him and develop him. Why have I suddenly been given this task of
> actually meting out some discipline?' (You think), 'Don't tell me. Just deal with it. Nine to four.
> School. Deal with it'. I find that a bit disturbing (that) automatically I feel compelled – I must do
> something about it. Ultimately it makes me an antagonist (and) I'm not comfortable with that. (Albert
> Park School, Mr and Mrs Rowe, parent interview, July 1994, Year 5)

I think we've got enough on our plate without every minute of the day thinking, Oh he's got to improve. I mean, you can end up putting him under so much pressure.... and it's not (just) a case of I'm trying to sit him down saying 'do your homework'. (The trouble is) he doesn't know about study skills. He doesn't know anything about setting out conclusions, What do you want to say? What do you want to show? It's no good you just writing a few pages if you mean absolutely nothing by it. I don't think he's been taught that. They haven't been prepared for study. But I'm not going to ... I shouldn't be too critical because, you know, they're good teachers, but I look after children with *learning* difficulties and I expect far more from them! (Albert Park School, Mr Rowe, parent interview, November 1994, Year 6)

12.8   DYNAMICS OF PARENTS' STRATEGIC ACTION

As we have stated above, there was nothing fixed and inevitable about parental patterns of response. As with the children's career strategies, the dimensions of conformity do not describe *parents*. The model of 'dynamics of pupils' strategic action' in Figure 12.2 shows the gap between conformity and other strategies as potential sites of tension for, in this case, home–school relationships. As described in Chapter 11, assessment is a multidimensional process and parents too made assessments of teachers. Redefining was not, therefore, constantly necessary but a strategy that could be used according to the degree of confidence felt in a particular teacher's approach as well as according to any objective measure of attainment. As the data has suggested, parents often attempted redefining, especially in the early years of their child's education. Mismanaged, these attempts could be labelled deviant by the school and antagonistic relation-ships developed. As we have also seen, failure to redefine came about as a result of unresponsiveness on the part of the school to parental attempts to influence outcomes for their child.

Something of the dynamics of one parent's strategies through her daughter's career through Greenside Primary School is set out below. We have described above how Mrs Morley's attempts to 'redefine' teachers' expectations for her daughter were actually realized as strategies of 'anti-conformity' as they became increasingly interpreted by teachers at Greenside as 'deviant'. From those early antagonistic relations with school Mrs Morley began in Year 1 (age 6), a gradual withdrawal from involvement in her daughter's schooling which culminated by Year 6 (age 11) in an almost complete separation of home and school concerns and experience for Harriet and her mother.

AP	Tell me a little bit more about how you see her self confidence with maths.
Mrs Morley	Well really, not being in the classroom, I can't say, and I always find it very difficult to find out exactly what is going on because if you ask too many questions you're labelled anxious. So I can't tell you.
	. . .
	At one time I was helping her to chose the (reading) books but that went out of my control completely. And I didn't find the books very good that she was bringing home. It makes it sound as if I am very pushy and anxious but in the end I thought, I can't. I won't do anything at all. Just let it slip.
AP	So really, your policy over the year was to 'keep your head down', in a sense?
Mrs Morley	Yes. I mean, I wish that teachers would appreciate parents who are anxious to find out what their children do. Why don't they? Tell me.

(Mrs Morley, parent interview, July 1989, Year 1)

In time Mrs Morley moved to a position of 'nonconformity', adopting a measure of indif-ference to school agenda and assessments. For instance, Mrs Morley was not confident that Harriet was doing as well in maths as teachers reported. She explained:

Well, you know, they always write really nice reports but I imagine they probably do for most people and I honestly don't think Harriet's got much of a clue in her maths and yet they all say she's got a good grasp. But delve below the surface and she knows very little. (Mrs Morley, parent interview, July 1993, Year 5)

Some of Harriet's maths improvement in school her mother believed was due to the extra tutoring they now were paying for, but which Harriet was resisting. Although concerned about Harriet's maths, Mrs Morley now expressed a more philosophical perspective on the children's education. She thought that, with a busy family life that did not leave a lot of time for over-close supervision of learning, they were, as parents, probably not 'pushy' enough to see high academic success coming from their children. For the same reason she felt relatively relaxed that (all three children) did less homework than they should have done and she understood their perspective if they wanted a less 'chasing around' and demanding life than they saw their father lead. (Reproduced from *The Social World of Pupil Career*, Pollard and Filer, 1999: 225–79)

12.9   DISCUSSION

We have documented the ways in which families variously act upon, contest, challenge, support or ignore the official and unofficial voices of both teacher and standardized assessment. In so doing, we have emphasized the significance of how families interpret and give meaning to assessment outcomes.

The longitudinal nature of the *Identity and Learning Programme* enables us to trace the *dynamic* development of families' characteristic repertoires of strategic involvement and influence in shaping school assessment outcomes and in mediating and interpreting them with their children. It provides an analysis over time – beyond a simple comparison of the two schools. In so doing, it extends a structural analysis of class-based differences to show how variations both exist and develop. In particular, we would argue that the dynamics of home–school relationships cuts across the structural analysis of power inequalities of working and middle classes (Vincent and Tomlinson, 1997).

In so doing, our analysis problematizes simple dichotomies of 'supportive' or 'problem' families which prevail in public and political discourse and among practitioners.

We see greater understanding of the importance of family contexts and parental perspectives as a basis for a more holistic, collaborative and reflexive approach to assessment. Assessment policy in England has, for some years, been based on misconceptions of 'what parents want'. There is plenty of evidence that parents are more sophisticated in their understanding of what is important in education, and potentially more willing *partners in learning* than their positioning as 'consumers' allows. Unfortunately, whilst government policy remains driven by the ideology and discourse of performance (Broadfoot and Pollard, 2000), teachers are likely to remain within its yoke and parents will remain as clients.

However, like the many other studies we cite here, our study shows the enormous potential of parents for facilitating children's learning in more holistic ways. In particular, parents may be more able than teachers to sense emotional issues in learning, to notice changes in attitudes over time and to monitor motivation, interest and commitment in different subjects or areas of skill development. Personal interest, individual attention, deep knowledge and sensitivity are all on the parent's side as a teacher of their child. But this potential must also be harnessed into an active, collaborative partnership between parents and their children and teachers. In this, mutual understanding of motivations, perceptions and the strategic and dynamic nature of home–school relationships is a precondition. The analysis offered in this chapter is a contribution to this goal.

12.10   CONCLUSION

This chapter has presented an analysis of case-study data relating to parents' strategic action in mediating and interpreting teachers' assessments of their children. It further illuminates our concept of 'transformative processes' developed through Chapter 11 with regard to processes that teachers' initial assessments are subject to, before recursively affecting children's identities as pupils.

In this analysis we have adapted our conceptions of the *dimensions and dynamics of strategic action* developed in relation to *pupils* for *The Social World of Pupil Career*. The typology and model presented there provides a useful analytic framework through which we can also characterize the strategic action of *parents*, as interpreters and mediators of assessments and school experience generally. They enabled us to cut across the more usual social-class based analysis of home–school relationships in comparing the strategic approaches to teachers of Greenside and Albert Park families. It enabled us to show parents, like pupils, to be in dynamic interaction with successive teachers, changing their orientation and patterns of response where they become more or less viable in new settings and relationships (Pollard and Filer, 1999: 296–301). The resulting analysis can also be set against simplistic assumptions and caricatures of parents as 'lacking interest' or 'pushy', 'supportive' or 'non-supportive'.

Numerous studies show the potential that parents have for contributing to school understandings of their child's achievements and that they would like a more active role in assessment processes. However, in the absence of support for parents as co-constructors of shared understandings, it will remain the case that the power to influence teachers' perceptions and actions will continue to be held by those parents who can employ the most successful strategies for intervention.

In further reinforcing the argument for a more cooperative, collaborative approach to home–school understandings of children's learning and identity, we can do no better than to return readers to our discussion in Chapter 3.3. There we problematized teachers' claims to 'whole child' knowledge in assessing their pupils, in posing the question: 'What is involved in a teacher knowing a child?'

Part Four

Reflecting

Chapter 13

Summary and Conclusion

13.1   THE SOCIAL WORLD OF PUPIL ASSESSMENT: A SUMMARY

This book presents a holistic, sociological analysis of primary school assessment practices. Set in a period of centralized policy making, public debate and immense educational change, our work focuses on the perspectives of pupils, teachers and parents and the educational contexts and processes within which they act.

We presented our analysis by posing 'questions concerning social influences on assessment', set out in a simplified form in Figure 1.1 (p. 9), and we offered a more elaborated interpretation of the questions in our model of 'cycles of assessment in a social context' (see Figure 4.1, p. 51). In Chapter 2, the first and important question on the model concerning 'Where and when is the assessment taking place?' was addressed. Thereafter, Chapters 3 to 12 were organized in pairs of theoretical and case-study chapters, each exploring successive key questions for enquiry.

Thus, in Chapter 2, we described some of the impact of extensive changes affecting all aspects of teachers' work in primary school classrooms through the period of the study. These changes were experienced at Albert Park and Greenside Schools, as they were in schools throughout the country, as challenges to teachers' ideologies, established ways of working and ways of assessing the learning of their pupils. The Albert Park cohort, which is the prime focus of this book, were the first to experience the National Curriculum and its assessment provision and the first cohort to experience SATs at Key Stage 1 when they were seven. The impact of those changes and challenges were therefore most profoundly felt by the teachers whose assessment practices focus in the case-study chapters of this book.

In Chapters 3 and 4 we explored the question of 'Who is being assessed?' through a consideration of 'identity'. In particular we discussed ways in which children's identities as pupils and their strategic responses are continuously and dynamically shaped through successive school settings and the day-to-day acts of assessment within them. Indeed, we set out our conceptions of some of the complex sources and dynamic influences of biography, people and settings on pupils' evolving identities and strategic responses. In the light of this interactive complexity and drawing on case-study data and findings from *The Social World of Pupil Career*, we were led to problematize what might be involved in a teacher 'knowing' a child. Thus we questioned assumptions embedded in notions of a 'whole child' approach to learning and assessment, with its suggestion of a child as a knowable entity, accessible for teacher interpretation. We discussed ways in which judgements that teachers make have been shown to arise, and be inseparable from, the particular classroom settings they create. To illustrate this argument we presented data from our longitudinal tracking of children's experience in home, playground and classroom contexts at Greenside and Albert Park Schools, which has generated a wealth of data concerning the *different ways* in which successive teachers 'knew' the same children.

What Chapter 3 began to argue, therefore, is that teachers' experiences of pupils and the different interpretation they put upon their behaviour, relationships, attitudes to work and intelligences are, in part, features of the classroom contexts that teachers themselves create. Teachers' presentation of educational knowledge and the social, emotional and organizational aspects of classroom life they create can have dramatic effects upon pupils' engagement with learning and classroom relationships, and hence upon the assessments that flow from those engagements and relationships. This is a key conclusion, one that is developed through the book and further illustrated through detailed case-study chapters.

In problematizing 'whole child' approaches to classroom assessment we do not suggest that teachers should abandon attempts to identify the background and causes of individual pupils' underachievement or disaffection. Rather a major finding from the *Identity and Learning Programme* as a whole concerns the importance of valuing and respecting children's individual identities and distinct approaches to learning as contextually realized. We set out the significance of allowing individual children to incorporate and maintain distinct identities within and through their classroom learning and the value of trying to access the perspectives of those children who experience and present difficulties through their acts of resistance and withdrawal. These studies show that changes to aspects of the learning context or relationships that are problematic for a child can have dramatic effects upon a pupil's engagement in learning and relationships and hence upon teacher perceptions and assessment of that child.

Thus, in addressing the question of 'What is involved in knowing a child?', we distinguished between the 'whole child' understandings that we have problematized above, and those arrived at through classroom research. We problematized the assumption that knowledge of individual pupils' attitudes, motivations and emotions can be 'read off' by teachers. An approach towards gaining 'holistic' knowledge involves, rather, an *active intent* on the part of teachers to understand a child's responses and relationships *in the context of classroom settings*. That is, it involves teachers in reflection on their own practice, in accessing pupil perspectives and in the creation of facilitative social relationships.

Chapter 4 is the second chapter concerned with the question of 'Who is being assessed? and through it we illustrate the issues raised in Chapter 3. In particular, we tracked some of the social influences of families, peers and teachers in shaping the assessment experiences of one child, Elizabeth, through successive classroom contexts at Albert Park School. The data shows how Elizabeth's identity, her classroom relationships and approach to classroom tasks were experienced and interpreted by different teachers and ways in which their assessments of Elizabeth were interpreted and mediated in the contexts of important family and peer-group relationships. We also presented the model of assessment in a social context (Figure 4.1), which bears a direct relationship to the 'Question concerning social influences on assessment' which were presented in Figure 1.1. It represents an abstraction of the details of Elizabeth's experience over the seven years as presented in the chapter. As in the similar models developed for earlier *Social World* books (1996, 1999) it is an expression of recursive cycles in which identity, teacher practices, peer and family cultures and the interpretations and mediations of teachers, family and peers feed into, reinforce and condition each other.

In problematizing what is involved for a teacher in 'knowing' a child we argued for a reciprocal understanding of the distinctive nature of teachers' individual identities and practices. Thus our initial question for enquiry, 'Who is being assessed?', was followed by one that asked 'Who is assessing?' In Chapters 5 and 6, therefore, we extended our analysis of the social contexts of classroom assessment set out in Figure 4.1 with a focus on 'pedagogy'.

In Chapters 5 and 6 we continued to argue that accounts of 'identity' have to synthesize the internal and personal concerns of individuals with the external influences of cultures and the expectations of appropriate groups and the wider society. However, we now applied it to issues of 'teacher identity'. We used the concept of 'coping strategies' and focused on factors that we see contributing to teachers' individual pedagogies. 'Role expectations', 'institutional settings' and 'self' were seen as the internal concerns and external influences which influence teachers' constructions of their pedagogic practices. We also considered some ways in which role expectations underpinning national assessment requirements conflict with existing and well-established role expectations held by many primary school teachers in England. An important aspect of coping in classrooms is concerned with the maintenance of integrity and a sense of autonomy and 'self' by teachers. Thus our question 'Who is assessing?' enabled an appreciation of the personal and the contextually specific ways in which teachers reconcile national and school-level requirements for change with the need to maintain personal integrity and a sense of 'self' in the classroom. Since the introduction of national assessment in primary schools, teachers have experienced increased pressure to produce 'evidence' and general expectations of formality and transparency in assessment practices. Stresses have increased where loss of autonomy and pressure to change their methods conflict with existing traditional role expectations which teachers have not abandoned. Despite the pressure for change, for many primary school teachers there is still a deep commitment to the 'whole child' and the fulfilment of a wide range of personal, social, moral and emotional, as well as cognitive, objectives.

However, to understand what 'coping' means to any particular individual we need to know much more about that teacher and the subjective interpretations which each individual makes of the contexts in which they find themselves. An example of just such an analysis in relation to one teacher's biography, values and practice, as well as on her pupils and the school setting, was offered in Chapter 6. That chapter presented a case-study analysis of some of the professional and social influences shaping the classroom practice of the Year 1 teacher at Albert Park School. In it Ann Filer described that teacher's perspective on the origins of her well-established practices and her perception of the threats to its integrity as she coped with the demands of national assessment. Filer showed the coping strategies of different groups of pupils, as they 'mesh' (Pollard, 1983) with those of the teacher, bringing about a differentiating effect on the progress of different groups of pupils. Both the academic and 'social diagnostic' (Filer, 2000) assessments made by the teacher are shown to contain elements of the teacher-organized context in which they were produced. Thus Chapter 6 further illustrated our argument that the 'whole child' as a subject for assessment has to be understood as the child *in context*. It illustrates in detail Leiter's (1974) conclusion that:

> Social types are not just a mere overlay on the setting by the teacher, rather they are an inseparable part of the setting. (123)

This is an area of key importance for understanding classroom assessment processes and outcomes. In *The Social World of the Primary School* Pollard suggested that favourable or unfavourable typifications will be made according to the extent to which qualities in children enable teachers to cope and reward their sense of self. Thus, as we suggested above, these kinds of social assessments that teachers routinely make of pupils are not the neutral forms of diagnostic 'knowledge' that teachers often present them as. Nor, like other assessment processes, are they always beneficial in their outcomes. A key finding of the *Identity and Learning Programme* as we have illustrated in our case-study accounts in Chapters 3 and 4, is that such assessments have an important role in shaping successive classroom, peer-group and home relationships and in individual children's approaches to learning.

In using the concept of the meshing of teacher and pupil coping strategies, Chapter 6 also shows ways in which achievement outcomes should be seen as the *joint achievements* of teachers and pupils, rather than as attributes attaching to particular children. Thus, the value of a holistic analysis such as this of the origins and effects of teacher-coping strategies lies in its power to reveal the distinctiveness of pedagogic contexts and the different and differentiating affects of those contexts on individual pupils and groups of pupils. In this, as with each of the detailed case-study chapters presented through this book, perhaps the greatest value of holistic analysis lies in drawing attention to the tacit contribution of teacher practices in the production of classroom assessment outcomes.

In Chapters 7 and 8 we explored the question of 'What is being assessed?' These chapters challenged simplistic representations of assessment in which pupils' responses are presented as self-evident products of existing ability, which can be revealed through assessment tasks or teacher questions (Mehan, 1973). Rather, we explored pupils' responses to task expectations as complex in their origins and bound up in multiple social and cultural understandings and relationships that shape and condition their production. We discussed ways in which the activities, materials and questions of testing are not neutral tools for scientifically measuring pre-existing knowledge and skills but can be seen as expressions of power relations that embody hidden values, social and cultural expectations and bias. A consideration of such power relations highlights the fact that, as well as having educational purposes, assessment fulfils a range of political and social functions within modern societies. These wider functions are concerned with social differentiation and reproduction, social control and the legitimation of particular forms of knowledge and culture of socially powerful groups (Broadfoot, 1996; Filer, 2000).

Through Chapter 7, we explored a range of contexts that research shows are important to the development of children's personal and biographical understandings and learning. These wider sociocultural contexts are powerful in shaping children's spoken and written responses, the manner of their presentation and levels of social or emotional involvements in tasks. Classroom responses are, for example, embedded in and conditioned by gender, ethnicity and social class. Thus, we argued, meanings are located in multiple contexts beyond the immediacy of assessment situations. Home, peers and community are ever-present, evaluative and relational contexts within which children locate their responses to classroom tasks and shape and communicate their developing sense of self.

In particular, in this chapter and through Chapter 8, we considered ways in which pupils' meanings and expectations embedded in peer-group relationships are often in dynamic tension with those derived from official classroom, biographical and wider sociocultural expectations.

Thus, ultimately, this pair of chapters reminds us that in observing the responses of individual children to assessment tasks or test item we should always ask the provocative question: 'What *else* is being assessed?'

Chapter 8 presented an extended analysis of classroom talk in the context of Year 3 National Curriculum assessment of 'speaking and listening'. Ann Filer argued that National Curriculum requirements for 'speaking and listening' are based on a model of 'communicative competence' (Hymes, 1971) that fails to address the social complexity of classroom language and assumes a 'performance' model of language and the development of an ideal and efficacious speaker. Her analysis of children's accounts of their 'news' telling uses an alternative model of language; one that enables us to see classroom talk in terms of 'meanings' and 'functions in a social system' (Halliday, 1978). This allows us to see pupil purposes beyond the immediate and obvious imperatives to fulfil teacher and task requirements. Through this analysis we see tensions between functions related to teacher requirements and a range of social functions *vis-à-vis* an audience of peers. It shows how pupil responses are embedded in the wider contexts of the socio-economic circumstances of their families and community, in peer affiliations and statuses and classroom identities. It again shows how pupil responses are embedded in the wider contexts of the socio-economic circumstances of their families and community, in peer affiliations and statuses and classroom identities. Further, it illustrates the challenges to identity, self-image and interests-at-hand of pupils where there is a tension between fulfilling teacher expectations, demonstrating state policy definitions of 'speaking and listening' skills and fulfilling real social functions *vis-à-vis* an audience of peers.

Again in these chapters, we argued that requirements for increasingly formalized classroom assessment and recording procedures often serve to obscure the reality of classroom life and the underlying nature of assessment practices. The issues highlighted show how the 'scientific' paradigm of testing disguises values and power relations, bias, inequalities and the sociocultural expectations of testers and the tested. Rather, we argue that classroom assessments, from the most informal to the most formal, are interpretive processes. Knowledge, skills and performance are inseparable from social and cultural attributes and learning, gender and ethnicity. The relevant 'context' of influence is not to be taken simply as the immediate social or physical environment of an assessment activity but to include the wider contribution of family and peer affiliations, sociocultural biography and individual identity.

Through Chapters 9 and 10, in exploring the question of 'How does assessment function in classrooms?' we focused on *classroom processes*. We drew on a number of theoretical perspectives and research findings, in particular those of Bernstein (1975), in analysing ways in which assessment and other classroom processes are bound together in patterns of authority and control. We contrasted ways in which particular forms of assessment give rise to particular patterns of teacher–pupil relationships and interactions in the teaching process and particular goals for learning. We analysed ways in which such patterns associated with 'performance goals' can act to polarize pupils' attainment and promote 'learned helplessness' in some children. In particular, we considered some important ways in which contrastive forms of teachers' language in assessing pupils can act to promote or inhibit pupils' responses. In this we addressed processes of cultural reproduction arising from pupils' differential access to culturally specific forms and patterns of interactions used in teaching and assessment.

In Chapter 7, as outlined above, we discussed pupils' purposes *vis-à-vis* an audience of peers which go beyond fulfilling the requirements of a particular task or teacher expectations. Similarly there are well-established understandings regarding ways in which teachers' language, when assessing pupils, simultaneously fulfils a range of pedagogic purposes. From the late 1960s and through the 1970s, there was much research interest in demonstrating ways in which classrooms were inadequate contexts for assessing children's verbal competence. Our review of such research into classroom processes in Chapter 9 demonstrates that the message which historically has emanated from sociological and sociolinguistic studies of assessment and classroom processes has been forgotten. The present preoccupation with the *content* of assessment, with 'evidence' and the 'ticked boxes' or their equivalent, relating to many and varied Statements of Attainment, is obscuring what we know about *process* (see also Filer 1993a, 1993b, 1995).

Chapter 10 is the second in the pair of chapters exploring functions of assessment and ways in which they are bound up with other classroom processes. In it, Ann Filer presented a comparative analysis of two classes at Albert Park School as language environments. Teacher talk was seen to be concerned not simply with processes of instruction and for ascertaining what pupils know or understand but as the simultaneous medium of both the pedagogic control of knowledge and the particular patterns of social interaction through which that control is maintained. Bernstein's theory of 'the framing of educational knowledge' was used to conceptualize these simultaneous functions of teacher language and a comparative analysis was made of the different patterns of control and forms of interaction of the two teachers. The importance of these different forms of control and interaction was shown through a contrastive analysis of the quantity and distinctive quality of verbal responses each evoked from the pupil cohort. The analysis of a case study of one child sets out in some detail the potential impact of different patterns of language and control on the assessments made by the teachers that used them.

Whilst the analysis in Chapter 10 related to the assessment of 'speaking and listening' it also, of course, has implications for other classroom assessments where pupil knowledge or understanding is inferred by teachers from verbal responses to their questioning.

Perhaps the most significant implication of this analysis is that it illustrates ways in which children's classroom language is conditioned by patterns and forms of control which are embedded in teachers' everyday routines and interactions with pupils. This has implications for ways in which we approach and interpret all classroom assessments involving teacher–pupil talk. As Bernstein (1990) pointed out, in their classroom talk, teachers are not culture free, ideal speakers. No one is. Teachers do not represent or provide a neutral linguistic background against which children can be assessed.

The issues which we addressed in our final pair of chapters relate to the processes to which *initial* assessment outcomes are subject before recursively affecting individual pupils' social and academic identities and sense of selves as learners. Thus our question, 'How are assessments interpreted and mediated?' was concerned with the possibility of what we have termed 'transformative processes'. Through this pair of chapters we introduced the concept of an 'audience' of families, peers and local communities who are active in the lives of individual pupils, interpreting and mediating, supporting or challenging the official and unofficial voices of school assessment. In this we drew attention to the sociocultural and professional power relations through which professionals, gatekeepers, policy makers, journalists and others legitimate, control and disseminate assessment outcomes and delimit 'audience' powers to interpret, mediate, contest and contribute to assessment outcomes.

In particular we drew on our own research and that of others in presenting an account of the gap between the rhetoric and the reality of parental power and involvement and between their *actual* and *potential* role in relation to school assessment practices. In a policy context which fails to fully value the educational application of parental knowledge and has a limited appreciation of their contribution to their children's learning, the power to intervene and influence assessment outcomes remains with those who can employ the most successful strategies. Through these chapters we also concluded that the current policy and government discourse that positions parents as consumers of assessment outcomes fails to capture their potential for contributing in more active and collaborative ways in the assessment of their children.

However, as we also discussed in Chapter 10, power and control are not absolutes in classrooms or in state policy within democratic government. Outcomes can be subject to contestation depending on perceptions of the '*legitimacy*' of systems of assessment and this important issue of 'legitimation' does not just relate to systems of mass assessment. Indeed, we illustrated how parents evaluate ongoing assessments of their child's attainment in the context of a *particular teacher's class*. In this they draw on their own evaluations of their child's capabilities and potential and make decisions to support or challenge the day-to-day judgements teachers made of their children. Thus our case studies in Chapter 12 showed assessment as a multi-dimensional process, whereby individual pupils' perceptions and responses to assessment practices and outcomes are differentially shaped within a matrix of family, peer-group, school and community perceptions, expectations and relationships. It presented an analysis of the strategic approaches of parents at Greenside and Albert Park Schools as mediators and interpreters of assessments of their children as they progress through primary school.

In developing the concept of an 'audience' for assessment, we highlighted how families variously act upon, contest, challenge, support or ignore the official and unofficial voices of both teacher and standardized assessment. In so doing, we emphasized how families interpret and give meaning to assessment outcomes. Indeed, throughout the longitudinal development of the *Identity and Learning Programme* we have traced the *dynamic* development of families' characteristic repertoires of strategic involvement and influence in shaping school assessment outcomes and in mediating and interpreting them with their children. Thus we have been able to provide an analysis over time of the dynamics of home–school relationships that cuts across the more usual structural, class-based analysis of power inequalities of working and middle classes in relation to schools. In so doing, our analysis problematizes simple dichotomies of 'supportive' or 'problem' families which prevail in public and political discourse and among practitioners. We see greater understanding of the importance of family contexts and parental perspectives as a basis for a more holistic, collaborative and reflexive approach to assessment.

CONCLUSION

In the Introduction of this book, we suggested that we would show 'objectivity' in educational assessment practices and outcomes to be an illusion. Indeed, we made three specific state-ments:

- individual performances cannot be separated from the contexts and social relations within which they are embedded;
- assessment techniques are social processes and are vulnerable to bias and distortion;
- the 'results' of assessment take their meaning for individuals via cultural processes of interpretation and following mediation by others.

We have illustrated our arguments by drawing on data from the *Identity and Learning Programme* and other research and have constructed a more abstract theoretical model of the social processes which, we would argue, *inevitably* contribute to any assessment process when seen holistically. Ethnography is a good, inductive method for generating such analyses and we believe that further research evidence will gradually accumulate to reinforce these basic propositions.

In concluding this book, we want to draw attention to two consequential policy issues of particular importance.

First, a significant equity issue is raised if it can be shown that standard assessment practices systematically disadvantage particular social groups. In the case of the UK, evidence of differ-ential performance in relation to gender, ethnicity, disability and social class is well established (see e.g. Wood, 1991; Gipps and Murphy, 1994; Black, 1998) and we believe that our work highlights some of the key social processes that yield such patterns. The same arguments apply to the more pragmatic concerns that education systems should contribute to the fulfilment of national potential and that educational institutions can be reliably compared and held account-able on the basis of standard performance data. Many researchers have argued that this belief is misplaced (see e.g. Slee *et al.*, 1998; Thrupp, 1999) and, in a sense, the public 'knows' from personal experience that such comparisons are unjustified. However, the assumption of compa-rability remains deeply and unquestionably embedded in everyday social practices. It is a task of the sociology of educational assessment to question such assumptions.

Second, we have shown how the outcomes of assessment practices are deeper and more enduring than simple signs of marks, grades and statements of academic achievement. Official assessment also affects each pupil's motivation, self-esteem and sense of self as a learner. Claxton (1999) has coined the term 'epistemic identity' to describe a pupil's belief in his or her self as a learner, with associated views of knowledge and knowing, and we know from Dweck's (1999) work that self-belief is vital in developing a forward-looking, problem-solving 'mastery' orienta-tion. Such attributes are closely associated with the new type of flexible, resourceful and self-confident learners whom we are told are required in the new century. If the state schooling system is to produce such learners, then a rethink of the use of assessment is essential. All the evidence suggests that a categoric system of classification, predominantly used summatively, is likely to reinforce conservative approaches to learning and will produce highly differentiated outcomes (Pollard and Triggs, 2000). From the sociological point of view, social divisions will tend to be reproduced as a relatively small group of academically successful, self-confident learners move through to key positions, and the majority take less fulfilling roles in the economy and elsewhere. Conversely, a more flexible mode of assessment, used formatively (Torrance and Pryor, 1998), has the potential to reinforce a wider range of skills, capabilities and even 'multiple intelligences' (Gardner, 1983 and 1993) and thus to develop self-confidence among many more learners. The outcome could be a larger, more diverse, capable and confident workforce which would be well placed to engage with future challenges. The social trend would be one of inclusion, with greater recognition of diversity and many forms of talent. On this, there is an unfortunate tension between the rhetoric and the reality of government policy in the UK and elsewhere.

References

Adams, N. (1997) 'Towards a curriculum of resiliency: gender, race, adolescence and schooling', in C. Marshall (ed.) *Feminist Critical Policy Analysis: A Perspective from Primary and Secondary Schooling.* London: Falmer Press.

Alexander, R., Rose, J. and Woodhead, C. (1992) *Curriculum Organisation and Classroom Practice in Primary Schools.* London: DES.

Allatt, P. (1996) 'Consuming Schooling: choice, commodity, gift and systems of exchange,' in S. Edgell, K. Hetherington, and A. Warde (eds) *Consumption Matters: the production and experience of consumption.* Oxford: Blackwell.

Ball, S. J. (1981) *Beachside Comprehensive: A Case Study of Secondary Schooling.* Cambridge: Cambridge University Press.

Barber, M. (1996) *The Learning Game.* London: Gollancz.

Barnes, D. (1969) *Language, the Learner and the School.* Harmondsworth: Penguin.

Berger, P. and Berger, B. (1976) *Sociology: A Biographical Approach.* London: Methuen.

Berlak, H. (1995) 'Culture, imperialism and Goals 2000', in R. Miller, *Educational Freedom for a Democratic Society: A Critique of National Goals, Standards and Curriculum.* Brandon, Vermont: Resource Centre for Redesigning Education.

Berlak, H. (2000) 'Cultural politics, the science of assessment and the renewal of public education', in A. Filer (ed.) *Assessment – Social Practice and Social Product.* London: Falmer Press.

Bernstein, B. (1971) 'On the classification and framing of educational knowledge', in M. F. D. Young (ed.) *Knowledge and Control.* West Drayton: Collier Macmillan.

Bernstein, B. (1975) *Towards a Theory of Educational Transmission. Class, Codes and Control: Vol. 3.* London: Routledge.

Bernstein, B. (1990) *The Structuring of Pedagogic Discourse. Class, Codes and Control: Vol. 4.* London: Routledge.

Bernstein, B. (1996) *Pedagogy, Symbolic Control and Identity.* London: Taylor & Francis Ltd.

Black, P. (1998) *Testing: Friend or Foe? Theory and Practice of Assessment and Testing.* London: Falmer Press.

Blumer, H. (1969) 'The methodological position of symbolic interactionism', in *Symbolic Interactionism: Perspectives and Method,* New Jersey: Prentice-Hall. Also reproduced in M. Hammersley and P. Woods (eds) (1976) *The Process of Schooling.* London: Routledge and Kegan Paul.

Boggs, S. T. (1972) 'The meaning of questions and narratives to Hawaiian children', in C. Cazden, V. John and D. Hymes (eds) *Functions of Language in the Classroom.* New York: Teachers College Press.

Bourdieu, P. (1986) *Distinction: A Social Critique of the Judgement of Taste.* London: Routledge and Kegan Paul.

Bourdieu, P. and Passeron, J. C. (1977) *Reproduction.* London: Sage.

Breakwell, G. M. (1986) *Coping with Threatened Identities.* London: Methuen.

Broadfoot, P. (1996) *Education, Assessment and Society*. Buckingham: Open University Press.

Broadfoot, P. and Pollard, A. (1996) 'Continuity and change in English primary education', in P. Croll (ed.) *Teachers, Pupils and Primary Schooling*. London: Cassell.

Broadfoot, P. and Pollard, A. (2000) 'The changing discourse of assessment policy: the case of English primary education', in A. Filer (ed.) *Assessment: Social Practice and Social Product*. London: Falmer Press.

Bruner, J. (1986) *Actual Minds, Possible Worlds*. London: Harvard University Press.

Caldwell, B. J. and Spinks, J. M. (1988) *The Self-managing School*. London: Falmer Press.

Cazden, C. (1972) *Child Language and Education*. New York: Holt, Rinehart and Winston.

Chomsky, N. (1965) *Aspects of the Theory of Syntax*. Massachusetts: Massachusetts Institute of Technology Press.

Clarke, A. and Clarke, A. (1996) 'Varied destinies: a study of unfulfilled predictions', in B. Bernstein and J. Brannen (eds) *Children, Research and Policy*. London: Taylor & Francis Ltd.

Claxton, G. (1999) 'Fishing in the fog: learning at the confluence of cultures', paper given at The Culture and Learning in Organizations autumn seminars, Graduate School of Education, University of Bristol, 3 November.

Collins, J. (1996) *The Quiet Child*. London: Cassell.

Cooper, B. and Dunne, M. (2000) 'Constructing the "legitimate" goal of a "realistic" maths item: a comparison of 10–11 and 13–14 year olds', in A. Filer (ed.) *Assessment – Social Practice and Social Product*. London: Falmer Press.

Crooks, T. (1988) 'The impact of classroom evaluation practices on students', *Review of Educational Research* **58**(4), 438–81.

Crozier, J. (1997) 'Empowering the powerful: a discussion of the interrelation of government policies and consumerism with social class factors and the impact of this upon parent interventions in their children's schooling', *British Journal of Sociology of Education*, **18**(2), 187–200.

Delamont, S. (1983) *Interaction in the Classroom* (1st edn 1976). London: Routledge.

Delgado-Gaitan, C. (1996) *Protean Literacy: extending the discourse on empowerment*. London: Falmer Press.

Department for Education (1994) *General Requirements for English relating to Key Stages 1 to 4*. London: HMSO.

Department of Education and Science (1984) *Better Schools*. London: DES.

Department of Education and Science (1988) *Science at Age 11: A Review of APU Survey Findings 1980–1984*. London: HMSO.

Department of Education and Science (1992) *The Parents' Charter*. London: DES.

Desforges, C., Hughes, M. and Holden, C. (1994) 'Assessment at Key Stage One: its effects on parents, teachers and classroom practice', *Research Papers in Education*, **9**, 133–58.

Desforges, C., Hughes, M. and Holden, C. (1996) 'Parents, teachers and assessment at Key Stage One', in M. Hughes (ed.) *Teaching and Learning in Changing Times*. Oxford: Blackwell.

Dumont, R. V. (1972) 'Learning English & how to be silent: studies in Sioux and Cherokee classrooms', in C. Cazden, V. John and D. Hymes (eds) *Functions of Language in the Classroom*. New York: Teachers College Press.

Dunn, J. (1988) *The Beginnings of Social Understanding*. Oxford: Blackwell

Dunn, J. (1996) 'Family conversations and the development of social understanding', in B. Bernstein and B. Brannen, *Children, Research and Policy*. London: Taylor & Francis.

Dweck, C. (1989) 'Motivation', in A. Lesgold and R. Glaser, *Foundations for a Psychology of Education*. New Jersey: Erlbaum.

Dweck, C. (1999) *Self Theories: Their Role in Motivation, Personality and Development*. Philadelphia: Psychology Press.

Edwards, A. and Furlong, V. (1978) *The Language of Teaching*, London: Heinemann.

Edwards, A. and Westgate, D. (1987) *Investigating Classroom Talk*. London: Falmer Press.

Edwards, D. and Mercer, N. (1987) *Common Knowledge: The Development of Understanding in the Classroom*. London: Methuen.

Elliot, E. and Dweck, C. (1988) 'Goals: an approach to motivation and achievement', *Journal of Personality and Social Psychology*, **54**(1), 5–12.

Entwistle, N. (1992) *The Impact of Teaching on Learning Outcomes in Higher Education*. Sheffield: CVCP, Staff Development Unit.

Filer, A. (1993a) 'Contexts of assessment in a primary school classroom', *British Educational Research Journal*, **19**(1), 95–107.

Filer, A. (1993b) 'The assessment of classroom language: challenging the rhetoric of "objectivity" ', *International Studies in Sociology of Education*, **3**(2), 193–212.

Filer, A. (1993c) *Classroom Contexts of Assessment in a Primary School*. University of the West of England: unpublished thesis.

Filer, A. (1995) 'Teacher assessment: social process and social practice', *Assessment in Education*, **2**(1), 23–38.

Filer, A. (1997) ' "At least they were laughing": assessment and the functions of children's language in their "news" session', in A. Pollard, D. Thiessen and A. Filer (eds) *Children and their Curriculum: The Perspectives of Primary and Elementary School Children*. London: Falmer Press.

Filer, A. (ed.) (2000) *Assessment: Social Practice and Social Product*. London: Falmer Press.

Filer, A. with Pollard, A. (1998) 'Developing the "Identity and Learning Programme": principles and pragmatism in a longitudinal ethnography of pupil careers', in G. Walford (ed.) *Doing Research about Education*. London: Falmer.

Filer, A. and Pollard, A. (2000) 'Assessment and parents' strategic action', in A. Filer (ed.) *Assessment: Social Practice and Social Product*. London: Falmer Press.

Firth, J. R. (1957) *Papers in Linguistics 1934–1951*. London: Oxford University Press.

Fraser, S. (1997) 'Introduction to *The Bell Curve Wars*', in A. H. Halsey, H. Lauder, P. Brown and A. Stuart Wells (1997) *Education*. Oxford: Oxford University Press.

Gardner, H. (1983) *Frames of Mind: The Theory of Multiple Intelligences*. New York: Basic Books.

Gardner, H. (1993) *The Unschooled Mind: How Children Think and How Schools Should Teach*. London: Fontana.

Gewirtz, S., Ball, S. and Bowe, R. (1995) *Markets, Choice and Equity in Education*. Buckingham: Open University Press.

Giddens, A. (1991) *Modernity and Self Identity*. Cambridge: Polity.

Gipps, C. and Murphy, P. (1994) *A Fair Test?* Buckingham: Open University Press

Gipps, C., Brown, M., McCallum, B. and McAlister, S. (1995) *Intuition or Evidence?* Buckingham: Open University Press

Gould, S. J. (1981) *The Mismeasure of Man*. New York: W. W. Norton.

Halliday, M. A. K. (1978) *Language as Social Semiotic*. London: Edward Arnold.

Halliday, M. A. K. (1982) 'Linguistics in teacher education', in R. Carter *Linguistics and the Teacher*. London: Routledge and Kegan Paul.

Hammersley, M. (ed.) (1999) *Educational Research: Current Issues*. London: Paul Chapman in association with The Open University.

Hargreaves, A. (1978) 'The significance of classroom coping strategies', in L. Barton and R. Meighan (eds) *Sociological Interpretations of Schooling and Classrooms*. Driffield: Nafferton

Hargreaves, A. (1994) *Changing Teachers, Changing Times: Teachers' Work and Culture in the Postmodern Age*. London: Cassell.

Herrnstein, R. and Murray, C. (1994) *The Bell Curve: Intelligence and Class Structure in American Life*. New York: Free Press.

Hirst, K. (1998) 'Pre-school literacy experiences of children in Punjabi, Urdu, and Gujerati speaking families in England', *British Educational Research Journal*, **24**(4), 415–29.

Hughes, M. (1996) 'Parents, Teachers and Schools', in B. Bernstein and B. Brannen (eds) *Children, Research and Policy*. London: Taylor & Francis Ltd.

Hughes, M., Wikeley, F. and Nash, P. (1994) *Parents and Their Children's Schools*. Oxford: Blackwell.

Huss, R. L. (1997) 'Teacher perceptions of ethnic and linguistic minority parental involvement and its relationships to children's language and literacy learning: a case study', *Teaching and Teacher Education*, **13**, 1–30.

Hymes, D. H. (1971) 'Competence and performance in linguistic theory', in R. Huxley and E. Ingram (eds.) *Language Acquisition: Models and Methods*. London and New York: Academic Press.

Jackson, P. W. (1968) *Life in Classrooms*. New York: Holt, Rinehart and Winston.

Jenkins, R. (1996) *Social Identity*. London: Routledge.

Johnson, M. and Barber, M. (1996) 'Collaboration for school improvement: the power of partnership', in D. Bridges and C. Husbands (eds) *Consorting and Collaborating in the Education Market Place*. London: Falmer Press.

Kagan, J. (1992) 'Yesterday's premises, tomorrow's promises', *Developmental Psychology*, **28**, 990–7.

Keddie, N. (1971) 'Classroom knowledge', in M. F. D. Young (ed.) *Knowledge and Control*. London: Collier Macmillan.

Labov, W. (1969) *The Logic of Non Standard English*. Washington, DC: Center for Applied Linguistics.

Labov, W. (1972) *Sociolinguistic Patterns*. Philadelphia: University of Pennsylvania Press.

Labov, W., Cohen, P., Robins, C. and Lewis, J. (1968) *A Study of the Non-Standard English of Negro and Puerto Rican Speakers in New York City*. Final Report of Co-operative Research Project No. 3288, Columbia University.

LaCelle-Peterson, M. (2000) 'Choosing not to know: how assessment policies and practices obscure the education of language minority students', in A. Filer (ed.) *Assessment: Social Practice and Social Product*. London: Falmer Press.

Lees, J. M. (1981) *Conversational Strategies with Deaf Children*. University of Nottingham: MPhil thesis.

Leiter, K. C. W. (1974) 'Ad Hocking in the School', in A. V. Cicourel (ed.) *Language Use and School Performance*. New York: Academic Press.

Lepper, M. R. and Hodell, M. (1989) 'Intrinsic motivation in the classroom', in V. Ames and R. Ames, *Research on Motivation in Education*, Vol. 3, San Diego, CA: Academic Press.

Licht, B. D. and Dweck, C. S. (1983) 'Sex differences in achievement orientation: consequences for academic choices and attainments', in M. Marland (ed.) *Sex Differences and Schooling*. London: Heinemann.

Lloyd, B. and Duveen, G. (1990) 'A semiotic analysis of the development of social representations of gender', in G. Duveen and B. Lloyd (eds) *Social Representations and the Development of Knowledge*. Cambridge: Cambridge University Press.

Madaus, G. (1994) 'A technological and historical consideration of equity issues associated with proposals to change the national testing policy', *Harvard Educational Review*, **64**(1), 76–95.

Madaus, G. and Horn, C. (2000) 'Testing technology: the need for oversight', in A. Filer (ed.) *Assessment – Social Practice and Social Product*. London: Falmer Press.

Maguire, M. (1977) 'Shared and negotiated territories: the socio-cultural embeddedness of children's acts of meaning', in A. Pollard, D. Thiessen and A. Filer (eds) *Children and Their Curriculum: The Perspectives of Primary and Elementary School Children*. London: Falmer Press.

Malinowski, B. (1923) Supplement to C. K. Ogden and I. A. Richards, *The Problem of Meaning in Primitive Languages*. London: Kegan Paul.

Malinowski, B. (1935) *Coral Gardens and their Magic*, Vol. 2. London: Allen & Unwin/New York: American Book Co.

Marshall, C. (ed.) (1997) *Feminist Critical Policy Analysis; a Perspective from Primary and Secondary Schooling*. London: Falmer Press.

Mead, G. H. (1934) *Mind, Self and Society*. Chicago: University of Chicago.

Meadows, S. (1993) *The Child as Thinker: The Development and Acquisition of Cognition in Childhood*. London: Routledge

Mehan, H. (1973) 'Assessing children's school performance', in H. P. Dreitzel (ed.) *Childhood and Socialisation*. New York: Collier Macmillan.

Mchan, H. (1979) *Learning Lessons: Social Organization in the Classroom*. Cambridge, MA: Harvard University Press.

Mills, C. Wright (1959) *The Sociological Imagination*. New York: Oxford University Press.

Mueller, E. C. (1971) *An Analysis of Children's Communication in Free Play*. Cornell University: unpublished doctoral dissertation.

Murphy, P. (1988) 'Gender and assessment', *Curriculum*, **9**(3), 165–71.

Nias, J. (1989) *Primary Teachers Talking*. London: Routledge.

Nicholls, J. (1989) *The Competitive Ethos and Democratic Education*. Cambridge, Mass.: Harvard University Press.

Nicholls, J. G. and Thorkildsen, T. A. with Bates, A. (1996) 'Experience through the eyes of quiet bird; reconnecting personal life and school life', in A. Pollard, D. Thiessen and A. Filer (eds) *Children and their Curriculum: The Perspectives of Primary and Elementary School Children*. London: Falmer Press.

Nyborg, H. (1988) 'Mathematics, sex hormones and brain function', *Behavioural and Brain Sciences*, **11**, 206–7.

Osborn, M. (1996a) 'Teachers mediating change: Key Stage 1 revisited', in P. Croll (ed.) *Teachers, Pupils and Primary Schooling*. London: Cassell.

Osborn, M. (1996b) 'Identity, career and change: a tale of two teachers', in P. Croll (ed.) *Teachers, Pupils and Primary Schooling*. London: Cassell.

Osborn, M., McNess, E. and Broadfoot, P. with Pollard, A. and Triggs, P. (forthcoming) *Policy, Practice and Teacher Experience: Changing English Primary Education*. London: Continuum.

OTA (Office of Technology Assessment), US Congress (1992) *Testing in American Schools: Asking the Right Questions* OTA-SET-519. Washington, DC: US Government Printing Office, Feb. 92.

Petersen, A. C. (1976) 'Physical androgyny and cognitive functioning in adolescence', *Developmental Psychology*, **12**, 524–33.

Philips, S. (1972) 'Participant structures and communicative competence: Warm Springs children in community and classroom', in C. Cazden, V. John and D. Hymes (eds) *Functions of Language in the Classroom*. New York: Teachers College Press.

Pollard, A. (1982) 'A model of coping strategies', *British Journal of Sociology of Education*, **3**(1), 19–37.

Pollard, A. (1983) 'Coping strategies and the multiplication of differentiation in infant classrooms', *British Educational Research Journal*, **10**(1), 33–48.

Pollard, A. (1985) *The Social World of the Primary School*. Renden: Holt, Rinehart and Winston. (Second edition 1996: London: Cassell.)

Pollard, A. with Filer, A. (1996) *The Social World of Children's Learning*. London: Cassell.

Pollard, A. and Filer, A. (1999) *The Social World of Pupil Career*. London: Cassell.

Pollard, A., Broadfoot, P., Croll, P., Osborn, M. and Abbott, D. (1994) *Changing English Primary Schools? The Impact of the Education Reform Act at Key Stage One*. London: Cassell.

Pollard, A. and Triggs, P. with Broadfoot, P., McNess, E. and Osborn, M. (forthcoming) *Policy, Practice and Pupil Experience: Changing English Primary Education*. London: Continuum.

Pollard, A., Thiessen, D. and Filer, A. (eds) (1996) *Children and the Curriculum: The Perspectives of Primary and Elementary School Children*. London: Falmer Press.

Pryor, J. and Torrance, H. (2000) 'Questioning the Three Bears: the social construction of classroom assessment', in A. Filer (ed.) *Assessment: Social Practice and Social Product*. London: Falmer Press.

Reay, D. and Ball, S. J. (1998) 'Making their Minds Up: family dynamics of school choice', *British Educational Research Journal*, **24**(4), 431–48.

Resnick, L. (1989) 'Introduction', in L. Resnick (ed.) *Knowing, Learning and Instruction: Essays in Honour of R. Glaser*. New Jersey: Lawrence, Erlbaum Associates.

Rutter, M. (1989) 'Pathways from childhood to adult life', *Journal of Child Psychology and Psychiatry*, **30**, 23–51.

Sinclair, J. M. and Coulthard, R. M. (1975) *Towards an Analysis of Discourse: the English used by Teachers and Pupils*. Oxford: Oxford University Press.

Slee, R. and Weiner, G. with Tomlinson, S. (eds) (1988) *School Effectiveness for Whom? Challenges to the School Effectiveness and School Improvement Movements*. London: Falmer Press.

Stafford, R. E. (1963) *An Investigation of Similarities in Parent–Child Test Scores for Evidence of Hereditary Components*. Princeton, New Jersey: Educational Testing Service.

Stenhouse, L. (1975) *An Introduction to Curriculum Research and Development*. London: Heinemann.

Strandberg, T. E. and Griffith, J. (1968) *A Study of the Effects of Training in Visual Literacy on Verbal Language Behaviour*. Eastern Illinois University.

Stubbs, M. (1986) *Educational Linguistics*, Chapter 1, 'Relevant Models of Language for Teachers'. Oxford: Blackwell.

Swann, M. (1985) *Education for All*. London: HMSO.

Task Group on Assessment and Testing (1988) *National Curriculum Report*. London: DES.

Thrupp, M. (1999) *Schools Making a Difference: Let's be Realistic* Buckingham: Open University Press.

Tizard, B. and Hughes, M. (1984) *Young Children Learning: Talking and Thinking at Home and at School*. London: Fontana.

Tizard, B., Mortimore, J. and Burchell, B. (1981) *Involving Parents in Nursery and Infant Schools*. London: Grant McIntire.

Tizard, B., Schofield, W. N. and Hewison, J. (1982) 'Collaboration between teachers and parents in assisting children's reading', *British Journal of Educational Psychology*, **52**, 1–15.

Torrance, H. and Pryor, J. (1998) *Investigating Formative Assessment: Teaching, Learning and Assessment in the Classroom*. Buckingham: Open University Press.

Troman, G. (1988) 'Getting it right: selection and setting in a 9–13 years middle school', *British Journal of Sociology of Education*, **9**(4), 403–22.

Tsoldis, G. (1988) 'Cultural affirmation: cultural approaches', in V. Foster (ed.) *Including Girls*. Canberra: Curriculum Development Centre.

Urdan, T. and Maehr, M. (1995) 'Beyond a two goal theory of motivation and achievement: a case for social goals', *Review of Educational Research*, **65**(3), 213–43.

Vincent, C. and Tomlinson, S. (1997) 'Home–school relationships: "the swarming of disciplinary mechanisms"?', *British Educational Research Journal*, **23**(3), 361–77.

Vygotsky, L. (1978) *Mind in Society*. London: Harvard University Press.

Walkerdine, V. (1988) *The Mastery of Reason: Cognitive Development and the Production of Reality*. London: Routledge.

Wegener, P. (1885) *Untersuchengen uber die grundfragen der sprachlebens*. Halle.

Wells, G. (1986) *The Meaning Makers*. London: Hodder and Stoughton.

Wells, G. (1992) 'The centrality of talk in education', in K. Norman, *Thinking Voices*. London: Hodder and Stoughton.

West, A., Noden, P., Edge, A. and David, M. (1998) 'Parental involvement in education in and out of school', *British Educational Research Journal*, **24**(2), 461–84.

White, R. T. (1992) 'Implications of recent research on learning for curriculum and assessment', *Journal of Curriculum Studies*, **24**(2), 153–64.

Wilder, G. Z. and Powell, K. (1989) *Sex difference in Test Performance: A Survey of the Literature*. New York: College Board Publications.

Wiliam, D. (1997) Review of Broadfoot (1996) 'Education, Assessment and Society', *British Educational Research Journal*, **23**(3), 396–7.

Willes, M. (1983) *Children into Pupils*. London: Routledge.

Winner, L. (1986) *Autonomous Technology: Technic-out-of-Control as a theme in political thought*. Cambridge, MA: MIT Press.

Wood, H. A and Wood, D. J. (1983) 'Questioning the pre school child', *Educational Review*, **35** special issue (15), 149–62.

Wood, R. (1991) *Assessment and Testing*. Cambridge: Cambridge University Press.

Woods, P. (1977) 'Teaching for survival', in P. Woods and M. Hammersley (eds) *School Experience*. London: Croom Helm.

Woods, P. (1979) *The Divided School*. London: Routledge and Kegan Paul.

Woods, P. (1983) *Sociology and the School*. London: Routledge and Kegan Paul.

Yates, L. (1997) 'Gender, Ethnicity and the Inclusive Curriculum: An Episode in the Policy Framing of Australian education', in C. Marshall (ed.) *Feminist Critical Policy Analysis; a Perspective from Primary and Secondary Schooling*. London: Falmer Press.

Young, M. F. D. (1976) 'School science: innovation or alienation?', in P. Woods and M. Hammersley (eds) *School Experience*. London: Croom Helm.

Name Index

Adams, N. 30, 49
Alexander, R. 13, 44, 113, 134
Allatt, P. 134

Ball, S. J. 71, 134
Barber, M. 131, 138
Barnes, D. 108, 109
Berger, B. 30
Berger, P. 30
Berlak H. 130
Bernstein, B. 4, 10, 102, 103, 104, 108, 113, 114,
    115, 117, 120, 121, 125, 126, 128, 155, 156
Black, P. 81, 82, 157
Blumer, H. 5, 57
Boggs S. T. 109
Bourdieu, P. 82, 128
Breakwell, G. M. 27, 28
Broadfoot, P. 8, 16, 31, 60, 81, 104, 105, 106, 128,
    130, 131, 132, 134, 138, 146, 154
Bruner, J. 30

Caldwell, B. J. 17
Cazden, C. 109
Chomsky, N. 88
Clarke, A. 29
Claxton, G. 159
Collins, J. 34
Cooper, B. 81, 82, 84
Coulthard, R. M. 108
Crooks, T. 106
Crozier, G. 138

Delamont, S. 119
Delgado-Gaitan, C. 132, 138
Desforges, C. 131, 138
Dumont, R. V. 109
Dunn, J. 30, 90, 110, 123
Dunne, M. 81, 82, 84
Duveen, G. 35
Dweck, C. 106, 107, 158

Edwards, A. 108, 110
Edwards, D. 30, 108
Elliot, E. 107

Entwistle, N. 106

Filer, A. 4, 5, 6, 7, 8, 9, 17, 31, 32, 34, 56, 58, 63,
    65, 73, 81, 83, 86, 97, 108, 110, 113, 114, 116,
    119, 125, 128, 130, 131, 133, 154, 155
Firth, J. R. 99
Fraser, S. 82
Furlong, V. 108, 110

Gardner, H. 158
Gewirtz, S. 134
Giddens, A. 29
Gipps, C. 31, 58, 59, 60, 81, 82, 157
Gould, S. J. 82
Green, A.
Griffith, J. 90. 109, 123

Halliday, M. A. K. 4, 79, 86, 87, 89, 91, 93, 96, 99,
    100, 109, 155
Hammersley, M. 5
Hargreaves, A. 10, 56, 61
Herrnstein, R. 82
Hirst, K. 132, 138
Hodell, M. 106
Horn, C. 80, 81
Hughes, M. 30, 90, 110, 123, 132, 134, 138
Huss, R. L. 132, 138
Hymes, D. H. 86, 87, 89, 100, 154

Jackson, P. W. 30
Jenkins, R. 3, 28, 29, 30, 55, 69
Johnson, M. 131, 138

Kagan, J. 29
Keddie, N. 108, 119

Labov, W. 90, 109, 123
LaCelle-Peterson, M. 130
Lees, J. M. 90, 123
Leiter, K. C. W. 32, 69, 71
Lepper, M. R. 106
Licht, B. D. 107
Lloyd. B. 35

Madaus, G. 80, 81

Subject Index

Albert Park Primary School viii, 5–7, 10, 12, 16–21, 36–7, 44, 51, 64–5, 87, 106, 113, 133, 134, 151
  families 16–17, 22–3, 37, 66, 97, 133, 138–9, 141–6
  head teachers 19–21, 22, 67–8
  suburb 66
Assessment: Social Practice and Social Product 7, 81, 130
'audience' for assessment 127, 129–30, 156–7
'authentic' assessment 58

biography 61, 79, 83, 154, 155
  pupil 32, 78, 82–3
  teacher 32, 44, 57, 62, 65, 66
  see also strategic biography

career *see* pupil career
classroom settings and practice 32–5, 43, 46, 48, 50, 64, 65–77, 79, 115–25; *see also* language, pedagogy, teachers
community 127, 130, 131, 133, 154, 155, 156, 157
coping strategies 4, 10, 32, 64
  teachers' 56–63, 64–73, 77, 112, 114, 115–16, 120, 153
  pupils' 64, 72–7
curriculum 14–15, 16, 17–19, 22, 34, 43, 102, 104, 109, 115, 117, 121; *see also* National Curriculum
cycles of assessment 9, 50, 151, 152

data gathering and analysis 5–7
diagnostic judgements 32, 43, 63, 69–72, 154; *see also* 'social diagnosis'
differentiation 8, 11, 30, 64, 72–7, 81, 84, 98, 100, 101, 103, 105–8, 109–11, 128, 153, 154, 158

Easthampton city 14–16, 51
  Local Education Authority 14–16, 17–19, 20, 23, 67
Education Reform Act 1988 13, 15, 58, 61, 113
ethics 6
ethnicity 10, 30, 49, 78, 82–3, 93, 98, 109–10, 130, 132, 154, 155

ethnography, longitudinal 4–5, 27, 28, 44, 46, 50, 61, 63, 139, 140, 146
  methodology 5–7

family 11, 28, 31, 44, 46, 127, 129, 131, 133, 152, 154, 155, 156, 157; *see also* Albert Park families, Greenside families, parents
formative assessment 15, 16, 63
framing of educational knowledge 103, 112, 114, 115, 116–20, 120–21, 156

gender 10, 30, 39–41, 42, 44, 45, 48, 49, 62, 78, 79, 81, 82, 86, 97, 98, 154, 155
Greenside Primary School viii, 5–7, 12, 15, 17, 21–2, 27, 32–4, 44, 51, 133, 134
  families 21–3, 133, 139, 141–6
  head teachers 21–2

holistic approaches to assessment 31, 32–5, 44, 58, 59, 62, 69, 151–2, 157

identity 3, 5, 9, 10, 27–32, 33, 34, 36–42, 48, 49, 51, 61–2, 69, 82–3, 100, 105, 129, 131, 134, 140, 151, 152, 153, 155; *see also* pupil identity, teacher identity, self
Identity and Learning Programme 3–7, 11, 28, 32, 34, 51, 61, 64, 69, 79, 82, 128, 129, 134, 152, 154, 157
ideology 101, 103–5, 108
inspection 15, 16, 21, 22, 60
interests-at-hand 4, 10, 42, 43, 49, 57, 67–9, 83–4, 100, 155
  model of 57

language 10, 83, 85, 86–100, 101, 103, 108–10, 113–14, 115, 116–20, 121, 122-6, 130, 154–6
learning 4, 29, 30, 34, 101, 102, 103–8, 134, 152, 155, 158
longitudinal analysis *see* ethnography, longitudinal

methodology *see* ethnography
motivation 105–8, 152, 158

National Curriculum 6, 10, 13, 16, 17, 20, 36, 58, 64, 65, 71, 72, 79, 80, 84, 87, 91, 99, 107, 113, 126, 151, 154; *see also* curriculum